AF540598

Housekeeping Hygiene and Sanitation

Housekeeping Hygiene and Sanitation

Rajendra Kumar Khatan

RANDOM PUBLICATIONS
NEW DELHI (INDIA)

Housekeeping Hygiene and Sanitation

ISBN 978-93-5111-546-5

Published in 2015 in India by

RANDOM PUBLICATIONS

Reprint 2018

4376-A/4B, Gali Murari Lal, Ansari Road
New Delhi-110 002
Phone : +9111-43580356, 011-23289044, 011-43142548
e-mail: sales@randompublications.com,
info@randompublications.com, randomexports@gmail.com

Type Setting by : Friends Media, Delhi-110089
Digitally Printed at : Replika Press Pvt. Ltd.

Preface

Modern day cleaning or housekeeping goes much beyond just keeping the place look clean and neat. It involves keeping it hygienically clean. This subtle difference between housekeeping and hygienic housekeeping requires minute understanding of the hygiene issues related to cleaning that are not immediately visible but have profound effect on the efficiency of the workforce in any workplace premises or the guestroom in a hotel. Housekeeping and workplace hygiene means providing adequate sanitation and hygiene facilities that are regularly cleaned and maintained so they do not pose a health and safety risk to employees. Workers need to have potable drinking water that is safe to drink, sanitary toilet facilities, safe food prepared in sanitary kitchens and served in clean canteens, and a work environment that is otherwise kept hygienic. Performing regular housekeeping and maintenance helps you identify potential issues and take preventative action before problems develop. Good housekeeping practices also help you control problems by eliminating tripping hazards, making sure floors are never slippery and keeping exit routes clear. A socially responsible company makes sure that none of its facilities and practices create a situation where workers are at risk due to poor housekeeping and workplace hygiene. This book will help you check whether there a risk of not meeting these standards in your current business operations and, if so, how to put controls in place to make sure your housekeeping and workplace hygiene needs are understood and controlled.

I would like to thank my team for standing beside me throughout my career and writing this book. My special thanks go to "Random Publications" who have published the book.

– Rajendra Kumar Khatan

Contents

1

Meaning of Housekeeping Department

The Housekeeping Department is one of the busiest sections in the hotel as far as the variety of functions performed, and number of staff working.

It is usually situated at the laundry room or any other convenient place close to Housekeeping Supplies. The Housekeeping Department is responsible for:

- Neatness and Cleanliness of all guest rooms and most public areas
- Maintenance of recycled and non-recycled cleaning inventories

Some of the functions might however be leased to a concessionaire. In this case, hotel shall still have a housekeeping department but to a minimum number of staff.

The Housekeeping Department is headed by an Executive Housekeeper. The procedure of cleaning guest rooms by the housekeeping department can be summarized in the following way:

- Checkout clerk contacts the Housekeeping Department that a room became vacant and needs cleaning.
- Housekeeping Department updates the room status from occupied to on-change and sends a room maid to clean the room.
- Room maid cleans the room and contacts the housekeeping department back about the latest status and condition of the room.
- If the room is out of order for any reason, then the Housekeeping Department deducts that room from those available for sale, until either scheduled to be extensively cleaned or post to the confirmation from the Maintenance Department that the deficiency was repaired.
- Housekeeping Department sends their inspectors to check whether the stated room has been cleaned to the hotel standards or not.
- If the room is cleaned to hotel's standards, the Housekeeping Department shall update the room status from On-Change to Clean and Available for Sale and communicate this to the Front Office Department.
- If the room is not cleaned to hotel standards, inspectors communicate to the Housekeeping Department that the room shall be cleaned again.

DEFINITION OF HOUSEKEEPING IN A HOTEL

Hotel housekeeping departments can be considered hotel ambassadors because of their dedication and responsibility in maintaining the hotel's image. Housekeeping performs detailed work in guest rooms and hotel areas to provide a clean, comfortable environment for hotel guests to enjoy. Through cleaning and organising public spaces, housekeeping departments ensure that what the guests see and experience result in a positive impression of the property.

FUNCTION

The primary role of the hotel's housekeeping department is cleaning guest rooms. Housekeeping works closely with front desk operations to communicate when rooms are clean and ready for guests to occupy. Although usually associated with cleaning and sanitising guest rooms, housekeepers are also responsible for other areas, such as public restrooms, convention space and offices. Housekeeping departments often manage laundry operations, which includes washing linens as well as employee uniforms. At some hotels, housekeepers are responsible for minibar inventory and room service.

TYPES

Housekeeping departments include a variety of job titles. The department will generally have a director of housekeeping, sometimes called the executive housekeeper. This employee is responsible for managing the department and its employees. Housekeeping departments also have supervisors who inspect work and several types of line staff, including room attendants, laundry attendants, turn-down attendants and public space attendants. In addition, other housekeeping employees run the department office by answering phones and dispatching attendants. In some hotels, the office personnel are responsible for managing lost and found items.

SIZE

The housekeeping department is often the largest employee department in the hotel. The number of employees is relative to the size of the hotel, and may be a combination of full-time hotel employees and temporary leased labour. The number of full-time employees is generally based on the average number of rooms one housekeeper can clean in one shift. The housekeeping department's full size is based on the rooms per housekeeper per day formula, but daily scheduling depends on occupied rooms and/or special projects.

SCHEDULE

Hotel housekeeping departments operate 24 hours each day, but the majority of employees work during the day. Day shift housekeepers are typically room attendants who begin cleaning rooms in the morning. The housekeeping schedule revolves around guest occupancy, so housekeeping departments are at their busiest between guest check-out in the morning and check-in in the afternoon. Turn-down attendants are scheduled for evening shifts, so they can perform nightly turn down in guest rooms. Laundry and public space attendants may work any shift.

TOOLS

Room attendants generally use a cart to hold their tools and supplies so they can bring the necessary equipment with them to each room. Carts are stocked with chemicals and cleaning supplies to clean surfaces in guest rooms and bathrooms. The cart also holds a vacuum cleaner, broom and trash bag. Although not brought to every room, carpet shampooers and ozone machines can be brought to rooms that require extra cleaning attention.

IMPORTANCE OF HOUSEKEEPING DEPARTMENT

- Housekeeping is the department that deals essentially with cleanliness and all ancillary service attached to that.
- The standard plays an important role in the reputation of the hotels. One feels comfortable only in the environment which is clean and well ordered, so cleanliness is important for health foremost also for well being.
- Accommodation in hotels tend to be the largest part of the hotel, it is the most revenue generating department, the housekeeping department takes care of all rooms is often largest department in hotels.
- The rooms in hotels are offered as accommodation to travellers/guest as individual units of bedroom. Some interconnected rooms are also made which will be helpful to the guest and families. Many hotels offer suits to the guest.
- Hotel offer laundry, dry leaning facilities for guest clothes, shoe polishing facilities also.
- Hotel aims to make environment comfortable and offer specialised service to the guest.

- Hotel offer guest the choice of specialty restaurant, coffee shop. The bar also sells liquors which generate the revenue of the hotel. They are available in banqueting, meeting and private party facilities.
- Revenue can be generated from conferencing, meeting, seminar etc.
- These days shopping arcade also found in hotels.
- A health club is a part of facilities of most large hotels especially resort hotels this also include swimming pool and spa facilities.
- Hotels try to make the ambiance as pleasant as possible by nice colour scheme, attractive furnishing and a well kept efficient staff.
- House keeping is the department determine to a large extent whether guests are happy during stay and in turn mankind they return to the hotel.
- The fine accommodation and service are provided to the guest so they are pleased with the hotel. The guest satisfaction is its primary object and the hygiene factor must always be present in the hotel.

In hotels major part of revenue comes from rooms, rooms which is not sold on any night losses revenue forever and reason for poor occupancy can be anything like hygiene factor, cleanliness, lack of modernising etc. hence main purpose is to improve whole appeal of the room. A guest spend more time alone in his room than any other part of the hotel, so he can check up the cleanliness he wishes to as some of the guest are more health conscious these days.

He may check up dusting, in-depth cleaning and losses confidence if properly not done *e.g.* If drawers are not cleaned he may generally won't feel like putting his clothes down.

Decent room supplies are service like quick laundry and dry cleaning service shows guest that hotel is considering his comfort and wishes to please him. not only this from the cleanliness of lobby, public area, restaurant, cloakrooms, the state and cleanliness of uniform the guest can judge a lot about hotel. it can be positive or negative judgement we can conclude that housekeeping department contributes greatly to all guest impression of the hotel.

LAYOUT OF THE HOUSEKEEPING DEPARTMENT

After understanding the organisational structure and functions of the housekeeping department, it is of utmost importance for you to know the layout of this department in a medium or large size hotel, irrespective of the location of a hotel. Layout also aims to convey important areas co-ordinated by housekeeping departments.

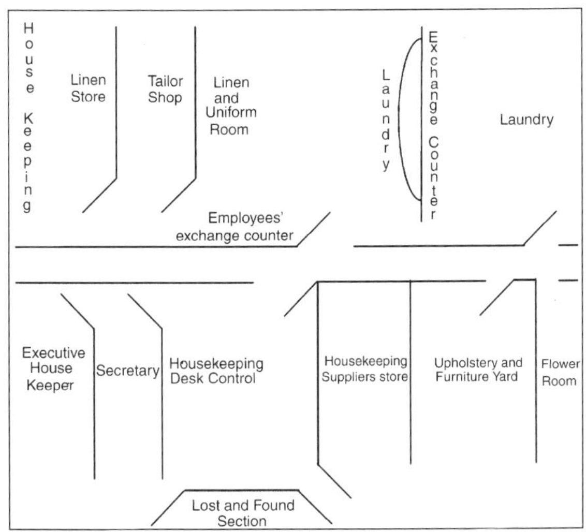

Fig. Operational Layout of Housekeeping Department

The layout given in Figure indicates the functioning departments of housekeeping like linen store supported by tailor's shop; laundry supporting the exchange counter; housekeeping desk control equipped with as many telephone lines as possible so that messages pertaining to the housekeeping personnel may be noted and passed down to them without any delay. Housekeeping also controls lost and found section, wherein all items lost or found by the guests are reported and recorded properly. To ensure smooth supply and functioning of housekeeping department its store shall be well equipped. Following items can be taken as a sample for this:

- *Night spreads*: 1 for every bed,
- *Sheets*: 2 for every bed,
- *Pillow case*: 2 for every bed,
- *Bath towel*: 1 for every guest,
- *Face towel*: 1 for every guest,
- *Hand towel*: 1 for every guest,
- *Bath mats*: 1 for every guest,
- *Mattress protectors*: Only a few to replace.

Upholstery and furniture yard is also an important section of housekeeping department with the prime duties to maintain and replace as and when furniture or any other replacement of furnishing is required in any room as is reported by room attendants. Another important part of this department is the flower room, equipped with a washing area and air conditioning to maintain freshness of flowers needed for decorative purpose. As far as ideal number of personnel to be deployed in each section of housekeeping is concerned following formula can be used as a sample:

- *Executive Housekeeper*: 1 for 300 rooms
- *Assistant Executive Housekeeper*: 2 for 300 rooms
- *Floor Supervisor*: 1:30 Morning Shift and 1:60 Night Shift
- *Public Area*: 1 for every shift
- *Linen/Uniform Room Supervisor*: 1 for every shift
- *Linen/Uniform Room Helper*: 1 for every shift
- *Room Attendant*: 1 for every fourteen rooms
- *Linen Attendant*: 1 for every shift
- *Housemen*: 1:60 rooms/per shift
- *Desk Attendant*: 1 for every shift
- *Tailor*: Subject to lo ad
- *Horticulturist*: One
- *Upholster* : One
- *Head Gardner*: 1 for every 20
- *Gardner*: 1 for each 450 sq. ft. of landscape area

ORGANISATION STRUCTURE OF HOUSEKEEPING DEPARTMENT

To run even a small hotel of 30 rooms you would require massive quantity of linen and a medium sized staff to keep it clean and hospitable for the guests. Within a hotel, the housekeeping department is normally the biggest department with a large number of staff members. Hence, housekeeping department of every hotel has an organised structure irrespective of its size. However, for smaller hotels organisation of housekeeping departments can be done in the manner given in Figure:

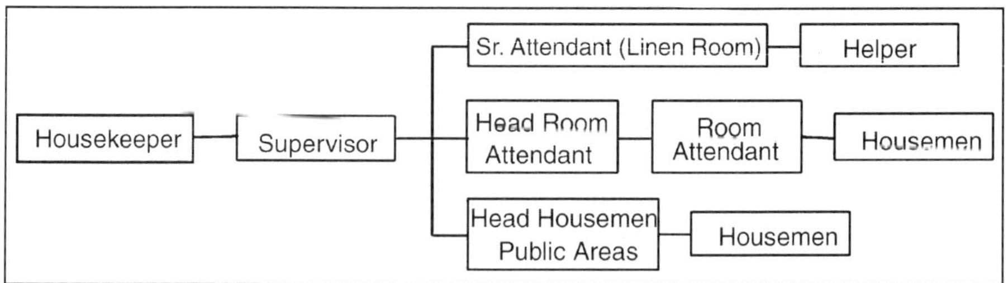

In any medium or large size hotel the housekeeping department is normally organised in the manner described in Figure. Some of their prime duties can be summarised as:

- *Housekeeping Manager*: Also known as the Head or Executive Housekeeper, is the one with ultimate accountability for the department in terms of staff deployment and development, operational standards and profitability. Delegation, community guidance and direction are key skills required in a successful housekeeping manager. As a whole, it is the housekeeping manager who owns the accountability for standards of cleanliness, maintenance and financial performance within the housekeeping department.

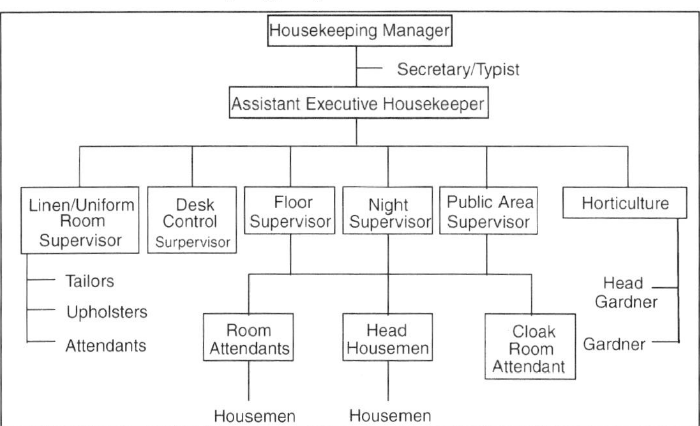

Fig. Illustrates that though the role of all Housekeeping personnel is Crucial, three are the key players, *viz.*, Housekeeping Manager, Floor Supervisor and Room Attendants.

- *Floor Supervisor*: Also known as floor housekeepers, is in charge of a floor or a specified number of rooms. His/her main job is to ensure the quality and efficiency of the room attendants. Once the room is checked and found to be upto mark it is "handed" over to the front desk for letting out to the guest. The floor supervisors also impart training to the new room attendants and re-training for the existing staff for corrective measures. They are also responsible for the equipments and costcontrol within their area, and liaison with other department like maintenance and front office. Management of linen, refuse and cleaning equipment is another duty of the floor supervisor. Sending soiled linen for cleaning and procuring clean linen for next day's cleaning of rooms is very important. Also the exact count of the linen needs to be maintained at all times in the linen closet.
- *Room Attendants*: Room attendants are also known as housekeeping assistants. They are primarily responsible for maintaining the high standards of cleanliness in each of the room assigned to them. Cleaning the room includes vacuuming the rooms, cleaning the toilets, checking and replenishing the used toiletries, changing the linens and towels and making sure that the general set-up of the room is correct. Reporting of the maintenance problems to the concerned department personnel is another key duty performed by the room attendants. At times guests place their queries regarding the local

amenities or about hotel facilities to the room attendants and while answering these queries they play their role in customer relations. All these duties are required to be performed in a specified time period as they are allotted fixed number of rooms to maintain.

FUNCTIONS OF THE HOUSEKEEPING DEPARTMENT

The extension of the housekeeping function outside the hotel bedroom normally includes cleaning of the bedroom floors and may also include the staircases, public cloakrooms and other public areas of the hotel. Many a times outside agencies are involved in cleaning the public areas such as the lobby and the restaurant area as well as the men's and women's restrooms. This activity is normally carried out at odd hours or at the times when public is not around this area. The standard of the cleanliness needs to be maintained and it's the duty of the executive housekeeper to see that pre-determined standards of cleanliness are maintained in all the areas of the hotel it be if the fire-exit stairwells and goods lifts or any other public area. To ensure this, the day of executive housekeepers begin with a round with assistant housekeeper of all such areas which is visited by the public. For this standards need to be set and once the standards are approved, the department shall strive hard to maintain them. Other function areas of the housekeeping department includes:

- *Lost and Found Department*: Many a times while cleaning a guest room attendant comes across some personal items of the guest left behind. The value of the personal item can vary from almost nil to thousands of rupees as in the case of Rolex watches, etc. All the articles found while cleanin g the rooms are, thus, handed over by attendants to the floor supervisor, who maintains a list of the found articles against the specific room number.
- *First Aid*: First aid as and when needed by the guests is provided by the housekeeping department which maintains the first aid kit.
- *Floral Arrangement*: Fresh floral arrangements all over the hotel are maintained by the housekeeping department. The private areas like guest bedroom or the public areas like the restaurants and the lobby floral arrangements are made by housekeeping department.
- *Laundry Services*: The laundry services extended to the guest are usually provided by the housekeeping. The laundry to be washed is collected from the guest room and washed, dried and ironed clothes are supplied back to th e guest room. Earlier, all the hotels had in house laundry services but nowadays many hotels have out-sourced this service, both for the hotel linen as well as for the guest laundry.
- *Purchasing*: This is one role of the housekeeping department where a lot of money transactions take place. This is one of the important areas which can affect the profitability of the hotel if various products

purchased and supplies are not well managed. The primary areas of purchasing that are under the control of the Executive housekeepers are:

- *Bedroom supplies*: *e.g.*, laundry bags, breakfast, cards, shoeshine, etc.,
- *Bathroom supplies*: *e.g.*, toiletries,
- *Linen*: bed sheets and towelling,
- *Tea and coffee making facilities*: *e.g.*, tea/coffee sachets, sugar, milk and biscuits,
- *Working replacements*: *e.g.*, shower curtains, crockery, glassware, vacuum cleaners, trolleys, etc.,
- *Cleaning supplies*: *e.g.*, air freshener, bleach, cleaning product, and
- *Uniforms*: *e.g.*, for the room attendants/porters.

It is necessary for the Executive housekeeper to ensure that the supplies and their consumption is monitored. The list of items in the purchasing list can be further classified into:

- *Consumable*: bedroom supplies, cleaning supplies and TCMF
- *Assets*: uniforms, working replacement and linen.

The Executive housekeeper would have different policies for these two distinct groups of purchasing. The actual consumption of the first group of purchases can be anticipated in line with the hotel occupancy. It is necessary to maintain a stock of these items so that the staff can put up their requisitions on a daily or weekly basis. The Executive housekeeper is thus required not only to ascertain the demands but also to control the use of consumable products by maintaining properly the invoices and requisition slips. The consumable products are many and if not properly monitored will obviously affect at large the profit statement of the hotel.

Today, computers are used for the purpose. "Assets", though not in true sense, like uniforms, etc. are not regularly used up and they do not need to be replaced daily. But it is the duty of the staff to maintain their uniform and turn up immaculately, daily. Other items like vacuum cleaners, crockery are phased out over a period of time and are recorded as depreciation. Hotel linen is very difficult to manage, as in a large hotel almost 5000 soiled linens are sent for cleaning daily. To count and counter check the linen from and to the laundry is a herculean task. Moreover, guests also tend to pilfer items like towels from hotels. To keep account of stock and maintain it and when necessary replenish it becomes the priority job for the housekeeping manager.

INTERDEPARTMENTAL COORDINATION

- *RandD and Marketing*: Your RandD Department works with Marketing to make sure your product line meets customer expectations.

- *RandD and Production*: RandD works with Production to ensure assembly lines are purchased for new sensor models. If Production discontinues a sensor, it should notify RandD. Production and RandD also discuss automation increases and their impact on revision dates.
- *Marketing and Production*: Your Marketing Department works with Production to make sure manufacturing runs are in line with forecasts. Marketing's market growth projections also help Production determine appropriate levels of capacity. If Marketing decides to discontinue a sensor model, it tells Production to sell all of that sensor's capacity.
- Marketing and Finance: Marketing works with Finance to project revenues for each sensor model.
- *Finance and Production*: Production tells Finance it needs money for additional capacity and automation. If Finance cannot raise enough money through stock, bonds and working capital, it can tell Production to scale back its requests, or perhaps sell idle capacity.
- *Finance and All Departments*: The Finance Department acts as a watchdog over company expenditures. Its job is to make sure the company does not run out of money. Finance should review Production's decisions. Is Production manufacturing too many or too few sensors? Does it need additional capacity? Has Production considered labour cost versus automation purchases? Finance should crosscheck Marketing's forecasts and pricing. Are forecasts too high or too low? Is pricing correct for the targeted segment? Finance can determine a range of possible outcomes for the year by changing Marketing's forecasts then checking. Lowering the forecasts will decrease revenue and increase inventory; raising the forecasts will increase revenue and decrease inventory.

2

Housekeeping Knowledge: Key Control

Key is a specially shaped and designed piece of metal or plastic/magnetic card used for opening and closing the lock.it is an essential too for lock.

In a hotel, it refers to the door lock key, which is primarily concerned for safety of hotel room contents and guest valuables.

The responsibility for handling key of the houseguest has always been with front office and housekeeping department. In all large, hotels the information desk holds the responsibility of issuing, retrieving and controlling room keys. Room attendants also handle room keys to prepare guest bedrooms. Hence, it is essential that strict control of keys is maintained regularly.

MANUAL/MECHANICAL KEY SYSTEM

The standard of manual key system in operation comprises of the following:

- Individual guestroom keys.
- Sub master key/floor key
- Master key
- Grand master key
- Emergency key
- Electronic/Magnetic Key System

CONTROL OF ROOM KEYS

Maintaining a strict control over the guest room keys is the responsibility of the information section. it is very necessary that a strict control be maintained for averting any mishaps. The information assistant keeps the keys into the correct slots of the key rack/pigeon hole.

For the security of both guest and the hotel, room keys issuing system must be very efficiently operated and controlled.the theft, loss or unauthorized duplication of keys could have serious security implication.

The system of key control is as follows:

- Know the different types of keys in circulation within the hotel.
- Keys should not be handed over to unauthorized personnel.

- Guests should be requested to handle their key cautiously.
- Guests should be urged to drop the keys at the'key drop slot' maintained at front desk each time they leave the premises upon their departure or for their own personal reasons.
- Identification should be sought and verified, if necessary, prior to issuing a key to a guest.
- key should always be placed in the correct hook/slot of the rack
- A regular inventory of keys should be carried out, and missing or damaged key should be reported immediately to the concerned authority.
- The master keys, when not in use, should be secured in a safe place.
- Key should be retrieved from the guests at time of check out.
- A logbook or control sheet can be used to monitor the distribution of keys.
- The keys of inter-connecting rooms should be kept secure and scheduled.

ISSUING KEY CARD

In many hotels, keys are stored in key rack located at the front desk. The rack consists of a number of'pigeon holes' large enough to hold regular size mail, with a key hook above. Each pigeonhole is clearly numbered by floor and by room in its console.

ISSUING KEYS TO INDIVIDUAL

Room keys are issued to guest on completion of the registration formalities. The room key may be issued to the guest personally, or to the staff escorting the guest to the room *e.g.* porter/bellboy. At all other times keys should only be issued to guest on presentation of identification, *i.e.* the key card.

ISSUING KEYS TO GROUP

For groups, keys may be organized in advance and distributed to its members in individual envelopes.

Table. Specimen of Key Control Sheet.

KEY CONTROL SHEET No................................							Date: ....
Key code	Name	Signature	Time out	Issued by	Time in	Signature	Received by

LOST AND FOUND MANAGEMENT

Lost and found refers to those articles which are unintentionally left or lost by a guest in the hotel premises.

Such articles can range from jewellery, costly electronic goods to simple garments etc. The hotel considers it duty to secure such articles until the guest claims them.

PROCEDURES OF HANDLING LOST AND FOUND ARTICLES

- It is general practice that any lost properties found in room/floor or the public areas should be handed over to the lost and found section of housekeeping department immediately
- The appropriate details should be entered into a slip, which is put along with the articles in a transparent bag.
- Control desk supervisor or assistant housekeeper fills up lost and found register.
- The article is sent to the lost and found section, where it is usually kept for a period of 6 months to one year or depending upon the policy of the management.
- Perishable articles or stuffs (non-valuables) are kept for a day, and then it is handed over to the finder or distributed to the concerned area staff after the set time.
- In case of jewellery (valuables) being found it is normally secured from 6 months to 1 year. If it is not claimed by the guest within the stipulated time, the item is sold and the housekeeping staff are distributing the amount.
- Incase the owner claims for the lost articles, proper identification is asked to establish the real owner. then the lost and found register is filled-up
- The signature if the guest is obtained and the article is handed over.
- The lost and found articles are normally disposed in the following ways
- The owner may come to claim or authorize someone on his. Her behalf to collect.
- It may be sent through the mail/courier as per the instruction of the owner
- If the article is not claimed within the specified time, it may be auctioned or given to the finder.

Table. Specimen of Lost and Found Slip/Form

Lost and Found Valuable/Non valuable No	
Finder's Name................................ Location /Room no........................... Description of article .... Name of the guest................................... Address... Signature of depositor	Date......................... Time......................... Signature of receiver
A. Received by owner Name................................ Address.............................. Date....................................	 Telephone No:....................... Signature............................
B. Dispatched by Post, Postal receipt No............. Name .... Address.............................. Date................................	 Telephone No....................... Signature............................
C. Retrieved by finder Name....................................... Cloak No....................................	 Signature............................ Gate pass No......................
Property handed over by Name................................. Signature.............................	 Designation........................... Date....................................

Table. Lost and Found Record.

No. Lost and Found Record								
Date / time	Received be Owner			Received by Finder			Dispatched by	
	Name	Address	Signature	Name	Signature	Gate Pass No.	Name.	Signature

PEST CONTROL

Pest conrol is a programme of eradicating pests. Pests are removed through pesticides.a pesticide is called a chemical used to control or eliminate pests. Insects are probably the larger pests.many insects transmit diseases such as malaria and typhus.some insects destroy or cause heavy damage to valuable vegetation. Other common pests include bacteria, fungi, rats and such weeds as poison ivy and ragweed.

Manufacturers use various chemicals in making pesticides:

- A pest is any organism that competes with humans, domestic animals. Or desirable plants for food or water.
- Injures humans, domestic animals, desirable plants, structures or possessions
- Transmits diseases and annoys humans or domestic animals.
- Pest control goals

- *Prevention*: Keeping a pest from becoming a problem
- *Suppression*: Reducing pest numbers or damage to an acceptable level.
- *Eradication*: Destroying an entire pest population.

COMMON PESTS AND THEIR CONTROL MEASURES

BED BUGS

These are tiny parasitic creatures that feed on the blood of human and other animals.

They are more of a nuisance than a danger, although they can cause severe irritation in some people, leading to loss of sleep and lack of energy particularly in children they hide in the crevices of beds, furniture, upholstery, wallpaper and skirting boards, emerging when hungry.

CONTROL MEASURES

Pouring boiling water into crevices is a temporary solution to get rid of bed bug. a thick application of kerosene of emulsion is also effective against bed bugs.

BEETLES

- *Biscuit Bittles*: these are brown with dense layer of yellow hairs on their body. They pests that attack cereal products and have even been known to infest poisonous substances such as strychnine.
- *Carpet Beetles*: these are the beetles that will attack furs, carpets and all kinds of woolen textiles. Carpet beetles are pests of animal and occasionally plant, products. They flourish in situations when they remain undisturbed-*e.g.* beneath carpets, around skirting boards and in wardrobes.
- *Control measures*: frequent vacuum-cleaning of fluff and dust is essential for control of these pests. in case of an infestation, insecticide powders may be sprayed in the affected areas.
- *Furniture Beetles*: This beetle makes its home in crevices and cracks of furniture made of unpolished wood.
- *Control measure*: the best time to apply insecticides to wood is around March o May, when the insects are near the surface of wood just before they emerge and so are more susceptible to the insecticide.
- *Cockroaches*: these are several pieces of nocturnal insect that spend most of the day hiding in cracks around drains or in other dark secluded crevices. Two common species of the cockroach are the German and the Oriental.
- Cockroaches carry food-poisoning bacteria in their bodies and are responsible for the spread of dysentery and gastroenteritis. They will

feed on almost anything, from faecal matter to food for human consumption.

- *Control measures*: cockroaches are the most difficult pests to eradicate.Proprietary cockroach-killer preparations may be used in the infested areas.however, pest-control experts need to be called if the infestation persists.
- *Fleas*: This area common nuisance. Even a vacant house can have a flea problem. They are usually laid in a host's bedding, hatching at room temperature in about 10 days.
- *Control measures*: on finding an infestation, the property should be sprayed with an insecticide that will kill adult fleas, their eggs, larvae and pupae. Pest-control expert should be called in to help with the problem.
- *Moths*: some of the moths species attack stores food products and are often found in houses, hotel kitchens, bakeries, grain stores and warehouses-anywhere that food is stored, especially dried foodstuffs such as grains, cereals, flours, nuts an so on..
- *Clothes Moths*: clothes moths in general are nocturnal insects and, although males and spent females sometimes come into the light, they are more likely to scuttle for cover that to fly into the open when disturbed.
- *Control measures*: cloth moth damage can be minimized by treating fabrics by mothproof finish.spray may be applied to carpets. Especially along and beneath the edges adjacent to skirting underneath furniture, and other likely areas of infestation where prolonged contact with humans or pet animals is unlikely-clothing and bedding should not be sprayed with insecticides.
- *Ants*: these insects generally invade in large numbers when they come in search of food, especially sweet substances.
- *Control measures*: they can be destroyed by placing tablespoonfuls of carbon bisulphde at the entrance.
- *Flies*: these filthy are dangerous to health as the contaminate food, causing diseases such as typhoid, cholera, dysentery and so on. They carry the disease germs on their legs and in their saliva. These are transferred to food on which they sit.
- *Control measures*: to eradicate flies, the first essential step is to destroy all possible breeding grounds early in the year before egg-laying begins. All garbage should be burnt. All dustbins should be covered. And a good standard of cleanliness for the surrounding should be maintained. Aerosol fly-killer sprays are also effective.
- *Mosquitoes*: these transmit diseases such as malaria, filarial and yellow fever. As life cycle of mosquitoes begins in water, do not allow water to stagnate in and around the property. The pits should not be open.

- *Control measures:* cover drains and pour kerosene oil onto these to prevent larvae from thriving there and growing into adult mosquitoes. Fine gauze on windows prevents the entry of mosquitoes. An effective, eco-friendly method for the control of mosquitoes is to place pots of water around the property for a week to two.during this time, the mosquitoes lay their eggs in the water. Before the eggs can develop, and however, this water is discarded, killing the larvae.
- *Mice and rats*: rats and mice both carry disease germs and may cause food poisoning, infection, jaundice and so. mice and can contaminate food stuffs, work tops and utensils with their urine, droppings and fur and are responsible for spread of many diseases, some of which can be fatal to humans.
- *Control measures*: the most effective methods of controlling these pests are poisoning, trapping, fumigating to eliminate their food supply and shelter and rat-proofing buidings.proprietary poisons are available to destroy rats and mice as well.
- *Fungi*: some fungi in the form of wet or dry rot can cause considerable structural damage to a property.
- *Wet Rot*: it is more likely to be found in kitchens, bathrooms and roofs. Outsides, it attacks window frames and sills, doors and door frames where water has penetrated the paintwork.
- *Control measures*: it is best to call pest-control firms to deal with wet rot.timber can be treated with water-repellent preservations to prevent wet rot.

SAFETY AND SECURITY

Safety and security are concepts often used interchangeably, and it should be understood that both are means of safeguarding human and physical assets.

The tern'safety' is with reference to such things as disasters, emergencies, fire prevention and protection, and conditions that provide for freedom from injury and prevent damage to property. The tern'security' is used with reference to freedom from fear, anxiety, and doubts concerning humans as well as protection thefts of guest, employee, or hotel property.

WORK-ENVIRONMENT SAFETY AND JOB-SAFETY ANALYSIS

The management of any place of work are legally bound to provide a hazard-free environment to their employees. The nature of work that the housekeeping staffs are involved in is such that employees may easily become accident-prone if they are careless with equipment, chemicals, or procedures.

Safety Management Programmes

The overall objective of a safety management programme is to eliminate hazards before they cause any serious accidents.

- There are 10 steps in the establishment of an effective safety management programme:
- Review work procedures and inspect work areas for safety hazards.
- Make departmental heads aware of the nature and variety of hazards.
- Establish a safety committee.
- Maintain accurate safety records.
- Conduct periodic in-house safety inspections.
- Train staff members to implement safety consciousness.
- Motivate staff members to be safety conscious.
- Investigate and analyses all accidents and injuries.
- Practice safety management and monitor follow-ups.
- Review the effectiveness of your own safety management programme.

Three Education of Safety

The safety of employees can be ensured by following the three Es of safety: education, safety engineering, and safety rules enforcement.

Safety Education

Safety programmes and policies can only be effective if the staff are trained to think and act safely at work. The best time to start educating employees on safety is during their induction into the establishment, so that they are well versed in safety rules and policies of the establishment before they start their job.

Employees should be encouraged to come up with ideas for inculcation safety into the hotel's methods too, and the best ideas should be put into practice and praised or awarded. The following should be ensured during training:

- Teaching safe methods, with particular emphasis on area of potential danger and how these can be guarded against.
- Demonstrating the use of safety equipment installed in the establishment, and the location and use of first-aid materials.
- Inculcating in people the ability to recognize the signs of hazards around them.
- Teaching staff the legal implications of non-adherence to safety procedures.

Safety Engineering

This involves the building in of safety features into the structure of the establishment-in the equipment, furniture, and fittings and in their proper arrangement within space. Equipment used by the housekeeping employees should be selected to ensure safety in design.

Safety Rules Enforcement

Rules, when not implemented or enforced are not effective. It is not enough to know about safety themes and procedures, but more important to motivate people to put the knowledge gained into practice. This does not come easily to all employees and therefore needs to be enforced by rule and practice.

Occupational Safety and Hazards Standards

Standard, universal laws on occupational safety and health (OSH) do not exist because of differences in local values and cultures. Therefore, differences in local and cultures. Therefore, different countries have developed their own standards on occupational health and safety management systems (OHMS) just as to their needs. India has published and follows the'IS 15001:2000 Indian Standards on Occupational Health and Safety Management Systems-Specifications and Guidance for Use', which is adapted to Indian needs.

The main emphasis of the system is on classifying work activities, identifying hazards, determining risks, deciding if a given level of risk is tolerable, preparing risk-control action plans, and reviewing the adequacy of action plans.

Job Safety Analysis

The executive housekeeper needs to develop a'housekeeping safety manual' for the use of all housekeeping employees. This manual should explain in comprehensive terms the safest methods of performing each task to accomplish a particular job. This has to be done for all the jobs carried out by housekeeping staff. For this purpose, the housekeeper, with the help of the supervisors, needs to carry out a job safety analysis. A job safety analysis is a detailed report that lists every job function performed in the housekeeping department and lists potential hazards, safe methods, tips, and'how-to's for each task involved in the jobs.

POTENTIAL HAZARDS IN HOUSEKEEPING

Due to the nature of the work performed by housekeeping staff, they may be exposed to many dangerous and unsafe conditions, or hazards, if they are not careful. To reduce safety risks, all employees should be aware of potential safety hazards. There hazards may include:

- Faulty equipment;
- Damaged flooring or chipped tiles;
- Slippery floors and spills not mopped up;
- Slippery guest bathrooms;
- Cracked or broken glass;
- Cleaning agents left uncapped;
- Non-adherence to instructions outlined in the materials safety data sheets (MSDS) for the use of cleaning chemicals.
- Handling corrosive cleaning agents with bare hands;
- Worn-out electrical insulation or fittings;
- Overloaded electrical sockets;

- Trailing equipment flexes;
- Worn carpets and rugs;
- Cleaning equipment left lying around;
- Unsafe use of ladders;
- Loose stair treads;
- Mixing certain chemical cleaners, causing undesirable/dangerous reactions;
- Cleaning agents dept in unmarked or wrongly marked containers;
- Incorrect use of trolleys.
- Incorrect methods of bending and lifting;
- Unsatisfactory hygiene and sanitation standards; and
- Incorrect posture.

SAFETY AWARENESS AND ACCIDENT PREVENTION

Safety awareness should be an ongoing programme at all establishments The management of all establishments should be aware of the laws concerning safe work environments and should be provided to all staff in order to raise awareness about safety. All employees should be aware of the potential hazards in their respective departments.

All heads of departments must ensure that employees follow safe job procedures, correct unsafe conditions immediately, and take adequate time to do the job so that accidents are not caused due to haste. The executive housekeeper should develop a comprehensive list of safety rules to be followed by all housekeeping employees. This can be part of the'housekeeping safety manual'.

BASIC GUIDELINES FOR THE PREVENTION OF ACCIDENTS

The following guidelines can be followed for the prevention of accidents:

- Always follow instructions when using any cleaning equipment.
- Replace caps on cleaning chemicals immediately and securely after dispensing.
- Label cleaning agents clearly.
- Keep floors clean and dry.
- Place warning and safety signs around the area while cleaning.
- Always dry hands before touching plugs, sockets, and electrical fittings.
- Mark faulty equipment as'out of order'.
- Dispose of rubbish carefully.
- Never place cigarette butts of sharp objects in the trash bag on the room attendants' carts.

- Open and shut doors carefully.
- Clean away broken glass carefully.

PROCEDURES TO FOLLOW IN CASE OF AN ACCIDENT

- When a guest or employee has met with an accident at the hotel, the procedure followed should be as follows:
  - With the help of another person, check if the victim requires any assistance.
  - Report the matter immediately to the manager concerned.
  - Either administer first aid (if you are trained to do so) or get help from trained personnel.
  - Transport the victim immediately to a hospital, if required. If the injury is serious, call an ambulance for the same. Follow all necessary first-aid measures until the ambulance arrives.
  - Fill in accident report form and hand it over to the manager concerned.

FIRE PREVENTION AND FIRE FIGHTING

Table. Format of an Accident Report form for Employees

Accident Report Form (for employees)
Name of the injured person..
Section..
Supervisor...
Date.............................Time of report..
Exten of injury..
Was hospitalization required?
Nature of the accident
Time.................................Place...
What happened/ cause..
....
Witness 1..
Witness2 ....
Supervisor's remarks..
Supervisor's signature

To understand fire prevention and fire-fighting, one must know how fires are classified.

Fires may be classified into four groups, based on their source of fuel:

- *Class A*: These are fires with trash, wood, paper or other ordinary combustible material as their fuel source.
- *Class B*: These are fires with flammable or combustible liquids as their fuel source.

- Class C these are fires involving electrical equipment.
- Class D These are fires with certain ignitable metals as the fuel source

Prevention of Fire

Fires may be prevented if fire hazards are identified and eliminated.

Some unsafe practices that may lead to fires are as follows:

- Guests smoking in bed.
- The hotel not providing sand urns or sufficient and appropriate ashtrays in rooms as well as public areas.
- Using high-wattage light bulbs in lamps.
- Leaving linen chute doors open.
- Storing rags and cloths with residues of cleaning polish still on them.
- Not unplugging electrical appliances when not in use.
- Using faulty electrical equipment or sockets.
- Leaving magnifying materials that are easily combustible.
- Using furnishing materials that are easily combustible.
- Each establishment must conduct fire drills on a periodic basis and ensure that all staff attend thee drills so that they know what is to be done during a fire emergency.

Fire Warning Systems

These may be electrically powered manually operated systems, automatic fire detection systems, or a combination of both. The usual components of such systems are discussed here:

- *Fire Alarms*: These can be set off by smoke detectors, heat detectors, sprinkler systems, or pull stations. The most common types of fire alarms are the ones operated by pull stations located in corridors, lobbies, and near elevators. The pull alarms themselves are red in colour, with a glass panel that needs to be broken to set off the alarm.
- *Sprinklers*: These are found in most hotel establishments, especially in corridors and rooms. They are situated on the ceiling and automatically spray water when the temperature rises above a certain level.
- *Smoke Detectors:* These are set off by smoke. The two types of smoke detectors available are photoelectric detectors and ionization detectors. Photoelectric detectors are alarms triggered off when smoke blocks a beam of light emanating from the detector. In the ionization type of smoke detectors, the alarm sounds when the detector senses a shift in electrical conductivity between two plates.

WHAT TO DO IN CASE OF FIRE EMERGENCY

In case a fire breaks out, follow the guidelines given below:

- Immediately switch on the nearest fire alarm.
- If possible, attack the fire with suitable equipment, remembering to

direct the extinguishers at the base of the flames. Do not attempt to fight a fire if there is any danger of personal risk.

- Close windows and switch off all electrical appliances, including fans and lights.
- Close the door to the affected area and report to your immediate supervisor for instructions.
- Carry out instructions-for instance, rouse guests in section and direct them to the nearest fire-escape route. Each guestroom should have the route to the nearest fire escape drawn out a displayed in a place where it is most likely to be seen by the guests.
- Report to the departmental fire representative for a roll call. The housekeeper on duty should check the list (in the form of the duty rosters) of the staff who are on duty so that all those on duty can be accounted for.
- Remain at the assembly point until instructed to do otherwise.
- Do not use the lifts.

FIRST AID

The initial assistance or treatment given to a casualty for any injury or sudden illness before the arrival of an ambulance, doctor, or other qualified person is called'first aid'. The notion offirst' aid itself signifies that the casualty is likely to be in need ofsecondary aid'.

PRINCIPLES OF FIRST AID

There are certain important principles involved in first aid. These are listed below.

The first aid provider must:

- Act calmly and logically;
- Be in control-both of himself/herself and the problem;
- Be gentle but fire, and speak to the casualty kindly but purposefully;
- Build up trust through talking to the casualty throughout the examination and treatment;
- Explain to the casualty what he/she is going to do;
- Answer honestly and say so in he/she does not know the answer (that is, avoid giving misleading information);
- Never leave the casualty alone and continue to talk to him/her until the ambulance or doctor arrives;
- Continuously reassure the casualty;
- Never separate a child form its parent or guardian;
- Sent the casualty to a hospital or doctor by the quickest means of transport;
- Always inform the police about serious accidents; and
- Inform the relatives of the casualty.

Do not:

- Touch a wound with your fingers or any instrument.
- Put an unclean dressing or cloth over wound.
- Allow bleeding to go unchecked.
- Move a patient unnecessarily.
- Remove clothing unnecessarily.
- Allow a patient with a fracture or suspected fracture to be moved until splints have been applied.
- Neglect shock.
- Risk burning a patient by using an unwrapped hot-water bottle or other hated object.
- Fail to give artificial respiration when needed.
- Fail to remove false teeth, tobacco, or any other eatables form the mouth of an unconscious person.
- Permit air to reach a burned skin surface.
- Wash wounds.
- Try to reduce dislocations, except of the finger and lower jaw.
- Leave a tourniquet on for over 20 minutes without loosening it.
- Forget to send for a physician.

3

Pricing

DECISIONS

No single pricing programme is suitable for all firms, since the complexity of pricing situations varies by product, cost, demand, and industry structure, and prices must relate to objectives, information, knowledge of alternative policies, and strategies and adjustments. The business executive is faced with the problem of establishing the best price under assumed cost-and-demand conditions. The lack of information, the dynamics of the market, and the problems of measuring both costs and demand make it a difficult task. Yet, estimates must be made of what management expects demand, cost, and competition to be under various conditions. Then it can develop pricing programmes that affect survival, profits, growth, volume, market share, R and D, and image.

A distinction is often made between price determination and price administration. The activities and focus of each are different. Price determination refers to the processes and activities employed to arrive at a price for a product. It includes consideration of relative prices of products within the same line, and differences in price for similar products of differing grades and qualities. Price administration refers to the activities involved in fitting basic prices to particular sales situations. For example, prices may be administered to bring them into line with such factors as geographic locale, functions performed by customers, position of distribution channel members, or special sales situations. Included in price administration is the determination of discount structures. Thus, price determination refers to the establishment of a "base price" that is adjusted through price administration to reflect varying sales and competitive situations. Six concepts and considerations useful in establishing prices are as follows:

- Pricing decisions should adopt a systems perspective. Executives must consider the whole marketing system-manufacturers, wholesalers, retailers, and consumers-and the impact at each stage.
- Prices must be related to market segments. The kind and strength of customer attitudes and the purchase desires of various market

segments affect the prices that can be charged, and customer acceptance of prices by a sufficient market sector is essential.

- The determination of the best price is usually impossible, and executives must often settle for satisfactory prices in view of profit and market-share objectives.
- Price is not to be considered merely as the result of costs; it is also a method of stimulating sales.
- Since they have both economic and political dimensions, pricing policies are more likely to be governed by tradition than by innovation. They are concerned not only with competition, elasticity of demand, marginal and average costs, industry structure, substitutability of products, and product and market characteristics, but also with numerous governmental constraints.
- Pricing policies must be reviewed and changed as basic conditions shift. This means that good pricing practices are research based.

What are the major pricing decisions to be made? They include determination of:

- Prices for each product or service.
- Discount structures.
- Price relationships among products.
- Price maintenance level.

These decisions should be based on information from market research, sales analysis, distribution cost accounting, standard costs, surveys, experiments, sales forecasts, simulations, and statistical techniques. The information required concerns competitive prices, cost data, demand estimates, product profitability, salesmen and customer reactions, and middlemen needs. But information about future demand schedules, future competitive reactions, and future costs is incomplete at best. Thus prices must be based on guesses and assumptions, yet they should be determined logically.

GOVERNMENT INFLUENCES

Price differentials are competitive weapons. To implement them, markets must be segmented and the bases for differentials established. The former requires consideration of demand elasticities; the latter has legal dimensions. Government involvement in pricing decisions takes a number of legal forms. Others include governmental pressure to prevent price rises, or even to roll them back in basic industries such as steel. Governmental involvement seems to relate price increases to the impact on inflation and increased productivity.

Such actions as withholding governmental orders or dumping metals from stockpiles back up such informal price control. Government has the influence to block or roll back price increases. Price differentials are subject to government scrutiny and regulation. They are established on the basis of quantity, distribution level, geo graphic area, and cash payment. Distribution discounts may be instituted on a net or list basis just as to distribution levels. Quantity discounts may be cumulative or non- cumulative, and may apply to part of a line or a whole line. Basing points, f.o.b. factory, and uniform delivered pricing are examples of geographic differentials. Discounts for cash are very common. Legally, price discrimination can be defended on the bases of meeting competition in good faith, of cost savings in dealing with different customers, and of promoting and not injuring competition. It is the effect of price discrimination, and not the act itself, that determines legality. The legal aspects of price discrimination and government involvement in pricing, particularly the provisions of the Robinson-Patman Act, arc. Although these legal constraints are significant in establishing price differentials, the practical guidelines are confusing and the economic consequences are mixed, since price discrimination can actually benefit society.

Both the Federal Trade Commission and the Justice Department are interested in pricing practices, particularly in the administration of prices. In the administration of price differentials, marketing managers must be concerned with legal problems of collusion and price discrimination as well as the impact on sales, profits, and competition. Undoubtedly more government involvement in pricing practice is the wave of the future. Price is the ingredient of the marketing mix that has enjoyed the most extensive economic analysis. In deciding marketing strategies, however, it cannot be separated from the other components.

The importance of price as a marketing factor varies with kinds of products and market situations. Sometimes non- price factors become more significant than price ingredients. Pricing programmes of firms, even within the same industry, vary greatly. Pricing strategies should consider both cost and demand conditions, and the dynamics of markets, thereby accounting for both internal and external variables.

Although the determination of an optimal price is usually impossible, a satisfactory one can be developed by analysis. The major pricing decisions include determining prices for each product or service, discount structures, price relationships among product lines, and price maintenance levels. Problems encountered in establishing prices relate to the inability to determine costs precisely, the difficulties of dealing with expectations, and the variations in impact of policies on different products in a company's product line. Marketing intelligence is a critical component of effective price determination.

ELASTICITIES

In addition to understanding the nature of demand, the measurement of various aspects of demand is basic to good pricing strategy. In particular, the measurement of price elasticities and buyer price expectations are significant. Elasticities vary with the substitutability and characteristics of products. The concepts of price or demand elasticity refers to the sensitivity of buyers to price changes. When small variations in price bring about relatively large variations in buyer reaction, the price elasticity is high. The situation is reversed for low elasticity.

Since various customers react differently to price changes, knowledge of demand elasticities helps to set prices. But the major problem is that detailed data are not available. Yet, several techniques can be used to approximate elasticities, including market tests, statistical techniques of historical or cross-sectional analysis, and surveys. Management need not determine precise elasticities; rather it needs reliable estimates and guides as to the break-even levels and likely profitability of price changes. There are two basic ways of measuring elasticities-cross-cut analysis and historical data. Cross-cut analysis pertains to a point in time. Examples are interviewing buyers, using panels, simulating price situations, and conducting pricing experiments. Often, companies conduct experiments by increasing or decreasing prices in test cities and analyse the impact on sales, market share, and profits. The problems of statistical interpretation are many, however. Historical data are analysed by time series analyses that portray the association between prices and sales over time; this method is widely used in estimating elasticities. Regression and correlation analysis are its major tools, and the analysis ignores factors other than price that affect demand.

PROBLEMS

What are the major problems in establishing prices? First, costs cannot be determined precisely. Second, management must deal with expectations-expected demand, expected costs, and the maximization of expected profits. This is particularly true of new products. Although cost estimates are more reliable than demand estimates, both are subject to wide error. They are based on the patterns of past data, which may deviate widely in the future, especially demand data, which incorporate a host of unpredictable market forces. Pricing must also be viewed from the perspective of a company's total product line, since products have complementary and competitive demands, joint and common costs, and by-products. Sometimes the demand for product A influences the demand for product B. This relationship is termed the cross elasticity of demand, with a negative cross elasticity referring to products that are complementary, a positive cross elasticity to substitutable products, and a zero cross elasticity to unrelated products. For example, an increase in the demand for pizza will increase the consumption of certain cheeses, while a large increase in the use of a company's brand R detergent may decrease the use of its brand S detergent.

Since market situations confronting products within a line differ, sellers have varying degrees of discretion in setting prices for particular items in a line, and should consider products both as separate entities and as members of a product set. Cost-plus pricing or uniform markups ignore individual product acceptance, market demands, and competitive conditions. In reacting to competitors' price changes, a company can sit tight, meet the change, or modify its own price or other elements of its marketing mix. Where customers consider not only price, but also availability, delivery, quality, service, and reliability, sensitivity to price diminishes.

When products are not homogeneous, companies have wider latitude in pricing situations. But when products are homogeneous and a price is cut, competitors may have to meet the reduction. Companies have the choice of following a price rise or not. Executives should study the reasons for price changes, their temporary and permanent effects, the impact on profits and. market share, likely industry response, and the alternatives available, before making decisions. Both purchasing situations and the decentralization of authority affect pricing policies. Prices may vary by the quantity purchased, and the purchaser's geographic area, trade position, and the functions he performs, as well as by the method and timing of purchases. In large, decentralized companies featuring profit-centre accounting, intra company pricing and transfer pricing, can influence product prices and raise significant conflicting problems. In some industries price changes in basic commodities occur frequently. Can computer programmes be developed to spell out the decision maker's thought processes in reacting to price changes? After studying a pricing executive in action over a period of time, one researcher developed a flow-chart programme that quite accurately predicted price reactions.

The programme included such information as personal biases and organizational influences in price reactions as well as market shares, anticipation of competitors' reactions, and intentions of the district office. The computer programme provided a simulation of the price-reaction process. Pricing policies are sometimes charged with emotion. Monopoly prices, price determination, and administered pricing are among the terms evoking emotional reaction. Also, the practice of price-cutting is often viewed with disdain or as an unethical practice by others in an industry, even to the point of indicating shoddy merchandise and service. Typically, new products have a monopoly position for a period a degenerative monopoly position.

Eventually competitors will develop competing and even improved products. The pricing executive must decide whether to charge relatively high or low initial prices, and the marketing consequences and related strategies are quite different in each situation. Obviously, regardless of economic models, it is difficult to establish an optimum price because demand and costs change over time. The attention usually settles on current profit maximization rather than on the long-run maximization; the whole life cycle of a product and the total product line, rather than a single item, must be considered in pricing; and price must be considered from the perspective of the total marketing mix. Where products are relatively homogeneous; several large firms constitute a significant part of the market; and buyers are well informed, then estimates of buyer reaction become a significant aspect of the pricing picture. So do competitive reactions that may be ferreted out by the use of marketing intelligence. Studies of what competitors have done in the past, coupled with detailed analyses of the current competitive situation, may furnish guides on what they are likely to do. This reasoning process, utilising subjective probability estimates, can provide decision makers with good guides for contemplated price changes. A specific illustration is seen in the following example: Since early 1955, the Everclear Plastics Company had been producing a resin called Kromel, basically designed for certain industrial markets.

In addition to Everclear, three other firms were producing Kromel resin. Prices among all four suppliers were identical; and product quality and service among producers were comparable. Everclear's current share of Kromel industry sales amounted to 40per cent. Four industrial end uses comprised the principal marketing area for the Kromel industry. These market segments will be labeled A, B, C, and D. Three of the four segments were functionally dependent in segment A in the sense that Kromel's ultimate market position and rate of approach to this level in each of these three segments was predicated on the resin's making substantial inroads in segment A. The Kromel industry's only competition in these four segments consisted of another resin called Verlon, which was produced by six other firms. Shares of the total Verlon-Kromel market currently stood at 70per cent Verlon industry, and 30per cent Kromel industry.

Since its introduction in 1955, the superior functional characteristics per dollar cost of Kromel had enabled this newer product to displace fairly large poundages of Verlon in market segments B, C, and D. On the other hand, the functional superiority per dollar cost of Kromel had not been sufficiently high to interest segment A consumers. While past price decreases in Kromel had been made, the cumulative effect of these reductions had still been insufficient to accomplish Kromel sales penetration in segment A. In the early fall of 1960, it appeared to Everclear's management that future weakness in Kromel price might be in the offing. The anticipated capacity increases on the part of the firm's Kromel competitors suggested that in the next year or two potential industry supply of this resin might significantly exceed demand, if no substantial market participation for a Kromel industry were established in segment A. In addition, it appeared likely that potential Kromel competitors might enter the business, thus adding to the threat of oversupply in litter years.

Segment A, of course, constituted the key factor. If substantial inroads could be made in this segment, it appeared likely that Kromel industrial sales growth in the other segments not only could be speeded up, but that ultimate market share levels for this resin could be markedly increased from those anticipated in the absence of segment A penetration. To Everclear's sales management, a price reduction in Kromel still appeared to represent a feasible means to achieve this objective, and perhaps it could still be profitable to Everclear. However, a large degree of uncertainty surrounded both the overall attractiveness of this alternative, and under this alternative the amount of the price reduction which would enable Kromel to penetrate market segment A. Formulation of the problem required a certain amount of artistry and compromise towards achieving a reasonably adequate description of the problem. But it was also necessary to keep the structure simple enough so that the nature of each input would be comprehensible to the personnel responsible for supplying data for the study.

Problem components had to be formulated, such as:

- Length and planning period;
- Number and nature of courses of action;
- Payroll functions; and
- States of nature covering future growth of the Verlon-Kromel market, interindustry and inter-Kromel industry effects of a Kromel price change, implications on Everclear's share of the total Kromel industry, and Everclear's production costs.

Initial discussions with sales management indicated that a planning period of five years should be considered in the study. While the selection of five years was somewhat arbitrary, sales personnel believed that some repercussions of a current price reduction might well extend over seven years into the future. A search for possible courses of action indicated that four pricing alternatives covered the range of actions under consideration:

- Maintenance of status quo on Kromel price, which was $1.00/1b.
- A price reduction to $.93/1b. within the next three months.
- A price reduction to $.85 1b. within the next three months.
- A price reduction to $.80/1b. within the next three months.

Inasmuch as each price action would be expected to produce a different time pattern in the flow of revenues and costs, and since no added investment in production facilities was contemplated, it was agreed that cumulative, compounded net profits over the 5-year planning period would constitute a relevant payoff function. In the absence of any unanimity as to the "correct" opportunity cost of capital, it was decided to use two interest rates of 6 and 10per cent annually in order to test the sensitivity of outcomes to the cost of capital variable.

Another consideration came to light during initial problem discussions. Total market growth over the next five years in each market segment constituted a "state of nature" which could impinge on the Everclear's profit position. It was agreed to consider three separate forecasts of total market growth, a "most probable, optimistic, and pessimistic" forecast. From these assumptions a base case was then formulated. This main case would first consider the pricing problem under the most probable forecast of total Verlon-Kromel year-by-year sales potential in each segment, using an opportunity cost of capital of 6per cent annually. The two other total market forecasts and the other cost of capital were then to be treated as sub-cases, in order to test the sensitivity of the base case outcomes to variations in these particular states of nature. However, inter-and intra-industry alternative states of nature literally abounded in the Kromel resin problem.

Sales management at Everclear had to consider such factors as:

- The possibility that Kromel resin could effect penetration of market segment A if no price decrease were made.
- If a price decrease were made, the extent of Verlon retaliation to be anticipated.
- Given a particular type of Verlon price retaliation, its possible impact on Kromel's penetration of segment A.
- If segment A were penetrated, the possible market share which the Kromel industry could gain in segment A.
- If segment A were penetrated, the possible side effects of this event on speeding up Kromel's participation in market segments B, C, and D.
- If segment A were not penetrated, the impact which the price reduction could still have oil speeding up Kromel's participation in segments B, C, and D.
- If segment A were not penetrated, the possibility that existing Kromel competitors would initiate price reductions a year hence.
- The possible impact of a current Kromel price reduction on the decisions of existing or potential Kromel producers to increase capacity or enter the industry.

While courses of action, length of planning period, and the payoff measure for the base case had been fairly quickly agreed upon, the large number of inter- and intra-Kromel industry states of nature deemed relevant to the problem would require rather lengthy discussion with Everclear's sales personnel. Introductory sessions were held with Everclear's sales management, in order to develop a set of states of nature large enough to represent an adcquate description ot the real problem, yet small enough to be comprehended by the participating sales personnel.

Next, separate interview sessions were held with two groups of Everclear's sales personnel; subjective probabilities regarding the occurrence of alternative states of nature under each course of action were developed in these sessions. A final session was held with all contributing personnel in attendance; each projection and/or subjective probability was gone over in detail, and a final set of ground rules for the study was agreed upon. A description of these ground rules appears.

CONSTRUCTS AND GUIDES

Although each pricing decision is unique, some constructs and concepts are useful in analysing pricing situations. The models of market structure, concepts of costs, demand concepts and the company philosophy of followership or leadership, are very helpful. With full knowledge of them, a "right price" can be established. But decision makers are confronted with incomplete or outdated information. The reasoning process they employ considers answers to two kinds of questions. First is "what if" or conditional reasoning. They assess possible courses of action, and the probable consequences of each. For example, if I change prices to A, what is the probability that competitors will meet the change, will not meet it, or will meet it partially, and what will be the consequences of each competitive reaction?

Second, there is a consideration of the relationship of price changes to changes in the other aspects of the marketing programme, advertising, distribution channels, product packaging, and personal selling. Prices may also be established through research. Various prices may be tested in limited areas and the "best" price selected. Research of customers' opinions and reactions to products is often sought as a basis for price. Sometimes products are tailored to meet predetermined price points, and product quality is changed so that prices can be maintained and product-line requirements and distributors' price points met. Although price is not merely the result of costs, price-cost factors are accorded major consideration. Moreover, since price affects volume, volume affects costs, and costs affect prices, the pricing decision is a circular one. Also, a variety of cost concepts may be applied. Prices can be based on total costs, average, or variable costs. The last basis leads to a marginal approach to costs. The major contribution of economic reasoning to the consideration of costs is the idea of marginal cost. Businessmen tend to rely more on an average cost approach to pricing than on a marginal approach.

Average costs, which are rarely pertinent to an optimal decision, satisfy the desire to "cover our costs and make a profit." In reality, this reliance on average costs can lead to a decision that can actually reduce sales, increase costs, and reduce profits. However, some executives advocate that sunk costs should be ignored. They are not affected by current decisions-nothing can be done about them. Yet it is also recognized that over the long run, they must be covered. A consideration of the impact of sales volume on costs provides a useful train of thought. For instance, price theory suggests a U shape for average costs-they decline to a point with increasing volume, reach their minimum, and then increase as volume increases.

This seems to make sense, since the concept introduces the notion of economies of scale and the impact of capacity on costs, indicating that volume beyond a certain point may increase costs. In addition to cost factors, pricing decisions in basic industries are greatly influenced by governmental considerations. Some industries such as steel are treated like public utilities and, sensitive to governmental reaction, must justify price increases. Although no laws exist that require governmental approval of price increases in these industries, such increases are judged as to their being warranted. A variety of pricing practices are of particular concern to certain industries.

For example, bidding is significant in defence marketing, hedging in commodity marketing, markdown in fashion merchandise, dumping in international marketing, price deals in food marketing, and loss leaders and discounting in retailing. In formulating marketing strategy, we have dealt with only the broader relationships of pricing to selected elements in the marketing mix. Price decisions in specific situations require both experience and practical knowledge. Theory alone will not suffice. In fact, where pricing is of critical concern, pricing specialists become necessary.Nonprice Competition

Given acceptable levels of prices, non- price factors can become most important. Yet, adequate economic theories of non- price competition are lacking. In marketing, great attention is given to such non price aspects as product-differentiation, branding, imagery, packaging, service, buyer behaviour, and styling. The most important factor in modern competition is not price, but product research and development, just as to a survey of more than 200 successful firms. Then come sales research and planning, management of sales personnel, advertising and sales promotion, product service, and finally, pricing. These non price factors, which are ignored in economic theory, must be considered in establishing pricing policies.

INFLUENCES

Since prices have great impact on both revenue and competitive reactions, pricing policies are usually determined at a high executive level. The pricing task involves not only a maze of variables but also conflicting situations. Conflicts exist among manufacturers and distributors, retailers and wholesalers, and consumers and retailers. For example, intermediate and ultimate customers weigh the prices they pay, competitors are influenced and react, suppliers watch margins carefully, financial institutions consider the impact on stock, and the government assesses competitive implications. Among the present and future external factors that influence pricing policy are number and concentration of competitors, the degree of competition, profitability, ease of entry, product heterogeneity, size, legal aspects, channels of distribution, elasticity of demand, total industry demand, kind and size of buyers, and spatial forces.

But basically these are handled through consideration of anticipated cost-revenue relationships. For in the long run, prices are constrained at their upper bound by market reaction and competition and at their lower bound by costs full or incremental. The latter are most significant in the immediate term, whereas total costs reflect a long-run situation. Prices may also be the result of competitive conditions such as total collusion or "cutthroat" competition. Either is unlikely for any protracted period of time, however-the former for legal reasons and the latter for economic considerations. Although precise cost information cannot be obtained, it is even more difficult to gain information about consumer reactions to prices. The latter is obtained from surveys, experiments, and observation. For example, consider the cost-price relationships of an automobile with its thousands of parts. What are the actual materials and labour costs of each? What is the overhead burden and how should it be spread? How are joint costs to be allocated? How many autos can be sold at each price? What are the price interrelationships among items of a product line? These are difficult problems to face.

But such costs, particularly increased costs, are price factors and the cost-price spiral is widely recognized. Also, as prices increase, sales may decline, which often results in increasing costs, since fixed costs are spread over fewer units. In reality, cost accounting of the marginal variety, which is advocated as a basis for pricing, is not often used. Both the ambiguity of costs and the difficulty of deriving the data make this impractical. In practice, the relationship of actual costs to prices may be rather loose, and in fact the prices of finished goods and raw materials or components can move in different directions. Prices should be based on both costs and market influences. In essence, maximum prices are governed by market factors and minimum prices by costs, and as they change, so should prices. The tendency exists, however, to maintain prices once they have been established. It should be noted that it is not the actual price or price change that is so significant, but rather the customer's perception and interpretation of these changes.

CONCLUSIONS

The pricing process is a central mechanism of a private enterprise or market system. Price adjustments facilitate the logical allocation of resources; both buyers and sellers use them to clear markets of gluts and to stimulate production when supply is short. A competitive price system features such adjustments to achieve maximum economic efficiency. From an industry's perspective, pricing can extend or limit markets; from a company's perspective, it can increase or reduce its share of the market.

Price is the ingredient of the marketing mix that has been subjected to the most intensive analysis-particularly by economists. But as an aspect of the mix, it cannot be divorced from other ingredients. It must incorporate and reflect them. Optimal prices cannot be established, and pricing remains an art with a host of factors to be evaluated for which there are no precise measures and weights. Although theoretical models exist for establishing optimal prices, in practice, theory does not enable managers to determine the correct price. Marketing management is guided by personal assessments of market conditions, costs, and competitive situations. The actual price established is usually the result of executive value judgments. Marketing managers may not share the economists' concern with price as the primary marketing factor. In a survey of 200 businesses, it was found that "business management did not agree with the economic views of the importance of pricing-one-half of the respondents did not select pricing as one of the five most important policy areas in their firm's marketing success." Consumers do not respond to price alone; they respond to value.

A lower price does not necessarily mean expanded sales. Moreover, marketing activities influence price. For example, governmental agencies have investigated advertising as a cause of higher prices. What is price? It is the amount paid to purchase something, or a monetary summation of the conditions that give value to a product or service. How important is the pricing decision? In microeconomic theory it has received great attention; in marketing, the significance of price varies among industries, competitive situations, and products. Pricing is significant where the market impact, profit results, or both, of price variations is great, and where firms have considerable discretion over the prices charged. In many instances pricing decisions are severely constrained and are sometimes relatively unimportant.

Large purchasers of industrial goods, for instance, may specify prices at which they will buy, determine product specifications, and send specifications to suppliers for competitive bids. For other products price may not be a relevant factor. In some technical areas where products require much research and development and involve much uncertainty, a cost-plus scheme may be used. In other situations, sellers may be almost completely free to set prices, while in still others, they may only be able to decide whether or not to sell at a price. Where industries are dominated by relatively few large firms, price is not usually the critical competitive variable. Each firm recognizes that price reductions will be met by the other large firms and the profits of all will suffer. Greater attention may then be given to non- price factors. In an economy of scarcity, price is accorded more attention than any other marketing factor. In an economy of abundance, non- price factors assume increasing marketing importance and products are differentiated on other bases than price. Style, colour, symbols, and brands become more significant and higher rather than lower prices may actually increase sales. For abundance brings widespread discretionary income, and price becomes a less significant component of the marketing mix than the economic literature might lead one to believe. Non- price competition and price confusion, rather than price clarity, now seem to be the rule.

Buyers are concerned not only with price, in their purchases, but also with service, status, and image. Low price alone does not result in a transaction. Consumers are not mechanical price calculators and price reactors, as so much theory leads one to believe. They do not know all the prices, for in reality, discounts, trade-ins, special deals, and premiums cloud the actual price. Prices are limited by direct and indirect competition, costs, and consumer reaction. Several disciplines help in improving pricing decisions. Economic theory affords guidelines and concepts of demand and elasticity. Accounting furnishes considerations of costs, break-even, and rate of return on investment.

Marketing adds to this a consideration and understanding of market behaviour particularly the role of consumers and intermediaries. Pricing is a sensitive and complex decision area affecting sales, costs, and profits for both industrial and consumer goods. For consumers, price reductions and increases have symbolic meanings. A customer may associate a price reduction with a reduction in quality, the anticipation of new models, or even lower prices or poor market acceptance.

Higher prices may indicate better quality, a good image, and good value. Customer perceptions of price are important. Whereas pricing is usually perceived as a short-run action, its implications can be long-run, even to the point of shaping industry structures. Markets that may be viewed as systems of information on cost and demand determine the appropriateness of prices. They contain signals that businessmen must decode. But market information is ambiguous, fragmentary, and imperfect; it contains much uncertainty and is interpreted differently by various executives. To those who can read the signals properly, increased profits are the results. But invariably, pricing decisions are wrong and must be altered, as is evidenced by changing list prices. Thus, pricing is a process of adjustment in which incomplete data are used for important decisions. As new information is gathered, the offering can be adjusted in two ways: alteration of the price, or alteration of the product to meet the price.

4

Creating and Delivering Superior Customer Value

TRANSLATING CUSTOMER NEEDS TO PRODUCT CONCEPT

We have already said that a firm must be able to assess what its customer value is—what its customers perceive as benefits received from the firm, versus what it cost the customers to access and receive those benefits. This assessment must be done both at the aggregate, segment level and at the individual, customer level, where appropriate. The aggregate, segment-level assessment orients the firm's thinking about overall product strategy. When a firm directly interacts with its customer, the individual, customer-level assessment helps the firm configure the product within that strategy to the individual customer.

In keeping with the view that a product is really a bundle of benefits, the core value in any product for any firm is the primary benefit that the firm provides. The supplementary product includes as parts of the solution additional benefits that augment the core product. Typically, a large part of the supplementary product is comprised of services. The example presents in a graphic this view of any product offering. For the most part, the core product is a commodity, as in the example of Commerce Bancorp. All banks offer deposits, withdrawals, and investments and banking products such as checking and savings accounts, and fixed and variable income securities, and today most banks offer mutual funds.

These products comprise the core product for banks. How these products are different from bank to bank is represented in the supplementary components of the total product. Commerce Bancorp offers free checking and money orders and does not compete on its lower interest on its savings accounts and CDs. Thus, Commerce Bancorp differentiates itself on a number of different supplementary benefits to the customer, ranging from the quality of its customer interactions to a number of facilitating services such as bathrooms in its branches. Similarly, most if not all banks have an online presence, but customers at banks like Allfirst Financial can talk with bank personnel via their home personal computer.

The hotel industry is one that grew out of its room-and-board days to a total product offering that today includes a multitude of facilitating services. "Room and board" was the commodity. As all hotels in a certain level, competitors in the same segment, began offering the same set of supplementary services, such as room service, meeting and conference rooms, a swimming pool, a gift shop, personal grooming salon service, business services, cable, or Internet service in each room, these became commodity and part of the core product. By March 2001, 78 precent of all Ritz-Carlton hotels offered highspeed Internet. While only two hotel chains—Omni and Westin hotels—have laptops available for guests, most hotels in that class offer two phone lines. Thus, over time, as competing firms add supplementary services, these previously differentiating value components become a commodity and lose their differentiating ability.

Consider the recent "advances" in the form of supplementary services in the hotel industry. Electronic kiosks can not only check you in with your room key and print your bill at checkout, but can also be an electronic concierge providing a guest with directions or maps to locations of interest. Human butlers are back in the hotel industry.

A growing number of hotels at the top end will provide a bath butler to prepare your luxury bath, a technology butler to solve your gadget problems, a private butler to pack your clothes or make your plans.

If you are traveling with a baby or young child, you can find a hotel that offers a room for a nanny and kiddie perks such as baby-sitting, some one to read a bedtime story with live actors, or toys and activities for the child. If you are bringing a pet along, some hotels will even offer you special pet services for a fee! Over time, hotels in the premium category will all be offering some or all of these supplementary features.

These features become part of the standard offering and reduce themselves into a commodity for that category of hotels. You can expect that the "technology butler" service will be adopted by hotels for the business traveller segment, briefly providing a differentiating feature only very quickly to become standard fare. In designing superior customer value, a firm must translate customer needs to the specifications of a solution in terms of core and supplementary benefits.

All hotels need not have the same core product. That statement might seem confusing. Consider the Station Inn, in Pennsylvania, between Pittsburgh, and Harrisburg. It sits 125 feet from the railroad tracks. Railroading buffs sleep at the hotel just to see the freight trains, about 60 of them in a space of 24 hours. Same industry as hotels—but a somewhat different core product. Precise definition of a product can only emerge from deep inspection of the "What business are we in?" analysis.

If product differentiation is derived from the enhancement that the supplementary product provides the core benefit, what constitutes supplementary product? Starting with the familiar: customer service is a common supplementary product (sometimes mistaken as the only element in the supplementary product). There are elements of the supplementary product, such as billing and payment that are also common to all firms. They are required to facilitate the core product. These must also be viewed as part of the supplementary product to the extent that they affect customer value. A firm can add to the customer value when its billing and payment process is customer focused or can detract from customer value if it is unpleasant in the customer's experience. Thus, there are some supplementary features that are found in all products that may not necessarily be recognized as such. Services marketing scholar Christopher Lovelock visualized this concept as a flower with petals. Think of the supplementary product as composed of elements of the total value bundle that facilitate and enhance (or detract from) the primary benefit sought in a product. Visualize these elements in three broad categories: facilitating services, quality of customer experience, and brand image.

FACILITATING SERVICES

Facilitating services are all those features of the product and activities of the firm that serve to facilitate the consumption of the core product. All firms have to provide some of these services at some level. Large retailers such as Sears, Walmart, and Lowe's will provide assembly and installation services for a fee and sometimes for no charge. Table outlines the four broad categories of facilitating services—complementary services, customer education, customer access, and customer service. Customer-focused firms differentiate themselves by excelling in these facilitating services.

Complementary services are those related to the consumption of the core product. Some are almost necessary, like the waiting area in a physician's clinic or parking facilities at a hotel. Passengers on long international flights enjoy a wide range of inflight entertainment activities such as films, TV channels, and even casino-style gambling or electronic shopping and services such as being able to rent a car or book hotel rooms from the technology at their seats. Some complementary services are product differentiators. For example, recognising that some of its customers were coming in to the bank to conduct their business bringing little children with them, some Wells Fargo branches have a play area with television cartoons, Nintendo, and the like—and even sells toys to children. Washington Mutual offers calculators, pens, and piggy banks for a small fee. To compete for advertising within its *Mutual Funds* magazine for instance, the publisher, Time, Inc. offers its advertising customers anything from primary research and use of its subscriber list to assistance in customising gifts and promotions to readers or sponsorship featured on special cover-wraps. These are examples of complementary services that help differentiate value created by different providers.

Table. Categories of Supplementary Product.

Facilitating Services	
Complemen-tary services	Services that are bundled with the core product such as the insurance feature for purchases made with an American Express card, or services such as free parking that facilitate the consumption of the core product
Customer education	and assistance to the customer, for example, on the use of the product information or about customer role in the service interaction
Customer service	Convenient locations and hours of access the service such as, for example, a wide variety of customer touch points and 24/7 access to customer
Customer Problem	Problem resolution that requires service personal attention as in product ailures, refunds or special customer situations.
Quality	
Quality of the product (core andsupplementary) as well as the quality of customer interactions—including such things as professionalism, courtesy,understanding and general empathy shown to the customer during all interactions	
Brand Image	
The image of the firm or the brand contributes to the value of the product such as the reputation and status of the firm, as well as any customer relationship benefits that might be accrued as a source of customer value	

Only with an intimate understanding of the customer's value chain consumption (and creation) activities can firms begin to see what opportunities there might be to facilitate the consumption of the core product. Sometimes complementary products are outsourced and provided directly to the customer by the supplier, as Wells Fargo did when it invited Starbuck's to open locations at some of its branches.

Ultimately, these complementary products ought to be consistent with the positioning strategy for the product. When a complementary feature is offered by all competitors in a particular product category, it becomes a commodity and part of the core product for that category and ceases to be a product differentiator.

Customer education is a form of facilitating service in that it provides information to the customer about the firm or the product in such a way that it facilitates the acquisition and consumption of the product. Instruction manuals and product support via telephone, fax, or the Internet are examples of customer education. Consider what some banks are doing to be more accessible for customers looking for assistance. Tellers and managers are dressed in khakis and casual shirts to appear approachable and friendly. Bank of America has tested concierges in their lobby to help direct customer questions. Home Depot provides free classes on home improvement projects. Once again, the service feature might be a necessary component of the total product, but how it is designed and delivered may be a source of product differentiation.

Customer access has to do with everything that the firm does to make its products available to the customer and to facilitate the acquisition and consumption of the product. The hours of operation and location are a simple example of customer access for a service. The various touch points that are available to the customer to access the services of the firm or to reach someone within the firm would be a measure of the customer access. The methods of billing and payment for the product would relate to access to the product and can be a product differentiator. For example, the convenience of payment by credit card was once a source of competitive advantage. Convenience and ease of use is a critical component of customer value for any product. Services such as financing options are also related to this idea of customer access. If these are not customer-focused, they will fail the customer and the firm.

Customer service is a key facilitating service and includes the commonly understood activity of businesses related to product complaints or failures, product returns, refunds, and such. The accommodation of special requests or adapting to unusual or irregular customer situations would be an example of customer service as well. Poor customer service reduces customer value and risks losing the customer.

QUALITY OF CUSTOMER EXPERIENCE

When the total product provided by all firms contains the same set of facilitating services, the product is not necessarily a commodity. The quality of the service offered remains a source of differentiation and therefore a supplementary feature of the product. Perceived quality enhances, and lack thereof reduces, the value of the core product. For example, even when Internet service is offered by all hotels, the quality of the customer experience with the Internet service is still a differentiator. One hotel may require you to get into a closet, fish out the cables and force you to shape yourself into a yoga pose to hook up those cables to your laptop, while another hotel may offer wireless Internet access from anywhere on the property. All airlines provide seating and, depending on distance and class, also provide meals and entertainment while transporting you from point A to point B. Differentiation in seating can come in legroom and comfort. First-class services can offer six and a half feet of seat length, single seats, pajamas, and privacy partitions between seats. The quality of the entire customer experience is most definitely a source of differentiation. In Chapter 10 we will look in more depth at customers' perception of quality.

Brand image is a supplementary feature of the product in that it adds to customer value. Brand image is the sum total of all the perceptions and attitudes about a brand. The image of the firm in the general media as well as for each individual customer provides a measure of the perceived quality of the product. The reputation of a firm is usually a result of the firm's product and actions. Where there is very little tangible evidence of the product, as in the case of Web-based services, an entire industry of so-called "reputation managers" has emerged. These reputation managers are Web sites that rate the reputation of others! A firm's image is an implicit source of differentiation in the market. Brand image is the ultimate differentiator. When all else can be seen as equal, the brand image captures the essence of the difference in customer value among the alternatives available to the customer.

Firms have to determine what their total product offering is and what it should be. The value bundle of core and supplementary product needs to be designed based on what the customers expect as standard from all providers of a solution in a product category. The supplementary product might also contain features that are sources of differentiation among solution providers reflecting the positioning strategy of the firm. Firms must constantly watch the various solutions that are being offered. Sometimes the threat of competition comes from newer business models. For example, online broker ETrade surprised the banking business when it began to open ATMs with new services. A deep and broad analysis of customer needs could reveal value-creating opportunities.

To determine how best to match the total product as the superior solution to fit customer need, the firm must understand the customer's value chain. This is an integral part of the product concept development of the customer-focused firm. A thorough understanding of the customer needs and the customer value chain will help the firm conceive its product from the customer's point of view. Firms that best relate their own value chain to the buyer's value chain, said Michael Porter, will enjoy a sustainable differentiation strategy.

The value chain is essentially a chain of value-creating and value-consuming activities, where the value created as output from one activity becomes the input to another value-creating activity that in turn creates value as input for another activity, and so on. Thus, any activity can be assessed by the value it creates versus the value it consumes. This is why activity-based costing practices make a lot of sense. As already said the value creating activities *within a firm* are those that contribute to the creation of either the core product or the supplementary product. The value created by these activities is derived by the processing of the productive factors of the firm—its people, facilities, and equipment. There may be assets or value components sourced from external suppliers or intermediaries that contribute towards producing either the core or the supplementary product. Some outsourced services may even be delivered directly to the customer. When any value component of the total product is outsourced, as in the case of a retailer offering customers outsourced financing options for purchases, or airlines outsourcing catering services, there is the obvious issue of quality assurance in the value creation that is outside the control of the firm.

Externally (to the firm) when you relate other firms' value-creation activities into a value chain, you see that the value created by one entity contributes to the value created by the next entity in the value chain. The same idea is referred to by economists, in the context of forecasting, as "derived demand." The demand for a product is dependent on the market for another product, such as aluminum and aircraft sales for example. We know a homeowner who gets a home improvement job done receives (customer) value from the home contractor who in turn is receiving value from the retailer who in turn receives value in the form of products and services from the supplier or manufacturer.

LOOKING FOR CUSTOMER VALUE OPPORTUNITIES

An understanding of the role that the firm's product plays in the customer's value chain could open up value-creating opportunities. A customer-focused firm has a detailed picture of the customer's consumption domain. When a firm views value consumption activities, it can see if there are other value creating opportunities that it can leverage from its assets. The watchmaker Swatch, for example, offers wrist watches with the technology that allows them to function as electronic passes at ski resorts in Switzerland or for public transportation in Finland. Wrist gadgets can now serve not only the function of telling time, but also making phone calls, playing music and videos, browsing the Internet, or sending e-maill.

This example defies categorization of product. What is the product? It is a wallet or a pocketbook, as well as a telephone, a personal stereo, a personal VCR, and an Internet communications device! The exercise of determining what revenue opportunities Swatch's value-creating assets would offer forces a complete redefinition of the product. As we saw the (product) solution is conceived to take advantage of opportunities to meet the needs in the customer's life with the assets that the firm has. Swatch has found a way to provide value to a recreational activity—skiing—and a functional activity—public transportation. It is contributing to the "customer access" components of the ski resort's and public transportation's product. By enabling customer access, information technology provides a whole range of supplementary benefits to a variety of products.

Contrast this with the example of a firm that does not understand the value of complementary product components and the customer's value chain. A customer came out of a movie theater in Kendall Square, Cambridge, and experienced a 40-minute ordeal trying to leave the theater's parking lot. She spent 30 minutes standing in line in frigid weather to pay the $2.50 parking fee and a further 15 minutes to exit the parking lot. When complaining to the management of the movie theater, she asked if she could pay the parking fee as she bought the movie ticket. She was told that the parking lot was owned by a different company and the theater would not take responsibility for the customer's bad experience at the parking lot. In contrast, the airline SAS has been known to provide an annual dinner to taxicab drivers in Stockholm because the SAS management wants the drivers to treat passengers on the way to and from the airport with professional courtesy and respect. Clearly, firms that are customer-focused conceive their product differently from other firms, because of their intimate knowledge of the customer's consumption activities.

Information about the customer's consumption cycle, therefore, is a key prerequisite to exploring the opportunities that might be tapped. As we saw in Chapter 4, an understanding of how the customer actually benefits from the solution and the information of how, when, where, and with whom the customer consumes the product should provide some interesting revelations of what the firm is doing and can be doing in the composition of the total product solution for customers. Thus, Procter and Gamble sends its researchers to homes to observe how people actually use laundry detergent. When Samsung was trying to break into the microwave business in the late 1970s and early 1980s, their design engineers observed homemakers shopping for microwaves at the retail store. You can stay ahead of the curve by offering value through supplementary product that your customer information tells you customers will be willing to pay for. Even if the value-producing feature or activity cannot be priced separately, you may be able to command a premium for your superior customer value. Being customer-focused is critical in identifying opportunities for establishing superiority in customer value.

All decisions about the product and, therefore, the value-creating activities of the firm are based on an understanding of the value-consumption activities of its customers. What are the decisions and what are the issues to be considered in determining the total product by a firm? The three major decisions constituting the product strategy are: the product concept, the operations design, and the value creation and delivery process alredy—displayed. The product concept defines the customer to be served and what value is to be provided. The operations design defines the productive assets of the firm required to create and deliver that value for that customer. Together, the product concept and the operations design define the scope and configuration of the productive assets that can be leveraged to produce the specific customer value that maximizes profits to the firm. The *value creation and delivery process* executes the product concept with the operations design. In developing the product strategy, the firm makes a fundamental decision in answering the question of how the product will be positioned among all potential solutions to the customer's need. This positioning question poses an asset- and market-based decision that comprises two perspectives.

- The *market-based perspective* looks outward at the market and asks what customer needs can be most profitably served by the firm.
- The *asset-based perspective* looks inward, at the firm's assets, and asks what assets of the firm can be most profitably leveraged by the firm.

The market-based perspective drives the product concept and the asset-based perspective drives the operations design. Thus, the initial step in developing product strategy involves two critical analyses. The product concept requires analyses of the various segments in the marketspace, while the operations design requires analyses of the firm's productive factors. These two sets of analyses are essential to determining what value-creating activities the firm should engage in to generate the maximum revenue from its assets.

A market analysis to determine what would be the most profitable segment mix for a configuration of the productive assets of the firm is the foundation for product strategy. First you need to identify the segments and the solutions that are currently available to the segments. The target market selection or the selected market segments to be served can be based on the profitability and size of each segment that the firm's assets are best positioned to serve. Here, a formal comparison of all the current solutions from the customer's perspective is necessary. Based on this analysis, the firm is able to determine what it can provide better than the alternative available to the appropriate target market, thus framing the firm's competitive advantage. Only after such customer needs analysis is it possible to specify what would be the desired customer value in the product offering.

The intended customer value in the product offering can now be translated into a detailed picture of the product concept—what the core and supplementary product ought to be. Remember that the customer value also reflects the customer's implicit assessment of the firm's solution compared to competitive offerings and, indeed, all solutions that are available to customers in the segment. To ensure that the product concept can effectively be superior customer value, the core product should combine the imperatives that have become commodities in the product category with the appropriate features in the supplementary product to reflect superiority in customer value. Thus, the product concept embodies the product differentiation and the superiority in customer value.

The operations design decision rests on how best the assets of the firm can be most profitably leveraged and follows a sequence of questions that pertain to the productive assets and capabilities of the firm and how they should be deployed: What people, facilities, equipment assets are needed to create and deliver the product? Which employees' skills and knowledge would be needed? When and where would specific human capital be needed and for how much time? Similar questions are asked about the facilities and equipment of the firm. Of course, when the asset or resource is not available within the firm, it seeks suppliers or outsources that part of the value creation. Ultimately, the question is what competitive advantage the firm is capable of and how the assets needed should be configured.

The process decisions are about determining the specific activities of the value creation and delivery. The process of making the product and delivering it to the customer must be detailed. The value creation and delivery activities required are set in a specific sequence as discussed in the next chapter. The firm must deliberate on the structure, content, and process of creating and delivering the product to the customer.

No product differentiation from supplementary product can be seen in isolation. If the total benefits from the product are not worth the costs that the customer incurs in acquiring and using the product, the product is likely to fail. The more carefully the firm designs the process with the customer in mind, the more likely the process ensures ease, convenience and quality for the customer. Thus, the customer-focused firm designs the creation and delivery process with the customer's percep tion of benefits and costs in the value consumption process.

Firms must also recognize that since customer value is dynamic, they need to continually monitor and improve this customer value. Ignorance of the need to innovate to sustain competitive advantage is a common mistake committed by the complacent firm. The argument is sometimes made that the firm's priority of customer focus minimizes the attention to innovation. Customer focus and innovation are not contradictory, an either/or strategic decision. Indeed, to be customer-focused would mean that the firm is continually looking for new ways and solutions to meet customer needs—and to be aware that customer needs evolve as well. Now we can know what the firm needs to do to ensure that it is creating and delivering customer-focused value that can be sustained. To sustain superiority in customer value the firm must ensure that management continually assess its market and its assets to ensure that the choice of customer and the value being created and delivered by the firm maximizes the profit goals of the firm. How well is the customer value in the product concept translated to the operations design and the value creation and delivery process? Is the superiority in customer value being executed. The answer lies in the customer's judgment. Customer-focused firms will let the customer decide whether the firm's value creation and delivery is customer-focused.

Continual customer satisfaction assessment information needs to be available for the customer-focused firm to improve by changing the product concept, the operations design, and the value creation and delivery process, or to continually reassess whether its assets and capabilities are being leveraged to realize the maximum profit potential. To ensure customer-focused value creation and delivery, firms must assess customers' perceptions of the benefits they receive as well as the costs incurred by them.

As an ongoing assessment of customer value, firms must continually assess customer needs and customer satisfaction. As customer needs change, the value bundle needs to be reviewed in terms of its product concept, operations design and delivery. An assessment of customer satisfaction presents an opportunity to improve customer value. The smart firm will continually monitor customer satisfaction to understand what customers perceive as the benefits they are getting from product compared to the costs that they incur. Based on customer satisfaction, does the value bundle need to be modified and redesigned? Are the assets and capabilities of the firm being leveraged for maximum sustainable profits? If the expected customer value cannot be delivered with the existing value-creating assets, then the firm has two choices. Either it acquires or outsources the required value-creating assets and capabilities, or it determines that the target market decision needs revisiting.

MANAGING CUSTOMER INTERACTIONS

The process of delivering value is a tricky and detail-rich exercise; it requires careful planning, using techniques such as blueprinting to visualize the entire customer experience. From the customer perspective, some service encounters are critical incidents requiring more attention than others. All service encounters must be staged for a customer-focused experience just as in the production of theater.

Why does Kimberly-Clark manage the discount retailer Costco's inventory of its diapers? The firm has a salesperson live near the Costco headquarters, and a data analyst responsible for overseeing stock at 155 Costco stores in the western United States. Similarly, Procter and Gamble stations 250 people near Wal-mart's headquarters in Bentonville, Arkansas. Large retailers are asking suppliers to more actively manage the movement of products from factory to retail store shelves. PandG estimates that stock-outs amount to 11 percent of an average retailer's annual sales. When firms like Kimberly-Clark pay more attention to how its immediate customers—the retailers—create value to their customers, they demonstrate that they are being customer focused. In fact, the Kimberly-Clark salesperson passed on information on how customers place packages in their shopping cart that played into package design for diapers. Wayne Sanders, chairman and CEO of Kimberly-Clark, attributes this change to the information age.

Prior to the industrial revolution, a service orientation and the individual-to-individual interaction was the predominant mode of competitiveness. Assembly-line production distanced the firm from the customer due to the sheer number of customers and the physical distance between the customers and the firm brought about by the wonders of modern transportation. Manufacturing goods became the engine of individual and collective (national) economic growth. Mechanization far outpaced services and replaced producer-customer interaction, relying instead on intermediary institutions to provide a specialized set of competencies that the producing firm lacked. Businesses lost sight of the customer. Now, information technology has brought this full circle, back to the customer.

We call it the information age because what has changed in our time is that new technology has revolutionized the way information is handled. Another equally significant revolution is the change in the customer's domain. Customers not only have access to more information on products and service offerings, they also have the ability to interact with the providers of products and services in ways not previously possible. Providers can also present enhancements to customer experiences from the functionalities presented by technology. Service providers must, however, also manage customer participation when they utilize technology. When firms take advantage of online marketplaces, it might be necessary to make changes in organizational structure so that value creation and delivery processes are adjusted to the addition of the online delivery. Two key technologies underlie this information age technology phenomenon: the Internet and wireless communications. What customer access to these technologies has done is to bring customer interactions to a new level and to the front and centre in how a firm deals with the customer. These interactions are essentially service encounters with the customer.

Much has been said about the service encounter—customer interactions with the firm. In a way, all customer relationship management (CRM) solutions are basically technology support to ensure that the firm maximizes returns from customers by enabling customer-focused interactions. The service encounter is truly "where the rubber hits the road"—where the prospects of customer loyalty are materialized or lost. It is where promises made in advertising are honoured or reneged on, and where expectations of customers are disappointed or met. It is where all the assets of the firm need to be brought to bear. Service encounters with the customers are also laden with the challenges of a product that is produced and consumed in real time, where failures are bound to happen. When the firm designs the value creation process with the customer in mind, it will be prepared for all predictable eventualities. When the service fails, smart firms have smart processes, that recover and learn from the failure. They have service recovery and knowledge management processes in place. As firms compete more and more on services, the management of the customer interaction becomes critical to ensure superiority in customer value. As the core product is a commodity, and most facilitating services approach the commodity state, the competitiveness comes from how the customer is treated by the firm at each and every encounter. This chapter discusses a method for designing the value delivery process with special attention paid to the service encounter and the critical incidents in the value creation and delivery process. A framework for designing the service encounter based on the theatrical metaphor is offered as a way to examine the customer focus of value creation and delivery.

Analysing customer interactions can be very rewarding. Amazon constantly tracks the reasons for every customer contact. It has made numerous changes to its value creation and delivery process based on customer input. The customer service function at Amazon is considered a research lab for ways to improve the Amazon customer experience. We can turn to the unique characteristics of services to obtain a clear understanding of what is involved in a customer interaction. Something intangible is always exchanged in the interaction (intangibility). Without a customer, there is no interaction and the separation of production and consumption is irrelevant (inseparability). To conduct the interaction, the firm has the resources and infrastructure in place that "perish" when not utilized (perishability). Each interaction is unique (variability). From these characteristics, as we saw in Chapter 3, emerge situations that are challenges and opportunities typical to the service firm. We need to keep these in mind as we design the process of creating and delivering customer value. At the most general level, all customer interactions occur in a certain place (or space), at a certain time, for a certain duration, between certain entities, in a certain manner for a certain purpose. Consider these as ingredients in a customer interaction and categorize them into elements of structure, content, and process. When the customer interaction is mapped onto the consumption activity cycle, the objective of the interaction becomes the driving force behind the design of the interaction in terms of its structure, content, and process.

- Structure relates to who or what entities are involved in the interaction.
- Content relates to the subject, the task, and its significance in the interaction.
- Process relates to the sequence of steps in the interaction.

The primary decisions that would configure the structure of the interaction involve the nature of the interaction—what entity should represent the firm, should the interaction be face-to-face or not, what technology can be utilized, where should it occur, and so forth. As a complementary question about the customer: What entities from the customer's domain are involved in the interaction? Similarly, decisions determining the content of the interaction should centre around the task and include what information should be required in the interaction, what should transpire between the parties, and what value should be created and consumed in the interaction. Decisions about process would include a script of the interaction and the roles of both parties in the interaction. Any of these decisions must be based on the information that the firm has about the customer's consumption cycle and on preferences regarding these dimensions of the interaction. For example, technology may provide the firm with scale economies, but the customer may want to disengage from the script and interact with a person instead. Ultimately, the important question is what value is being created in the interaction.

As we saw earlier the execution of the product concept as the delivery of the product involves a process, a sequence of activities. Therefore, designing the product must necessarily include a design of the delivery process. Lynn Shostack proposed a technique called "blueprinting" to detail the process design in the delivery of services. The service blueprint is a map or flowchart as a visual representation of the process of service delivery. Essentially, the blueprint design is diagramed in three steps. In the first step, all types of customer interactions with the firm are listed. Next, these interactions are arranged in sequence of occurrence. In the final step, processes within the firm that are required to create and provide each customer interaction are mapped. How and what information, materials, facilities and equipment, and people are processed must be included in the service blueprint.

The customer-focused blueprint is one that is designed with the customer in mind. With the activities in the customer's consumption cycle in mind, processes within the firm need to be designed in such a way that the desired value added in the solution is reflected at each and every encounter with the customer. Commerce Bancorp, for example, encourages its employees to make suggestions in streamlining the service delivery process. Commerce Bancorp employees receive a fifty-dollar reward for finding something about a process that does not contribute to customer value and instead is an impediment to serving the customer; the bank immediately adjusts its operations.

Even as a simple representation of the value creation and delivery process, the service blueprint has a variety of important strategic, analytical, and diagnostic uses. In designing the delivery of the product, it can be used to determine the uniqueness of the service process. When compared with competitive blueprints, where and at which points in the process the firm derives its competitive advantage and superiority in customer value become evident. Thus, the service blueprint can be used in a strategic analysis of the differentiating features and benefits of the service delivered by the firm. Only with such comparative analysis of the service blueprint is it possible to ensure that the value creation and delivery processes are commensurate with the superior customer value planned in the product concept and operations design.

The service blueprint has two major dimensions that characterize the nature and scope of the service delivery process: complexity and divergence. The complexity dimension reflects the number of steps or activities in the process. A highly complex service process has a great variety of activities during the series of customer interactions. Some of these activities occur in the front stage and some in the back stage, away from the customer's view. A so-called line of visibility determines what the customer sees or does not see. The customer-focused firm will need to examine everything that the customer sees and experiences to determine whether the service delivery at the service encounter is contributing to or detracting from customer value. The divergence dimension reflects the degree of flexibility at each customer interaction. The greater the divergence, the greater the customization built into the service—the greater the number of options the customer is given to choose from at each interaction. Therefore, supplementary product benefits such as customization must be mapped into the service delivery process. Complexity and divergence decisions will determine the position of the firm's offering compared to competitive offerings. Competitive blueprints can be compared to determine how competitive value bundles differ from each other. It becomes clear that the positioning of each competitive offering is reflected in the service blueprints.

The patient experience is very carefully orchestrated to support the entire concept of the "Shouldice Method." The surgical procedure itself is probably the least sophisticated element of the whole process. The recovery process is more important than the surgery. Every step in the blueprint is designed for a speedy recovery and an overall "enjoyable" experience—despite the anxiety and pain of the surgery. The method is known for a very low recurrence rate and high customer satisfaction. The hospital even has patient reunion parties each year that are sometimes attended by as many as a thousand former patients. For this service, its critical steps are not in the surgical procedure but in in the recovery process and the total customer experience.

All customer interactions depicted in the blueprint are not of equal importance in terms of criticality towards customer value—some are more important to the customer than others. It is imperative that the firm employ its knowledge of customer expectations so that the critical interactions are highlighted for priority when allocating resources of the firm. This is the primary application of the blueprint technique.

Jan Carlson, CEO of the SAS airline, popularized the notion of the "moment of truth" in services. While each customer interaction is a moment of truth, those product features and customer encounters with the firm that are considered critical to the satisfaction of the customer are considered *critical incidents.* The critical incident technique has been applied in the managing of services to understand what can make or break the customer's experience.

The method was initially developed for the U.S. Air Force in simulations to help in cockpit design and pilot training.

A simple question to the customer soliciting a verbal description of a typically satisfying and a typically dissatisfying experience with the product and firm would yield valuable information on what might constitute a critical incident. The incidents to which the customer attributes a satisfying or dissatisfying experience are those that are critical to customer satisfaction. When a particular point in the service delivery process keeps recurring in customer descriptions of satisfying and dissatisfying experiences, it becomes clear that it is a critical incident. These incidents can also uncover "failpoints"—points in the process that are especially likely to fail to perform as desired. Some are internal to the firm and cannot be obvious to the customer, while others occur during direct interactions with the customer. For each of these, the design of the process should ensure "fail-safe" methods and have a system recovery process in place. Fail-safe processes require a metric that triggers the recovery processes. Thus, benchmarking the performance at the failpoints is critical to the successful implementation of the product concept and operations design to deliver the desired customer value.

For firms that rely on intermediaries to bring the product to the customer, critical incidents may lie outside the firm's control. Consider, for example, what Handspring, Inc. does to make sure the customers of its products are served well at the retailer. The firm sends its employees from channel marketing posing as customers to retailers such as CompUSA and ensures that its product is stocked and well displayed and that the floor salespeople are presenting the product to the customer in the way Handspring had instructed them to do. Microsoft hands out a free Casio pocketPC to every sales rep who completes its training. These examples show an awareness that customer interactions at these intermediaries are failpoints and need to be monitored.

Critical incidents help in assigning the appropriate level of resources within the firm. Thus, the service blueprint is useful from a quality control perspective. Customer evaluations of a firm's service can be linked to specific customer encounters in the blueprints and all processes directly affecting or affected by the critical incidents must be monitored for quality. Customer-focused quality control efforts can be focused on critical variables that can be controlled. Service recovery procedures must be designed into the process at these points.

Interactive technologies provided by the information age revolution are now an integral part of the design of the value creation and delivery process. These technologies work through the three primary productive components of customer value—the people, the infrastructure in facilities and equipment, and processes and systems of value creation and delivery. Consider all the ways in which the customer can interact with a firm. Each touch-point can be made by the converging technologies of today. For example, in some interactions the location of either buyer or seller becomes irrelevant. Customers can interact by wireless or wired means, which can be by voice, video, or text, initiated by either party; they are constantly getting cheaper and better in features and functionality. The basic difficulty with any of this newer interactive technology is that the objective and role of the technology can be lost sight of and the technology itself become the focus. The final measure is whether the technology is contributing towards sustainable profits for the firm by improving customer value.

The benefits of interactive technology come in the form of efficiency and efficacy. Efficiency is reflected in increasing productivity and efficacy is reflected in improved customer value. Both of these outcomes contribute to the bottom line of the firm. For a firm competing on service, interactive technology is critical to sustain profits because of what it can do to customer value. Maximize the return from interactive technologies by deploying it at the critical points; prioritized by its customer value-creating power. For example, a common source of dissatisfaction and irritation to the customer is the length of waiting time before being served. Any point in the process where there is likely to be a wait is a potential critical incident requiring the firm's express attention. If there are interactive technologies that can be used to effectively manage the customer in these situations, customer value is not threatened.

All the service components in the total product, being susceptible to the inherent characteristic of being produced and consumed in real time, force customers to the experience of "wait." As we will see in the next chapter, demand and supply need to be matched as closely as possible. To avoid idle capacity, services adopt the queuing (and scheduling) approach to processing customers, resulting in a certain amount of wait before the process begins. In multi-stage processes, which many services are, in-process waits are common as well. The problem of course is that no one wants to wait. Customers will wait for a certain amount of time that is reasonable to them as per their expectations. What is reasonable is a very subjective judgment, of course—one that requires analysis of the factors that determine the perception of waits.

Maister's work on the psychological cause and effects of wait suggests a way to reduce the negative consequences where wait is a given.

- Preprocess waits feel longer than in-process waits. Allow the customer to begin the process by completing the first step in the value delivery process.
- Unoccupied waits feel longer. Keep the customer in wait occupied with activities, preferably related to the product or service.
- Uncertain waits feel longer. Keep the customer informed about how long the expected wait is to likely to be.
- Unexplained waits feel longer. Keep the customer informed about why they are having to wait.

- Inequitable waits feel longer. Serve customer based on priority, determined by what is considered just in the ambient society.
- Value of the service. Ensure that the customer value you are providing is clearly superior to any alternative.

The most important common thread through all of these suggestions is that they all have to do with managing the customer perceptions. The firm is better placed if the customer perceptions can be influenced favourably by managing customer role and expectations in the value creation and delivery.

To varying degrees, customers play a role in the production of products and not just in the consumption. Firms that realize this have paid serious attention to how the customer fits in the organization. In services, the role of the customer is abundantly evident. Customers engage in a coproduction role. In services or in the service component of the product, customers are coproducers in self-service configurations. All services as we saw earlier involve some kind of customer participation, as in the case of providing required information to the tax preparer, for example. Even when placing the order with the provider, the customer is essentially contributing to the production of the product by providing input into product specifications. When the customer is interacting with the firm and this interaction has some relevance to the production of the product, by definition we have the customer engaging in coproducing the product. Service firms instinctively manage the role of the customers in their participation in the service. Restaurants have menus, professors have syllabi, airlines have their method of emplaning passengers according to a certain priority, etc. Sometimes managing customer roles may be in the form of a complementary service. For example, Universal is experimenting with a calming zone adjunct to its roller-coaster rides, for people who need help with coaster-phobia before they get on the ride. UPS and other package delivery firms instinctively accommodate special customer requests as to where their packages should be deposited if the customer is not at the location of delivery.

It is a matter of perspective. If we take the notion of value creation a step further, we could argue that even in the case of packaged goods, the value hasn't really been created to the customer until the customer actually begins to use the product. Value creation and value consumption are both inextricably interwoven into a continuous and overlapping set of activities. This is an important issue in a service orientation. In the case of services, customer interaction is a given. And the firm must include the customer in the design of its operations. The customer-focused firm by always keeping the customer in central view manages the role of the customer in the value creation and the value consumption activities. For example, providing excellent product assembly instructions improves the value created for the customer in an "easy to assemble yourself" product. Conversely, even with a well-engineered product, poor instructions reduce customer value. Recent product innovation studies have shown that some firms are equipping customers with the tools to design and develop their own products, ranging from minor modifications to major new innovations. PTC (formerly Parametric Technology) is a world leader in computer-assisted-design (CAD) technology, whose software solutions bring suppliers and customers together so that a client can use the software during product development to virtually interface with upstream and downstream players.

Ultimately, anything that the firm can do to manage the customer's role in the value creation as well as value consumption process is an imperative for the customer-focused firm. As mentioned earlier, Procter and Gamble is recruiting families to allow a team of their ethnographer-filmmakers to observe their daily routines to get a better sense for how their customers use household products. The actual use situation says a lot about how a product should be designed. It would also be a way to learn how the customers should be instructed in the appropriate use of the product.

How does a firm take a systematic approach to managing the customer? First, the firm identifies all the activities that the customer enacts in the value creation as well as value consumption blueprint. Next, the firm scripts the role for the customer at each activity. Firms then have to determine how best to communicate and educate the customer in playing the appropriate role. Customers' performance of their roles will depend on their ability and inclination to perform those roles. The consumer's ability will depend on consumption skills that the customer's past experience may have provided. The customer's inclination will depend on the personal characteristics of the customer. Familiarity with the service and service provider could affect the ability and the inclination of the customer in the role performance.

In the case of services and the service components of a product, customer role is managed by the service provider. The service provider's production skills and motivation could affect the way in which the service provider manages the customer's role. The service provider's familiarity with the segment and the specific customer will influence the service provider's skills and motivation in managing the customer's role performance. The service provider's production skills are reflected in its operations and customer interaction skills. The personal characteristics of the service provider can affect the service provider's motivation. When designing the service delivery process, it is important that the firm incorporate these factors on the customer's role performance.

ATTRACTING CUSTOMERS

To maximize the total lifetime value of their customers, firms must proactively manage customer relationships. As seen proactive customer relationship management should seek customer appreciation from the heavy user and attract more interest from light users with better value bundles if they can contribute more in their lifetime value to the firm. This is in contrast to the firm that may have good customer service, for example, but in its reactive mode will leave the light user relatively indifferent to the firm and the heavy user susceptible to a competitor.

Most loyalty programmes involve some kind of reward for the continued patronage of their customers. Referred to as frequency marketing, continuity programmes, awards or points programmes, or simply loyalty programmes, the goal of these programmes is to market and manage relationships with customers. First instituted by American Airlines in the 1970s to get around government regulation that prevented price competition, now many firms' programmes attempt to solidify their relationships with its customers. The rewards or awards, as they are called, may come in the form of free products and services at the firm, or sometimes even free products from other firms. The smart firms impose restrictions on the use of these rewards, so that they are used to increase demand when and where needed. For example, the hospitality industry blocks out certain dates so that the promotions are targeted at different segments to entice customer utilization at low demand periods. The problem is that many of these programmes are misguided in design and implementation. One obvious omission is evident when the lifetime calculus is compared to the criteria for the rewards.

The rewards focus on revenues for the most part. That costs are taken into account is not clear at all. A recent *Harvard Business Review* article offers data that would be a surprise for managers who have not considered costs of serving the customer. Brand-loyal customers are not necessarily profitable customers. In their knowledge of their own value and indispensability to the firm, the brand-loyal customer could make costly demands of the firm. The firm, in doling out the goodies along with the product and other business favours, may actually be spending more than it recognizes as costs of serving that customer. The only criterion for these (brand) loyalty programmes should be that they should maximize the customer equity for each customer, based on the calculus of lifetime value that we have discussed. To be meaningful and powerful in managing relationships with the right customers, these customer acquisition and loyalty programmes must specify the following:

- Objectives of the programme
- Market and customer scope of the programme
- Value for customer scope of the programme
- Impact scope (costs, timing, impact on people, process, physical assets, other customers, publicity opportunities, etc.)

The objectives of the programme need to be stated in the context of customer relationship management. What is the expected value of the programme to the firm? What specifically must the programme accomplish?

Perhaps it is to shift demand from peak to low periods, to attract new segments, to get light users to become heavy users, to promote a new product offering, or some other specific objective. Without a known objective, no programme can be assessed on merit.

The next specific decision for customer relationship programmes is to specify the customer that the programme is intended for. Often, frequency programmes are so loosely formulated that the rewards are earned by the wrong customer. Consider this example of the unfortunate consequence of a poorly guided programme. One Mr. Phillips logged 1.25 million frequent flier miles—about $25,000 worth of airline travel—with an investment of 50 hours of his time and $3,140. Mr. Phillips took advantage of an offer he found on the package of a Healthy Choice frozen entrée: 500 American Airlines miles for every 10 UPCs, with early birds receiving a double count of miles! A Mr. Fisher participated in the same programme and got 12,000 Northwest Airlines Miles.

Even if the airlines got an awfully good financial deal with Healthy Choice, one must ask who the loyalty programme attracts—whether the airlines are in the grocery business or in the airline business. How do their returns from this investment compare with the returns that they would have achieved with programmes that targeted the frequent flier instead of the frequent grocery shopper? The objectives of the programme should determine the appropriate segment or customer for the programme. The problem with most programmes is that they don't take into account the profitability of the customer. Who should be the target of the programme? Not every customer is right for the firm, as we have seen, nor is every customer right for every programme. The best programme is one that tailors the award to the target customer. Thus, giant supermarket retailer UK-based Tesco mails 100,000 variations of promotions to its loyal customers. Further, some customers may be more costly to retain, while others may be increasing their profitability to the firm. As it is evident that firms need to look at the acquisition costs and retention costs of its customer base when determining the focus of their retention efforts.

The calculus of the lifetime value of a customer is clear in its indication of what needs to be factored into deciding to which customer to target the promotion. Low acquisition costs and low retention costs are realized from your most profitable customers. At the other end are your customers who were costly to acquire and cost you a lot to serve. Given the acquisition costs, the firm must keep a close eye on the customer's cost of retention. If the firm misjudged a customer's lifetime value or committed more resources to the acquisition of the customer than the revenue stream would justify, the firm has to either reduce retention costs or stop serving the customer if possible.

For the chosen customers, the firm needs to decide what they would do to motivate the customer to act. Customer knowledge should indicate what the customer is sensitive to, so that the value of the promotion can be appropriate for the specific customer or segment. The value of the promotion may be in the form of additional product, a complementary service, a straightforward price-break, or a discount for future purchases or a gift, among other things. Software firms are able to use lead customers in beta-tests and other benefits about new and innovative offerings before the rest of the market will find out, giving these B2B customers early mover advantage in their value chains in their industry.

Of course, a projected cost/benefit analysis is a must—what additional revenues have been realized and at what cost? For service firms, and where the programme is about service components, it is imperative that the promotion take into account what it would do to the demand patterns of customers. The last thing you want is for customers to strain your operation if your programme ends up drawing more customers during peak times when you are already at optimum levels of served customers. Any programme must consider the impact on other customers, on the staff, physical assets, and the delivery system or process. For example, a shortage of airline seats infuriates frequent fliers who, as brand-loyal customers, having diligently set aside miles for use on family vacations, find they are not able to use the miles because use of awards is limited to a certain proportion of the volume on each flight and are restricted to certain times and dates. Estimates are that about 10 percent of all miles flown on a carrier can be from people cashing in on these rewards. Does it make sense for frequent flier awards to range from personal digital assistants to designer watches? Are the costs and impact of these awards assessed? Another less obvious criterion is the potential for publicity in a promotion. A promotion that is newsworthy could attract the attention of a large number of potential customers and other stakeholders.

Firms must prioritize the management of customer relationships as a firm-wide imperative. Dell Computer, for example, has a "customer experience council" consisting of senior executives from each division or business line and major function that reports to a corporate vice chairman, no less. The council oversees measurement of several aspects of customer behaviour, including the effectiveness of its loyalty programmes. Dell even measures all the costs its customers incur in purchasing and using their products, including such things as shopping, ordering, installing, operating, servicing, and disposing of products. The real value of tracking these revenues and costs over the lifetime value of the customer is that it allows firms to understand their brandloyal customers and anticipate their future needs. Such management practices will be able to deliver benefits to the heavy user to maximize their lifetime value.

The lifetime value of the customer must be calculated for each customer—an assessment of revenues and costs over the lifetime of the customer's relationship with the firm. The investment in acquiring and retaining a customer must be made based on the customer's lifetime value to the firm. A continuous monitoring of up-sell and cross-sell opportunities could increase the lifetime value of the customer. The potential customer equity from each segment or customer should determine the extent of value-creating adjustments to be made in terms of delivery process or product outcome customization in terms of value or other benefits to the customer or in terms of adjusting the price and other costs to the customer. These changes in promotion offerings to acquire a new customer or remarket to a current or inactive customer will impact both costs and revenues and their effect on the lifetime value of the customer will determine subsequent investments in acquiring and retaining customers.

Maximising customer equity requires maximising customer satisfaction by providing superior customer value. Ensuring product quality as the key driver of customer satisfaction requires checking the links between the firm's assessment of customer expectations and its ability to translate that assessment into product concept, operations design, and execution.

The doorman greeted the guest as the taxi pulled up to the Windsor Court Hotel, a 324-room hotel in downtown New Orleans, one of 120 independent luxury hotels of Preferred Hotels and Resorts Worldwide. Later, the waiter at the restaurant in the hotel accommodated off-the-menu orders—but the waiters did not make eye-contact with the diners. The guest room did not have the current edition of the Yellow Pages. This guest was one of Richey International's hotel spies, who had just conducted the Preferred test for the hotel. He has determined based on his experience as a customer that this hotel had met 88.5 percent of the Preferred standards, passing the 80 percent minimum. Firms such as Preferred want an unbiased assessment of the quality of their product and hire independent quality assessment firms such as Richey International to do the benchmarking of its hotels.

MODIFYING CUSTOMER BEHAVIOUR

Why do customers perform those interactions when they do? What will it take to change their behaviour to perform those interactions during other times? In other words, what is their behaviour sensitive to? Essentially, this analysis is reflected in a change in customer value. Segments differ in price sensitivity; different segments will switch their interaction times at different price levels. Insofar as customer value is affected by price, pricing is a powerful tool to modify customer behaviour.

Firms can do this with adjustments to the value bundle, by manipulating elements in the supplementary product. Adjustments to benefits and costs as reflected in customer value can be analyzed for its effect on customer behaviour. In how it affects customer value, the amount of customer participation sometimes allows flexible pricing. Automation versus personalized service can be used to provide varying degrees of levels of service to the customer. Customers may choose the technology during peak periods such as in the case of the self-service checkout counters in many stores. Standardized versus tailored versions can be used to shift demand. Different versions of the product with different combinations of features using product bundling are effective demandshifting mechanisms. Firms in some industries do this instinctively without much sophistication while others such as airlines and hotels use very sophisticated methods. Firms that have a good customer understanding are better equipped to adjust customer value without losing superiority among its competitors.

Price promotions are powerful demand-shifting tactics. There are numerous examples of price promotions, from early bird specials to discounts during low periods. The problem with most price promotions is that they are not aligned with demand fluctuations, so that the effect on the customer is random—where the firm is simply hoping to build demand without a sense of timing and how it would affect demand fluctuation patterns. Unless the firm's assets always operate at the same level of capacity, every firm should be offering price promotions to bring in customers during periods when the assets are idle. Anything from customer convenience in payment such as interest-free deferred payment schedules to outright price bargains are common uses of pricing for this purpose.

Customer behaviour can be modified to the benefit of both the customer and firm with customer education on how demand fluctuations can affect their own customer experience. Different industries have different norms in the attempt to inform the customer about peak times so that those customers who would not want to be subjected to long lines and wait times can choose to interact with the firm during lowdemand periods. Most customer service phone lines will inform you of the expected wait times after you are greeted and logged in to their system. When there is an exaggerated peak and valley pattern, firms must find ways to educate customers to move their patronage to a different time or access point to help with the strain on capacity while reducing the risk of a poor customer experience that could be detrimental to customer loyalty and sustainable profits.

Customer lifetime value and customer preferences and priorities can and must be kept in mind when attempting to manage demand by changing customer value. Any type of membership benefits and loyalty programmes can be designed to essentially manage demand. The terms of the membership programme need to ensure that the firm is managing the use of its productive resources according to the lifetime value of the mix of customers being served. Any change in customer value with demand and supply management technique should be monitored for its impact on brand loyalty and customers' lifetime value to the firm.

Managers of firms competing on service will find that demand fluctuations are a definite predominant challenge. Demand must be managed by smoothing the demand fluctuations and making capacity adjustments in value-creating assets. The smoothing of demand requires building demand during low and shoulder periods and moving excess demand from the peak times to the low or shoulder demand periods.

When and why do the customers' consumption activities and demand fluctuate as they do? Demand analysis must include an understanding of customer behaviour and the profitability of the various customers and segments being served at different times during a demand period.

Thus, their sensitivity to various customer value changes would determine the appropriate demand-shifting actions that the firm might attempt.

Capacity management requires a cost-revenue analysis of the productive factors or the value-creating assets.

That analysis should focus on capacity utilization. What is the profitability of the value bundle created by capacity (assets) that was being utilized? Are the value-creating assets being used to serve the maximum profitable customer mix at any given time?

Table. Customer-Focused Analysis: Yield Management.

Elements for Analysis	Analytical Questions
Susceptibility to	What is the extent of variation in actual demand around the Fluctuating Demand:mean level of optimal customer demand levels?
Demand Analysis:	What are the patterns of demand? What is the segment mix in these patterns? Why do they interact when they do? What are the sensitivities of each customer/ segment towards demand management techniques that essentially change customer value? What is the profitability of the customer/segment?
Capacity Analysis:	At what points in the blueprint do the customer interactions occur in the blueprint? What is capacity of processes and resource allocation serving each customer interaction? What is the profitability of the value bundle or the contribution of the specific process towards cus tomer value? What should the priority of resource allocation be for the customer interaction processes and productive factors of the firm? What is the elasticity of the capacity for these productive factors?

CUSTOMER INTERACTION

The essence of customer-focused design of the value delivery process is in the design of the customer interactions that make up the blueprint.

Customer interactions have gone by various names in research on services—service encounters and moments of truth, for example. Designing the customer interaction requires analysis and decisions regarding three of the structural dimensions of the value delivery process: the process itself, the participants, and the physical facilities and equipment. Customer roles have to be defined so that customer participation can be designed into the delivery process as appropriate.

One useful framework that has utility in managing customer interactions is to view service encounters metaphorically as "drama." When firms and customers interact, firms try to put on the best performance—like theater. The firm's *actors* perform their roles for the *audience*, the customer. In any service, there are actors and audiences involved in producing *performances* in a *setting*. For example, restaurant customers are audiences with hosts and waitstaff as actors in the physical setting of the restaurant. Just as in theatrical production, there is a stage (the dining area) and a backstage (the kitchen); there are acts (welcome and seating, appetizers, main course, and dessert), scripts (menu and specials), props, and costumes. Each element is carefully choreographed to produce the intended impression on the audience. Any service provider can examine each of these elements and determine the exact impression that would be appropriate for each customer segment. The "drive-thru" or take-out type of fast-food restaurant confronts different impression management challenges compared to the sit-down type of restaurant.

Different types of services would require a different combination of these theatrical elements for the desired impression. Services rendered at arm's length over the telephone or by mail, such as in investment brokerage services or credit card services, would see these elements differently from the face-to-face setting of hotels or airlines. Internet "clicks" retailers would find a different set of issues compared to the "bricks" retailers. Hybrid retailers have to approach the issues differently for the two different settings.

In some cases, the performance is shared by a number of customers, as in a restaurant or a hotel or airline where customers share many aspects of the firm's productive factors—employees, facilities, and equipment. The setting dictates a shared product, and some aspects of the setting are visible (onstage) to the customer and some are invisible (backstage). Performers or actors (frontline employees) utilize scripts, costumes, and props in their performances. Every feature or theatrical element is carefully choreographed for the intended impression. Therefore, just as in theater, managers can focus on impression management for customer-focused business activities. World-class service firms like Disney employ a service orientation profile (personality and skills) in their hiring; they call their employees the cast and carefully train them in both operations and customer interaction skills. Disney's "guests" are treated in a customer-focused manner evident in the culture, in the way the cast is empowered and motivated to provide customer-focused performances.

What is the type of setting where the customer value is delivered? There could be no interaction necessary with the value provider at certain phases in the consumption cycle, and there could be phases of physical, face-to-face interaction, or electronics-mediated interactions. At each interaction, the value provider must determine the line of visibility between onstage and backstage, what is or should be visible to the customer. What is the process and duration of the various steps in the interaction, and what kinds of orientation must there be for the participants? What is the customer role in each setting, and are there other customers in shared experience? The following table presents the analytical questions based on the theater metaphor to determine whether the value delivery process is customer-focused.

Table. Framing the Customer-Focused Analysis.

Role of Theatrical Elements	Customer-Focused Analysis for Managerial Actions
Actors —who the actors are and how they play a role in creating the performance for the audiences with their respective scripts	What profile of each employee would What are appropriate criteria in selecting and hiring and trainin employees? What kinds of scripts are appropriate for each employee? Are the employees motivated to be customer-focused?
Audiences -who the audiences are, their preferences and biases and how they derive value from the various elements in the theatrical production	What is the profile of the appropriate customer? Are the needs of the customers and how the product works in the customer's consumption activity cycle clearly understood?
Setting —the constituent elements of each setting	What is the configuration of the setting? Are all of the tangibles that including costumes, props, make up the setting carefully décor, ambience, etc., and examined for the appropriate value it how they create the must add for the customer? desired impression for the performance
Performances —the various acts and scenes that make up the entire performance and how they create the desired impression for the audience	What are the various steps in the process of serving the customer? Are the acts and scripts customer-focused? Are the actors wellrehearsed and supported for their performances from backstage? Is the customer given the necessary instructions to get the most out of the solution?

Ultimately, all of the theatrical elements need to be carefully directed and choreographed to provide the appropriate impression. *Servicescape* is a term that refers to the immediate physical and social environments containing a service experience, transaction, or event. The servicescape plays a number of different roles such as packaging the value bundle, facilitating the value delivery activities, socialising the employee and the customer, and differentiating the product. Managers must understand which servicescape elements can be controlled for the desired behaviours from both employees and customers.

What is the role of each process in the value creation and delivery as seen by a firm with a customer focus? What should the structure and content of the process include by way of design? What are the critical points in the process for its meeting customer needs and preferences? The firm should have in place metrics and customer-determined benchmarks that will trigger recovery procedures, anticipating that the firm will sometimes fail the customer. Using the theatrical metaphor, any impression that the actor, the audience, the setting, or the performance imparts must be examined and managed by the firm. The focus is on the effect each customer interaction or service encounter has on customer value from the customer's point of view. Customer-focused firms design the value creation and delivery process with the customer in mind.

Value-creating assets are perishable in that when idle they incur costs without generating revenues. Demand and supply management is an imperative for any firm, especially those that produce services or whose products have a significant proportion of service components. Analysis of demand patterns and capacity utilization should drive yield management in a customer-focused firm.

Following the dot-com crash, four-star hotels and other premium services in the hospitality industry found themselves losing business as corporate expense accounts became slim. By mid-2001, in some locations, you could get a room at the Biltmore, the Ritz, and others like the Waldorf-Astoria and the Plaza in New York for less than at such budget hotels as Holiday Inn, Comfort Inn, or Best Western. In the previous year, hotel overbuilding had prompted analysts to warn of lowered revenue from lower prices. The dot-com boom had hotels already committed to expansion. Similarly, key players in the cruise industry, also "over-built" following an ambitious expansion spree, found themselves in a quandary. The number of berths among cruise ships worldwide was scheduled to increase by about 12 percent over a couple of years from the year 2000. Vacations on cruise ships could be had for bargain basement prices. Why are firms better off selling their product for such low prices? If your assets are idle, you are still incurring fixed costs. As long as the variable costs are covered, every additional revenue dollar contributes to the fixed costs and profits as contribution margin. This situation is especially common to service firms and to firms whose assets are being used to provide services directly to the customer. Every firm must continually assess whether its value-creating assets are producing maximum value at minimum costs.

Most firms instinctively reduce capacity during low demand periods and increase capacity during peak periods. The airline industry uses sophisticated methods to get customers committed early so that a certain level of demand is ensured for any given period. The 21-day and 14-day airfares ensure that airlines have a certain amount of capacity filled before prices are raised. Idle capacity is too expensive to carry. Hotels will charge you if you are a no-show and some will charge you a fee for a late checkout. Upscale restaurants, too, will charge for no-shows and require cancellations to be made 24 hours in advance, just as hotels do. Underutilized capacity could be disastrous for any firm, especially for assets that produce services. The hospitality industry is a perfect example of capacity-constrained services that have to address the challenge of perishable revenue opportunity from their productive assets. An important consequence of the inherent characteristics of services and of service components in products is that the product cannot be produced without customer interaction—production and delivery processes of services are idle unless a customer is being served.

For a number of reasons, fluctuating demand is an inevitable fact of life for businesses. There are times when demand exceeds supply and at other times supply exceeds demand. For firms that produce services, the demand-supply mismatch results in situations where revenues and profits are not maximized. Every firm seeks to generate the maximum profits from its assets; this goal requires yield management for long-term profit maximization. The firm needs to manage demand and supply such that it attracts and serves the segment mix that provides the maximum total profitability.

This chapter is about managing demand and supply so as to maximize the returns from value-creating assets. Patronage and capacity of productive assets must be managed for maximum profitability. The pattern of the flow of customers dictates the utilization of the productive factors of the services. Thus, the firm should attempt to smooth peaks and fill valleys of fluctuating demand patterns. The first section is about how to understand the demand patterns and to study the capacity of the value-creating assets. Next, a method for assessment of the revenue-generating utilization of the firm's assets is presented. Finally, ways in which the firm can improve the profitability of its value-creating assets are suggested.

The task for the firm with perishable assets is not just increasing demand, but increasing demand during low-demand periods. The key is in the timing of demand as much as in volume. The task may be more one of shifting rather than building demand. This is a daunting task, especially when the causes for demand patterns may be uncontrollable, such as weather or the school year and other institutionally imposed events such as filing taxes or reporting quarterly earnings. When the demand is predictable and some behaviour can be modified, firms must find a way to shift demand when and where possible. Before you attempt that, you need to have a sense for the profit implications of shifting demand, because the quality of demand is just as, if not more, important than its quantity. Quality of demand refers to how desirable the customers are. A firm should be relentless in making sure that the profitability of the mix of segments making up demand is maximized. Segments are selected to be served based on the long-term profitability of the customer. Therefore, demand management should consider the timing of the demand as well as the profitability of the demand being served at all times.

A measure of how well a firm is doing is the profits generated from its assets. In service firms, this is yield management, plain and simple. Yield management is practiced extensively by airlines and hotels in the service sector, for example, as they seek to maximize the returns from assets by maximising the utilization of capacity at maximum margins. Customer-focused firms base their yield management techniques of demand and capacity management on their knowledge of the customer behaviour without losing sight of creating and delivering superior customer value and sustaining profits for the long term.

Demand management should aim to manage volume and revenues generated by the firm for maximum long-term profits. Capacity management, at the same time, should aim to minimize the costs of production along with maximising utilization for maximum profits. When competing through service, the analysis required for customer-focused yield management is discussed. Customer-focused firms will seek to understand customer behaviour to manage customer demand. They will also seek to cost-effectively adapt capacity to the demand level without affecting the customer experience. The objective of yield management is to manage customer behaviour and the capacity utiization of the firm such that returns from assets are maximized.

MANAGING CUSTOMER RELATIONSHIPS

The task of creating and delivering superior customer value must be complemented with the selection of the appropriate customers and the effective management of relationships with those customers. Managing customer relationships should be guided by an understanding of what the customer's equity is to the firm. Customer equity, the value of customer to the firm, improves as superiority in customer value improves. Since customer equity is perhaps the firm's most valuable asset, the firm must continually seek to improve customer value for it best customers. A firm's potential return on customer equity should determine the investment it makes in customers. For its most valuable customers, the firm must guarantee superior service quality and customer service, with special attention to recovering from inevitable product failures when they occur.

Maximising long-term profitability comes from maximising customer equity—firms must maximize the lifetime value of the customer, including revenues, referrals as well as costs of serving the customer. Customer acquisition and retention efforts must be guided by the worth of the customer to the firm.

Maytag provides premium service to its premium customers—those who purchase the Neptune line of laundry machines. Neptune customers get a dedicated staff, a separate toll-free number and fast response on service calls. This is an example of the common business practice where firms allocate resources by the profitability and value of the customer. They utilize the opportunity in directly interacting with individual customers to determine customer profitability and allocate assets accordingly. And what are the benefits of the practice of differentiating among your customers?

Broadly referring to the practice as CRM can sometimes defeat its purpose by losing sight of the basic meaning of the term: managing customer relationships. Managing customer relationships would mean actively planning, organising, directing, and controlling a firm's business relationships with its customers. The term might be "new" in its current usage, but the business practice of managing relationships with customers is certainly not new. What has prompted the increased attention to CRM is new technology: how well firms can practice CRM has been advanced by information technology in the new economy. Technology brings with it the risk of missing the benefits of huge investment costs if used inappropriately, however. The benefits can seem so attractive that the costs are rationalized until the technology fails to deliver. The American Customer Satisfaction Index, a measure of customer attitudes towards about 200 companies from over 30 different industries, has actually shown a decline, while at the same time CRM technology investments had grown about five times. When used with a fundamental understanding of CRM's purpose, the benefits of CRM technology enabling the business practice of managing customer relationships are clearly powerful. Siebel, Peoplesoft, Oracle, and other CRM technologies are really customer information management or customer knowledge management systems. These systems gather data and convert it to knowledge that will help firms in their customer relationship management activities.

The most significant contribution of CRM technology to the practice of business is not the technology itself, of course. It is in what the technology does to the practice of managing customer relationships. Because technology has now made it easy to do all the tasks of gathering and analysing customer information, firms have been able to discover and realize the incredible benefits in proactively managing customer relationships. For example, Continental Airlines' customer information system allows its staff to mine data on passenger profitability and is also able to suggest remedies and perks for special requests or complaining customers.

Customer benefits from relationships with firms have been conceptualized under three categories: social, psychological, and customization benefits, in a two-part study using interviews and surveys. Financial services such as brokerage and banking are heavy users of CRM technology. Deregulation and information technology have effectively blurred the boundaries between those two once-different financial institutions. They have had a heavy reliance on information because these are primarily knowledge businesses. "Signature"-level customers at Charles Schwab wait no longer than fifteen seconds to reach a customer service person, whereas other customers can wait ten minutes or more. Some banks have coded their customers so that customer service reps can decide on rates and fees depending on the customer's profitability code. Centura Banks rates its customers on a profitability scale of 1 to 5. The most profitable customers get service calls from staff and an annual call from the CEO.

Attrition rate at the bank is down 50 percent in four years, and—more interesting—the percentage of unprofitable customers has gone down from 27 percent to 21 percent. The hospitality industry was able to slash 50 percent of its promotion programmes and increase response rates by 20 percent with a good database of response behaviour from its mailing list. CRM systems have provided firms with the data they need to determine the revenues and costs to serve at the individual customer level, allowing firms to prioritize their allocations of value-creating assets and resources to the more profitable customers. According to AMR research, the CRM market grew from $200 milllion to $1.1 billion between 1994 and 1997, and is expected to reach as much as $16 billion—an indication of how much firms want this technology to manage customer relationships. A firm's knowledge about its customers has allowed it to adjust customer value based on the profitability of the individual customer.

Just as with power, information technology has to be used judiciously. Discriminating against less profitable customers can seem unreasonable to all paying customers and could backfire with publicity. ATandT withdrew its minimum usage charges for its basic-plan customers who were unprofitable. GE Capital tried to charge credit-card users who were not accruing a minimum level of interest charges and ended up having to sell its credit card business. When used appropriately at the individual level, information technology can be very rewarding. Capital One's senior vice-president for domestic card operations, Marge Connelly, says, "We look at every single customer contact as an opportunity to make an unprofitable customer more profitable."

CRM systems are not just about profiling customers and loyalty programmes. To derive maximum benefits, one must broaden the thinking about CRM technology. The technology should be viewed as knowledge-based systems that seek to prioritize commitment of a firm's assets and resources to the more profitable customers while enhancing the relationships with ALL (right) customers. Pricing may not be the appropriate means to deal with the unprofitable customer. CRM systems give the firm access to information that may reveal other ways to manage the unprofitable customer. *Enabling* the managing of customer relationships is the goal of the CRM system. Managing customer relationships is about selecting, acquiring, retaining, and enhancing relationships with customers by using an intimate knowledge of the customer's consumption domain to maximize the return on the firm's assets. With CRM systems, firms have the knowledge and the technological capability to identify, retain and enhance more desirable customer relationships.

This chapter covers issues regarding which customers to acquire and retain for maximum sustainable profits. How do you assign value to customers and what is involved in that evaluation? Who is the right customer? Who should be in your customer portfolio? Firms look at customers as investments. How do you value these investments? Or, What is the equity of your customers?

SELECTING THE RIGHT CUSTOMER

Markets consist of customers with diverse needs and differences in customer profitability. When serving multiple groups of customers, the goal must be to maximize the profitability of the combination of segments. When different segments are targeted, the firm essentially has a portfolio of customer segments—just as investors have an investment portfolio that maximizes returns at a certain level of risk, firms manage customer portfolios for maximum profits. In other words, this is the selection of customers at any point in time, compared to other segments, from which the firm can generate maximum profits. Firms must attract these most profitable customers and then must establish systems and procedures to retain them.

Most firms serve different segments depending on how the definition of segment is aggregated. The "segment-of-one" used in common business parlance to refer to customization at the individual level is really a maximum disaggregation of a market segment. As we saw in the preceding chapter, most firms facing fluctuating demand and experiencing peak, shoulder and low periods of demand find it inevitable that, at different times, different segments must be served. Of course, each of these segments must have a compatible fit with the overall corporate image as well as a compatible fit with the products, services, employees and other customers. The question is, are they selected based on their combined long term value to the firm?

Most firms forecast the volume and revenues from various segments at certain price points at different times in the purchase cycle. In the typical firm, sales and communications efforts follow these underlying assumptions in pricing and in messages targeting sales prospects. The typical firm then attempts to formalize advertising campaigns to reach as many people as possible in the case of packaged goods. In the case of business-to-business services, the salespeople focus on making a sale. Most firms then struggle to orchestrate all these messages for acquisition of the customer in a coordinated fashion. Much less attention is paid to the retention of the customer. Barring the well-run operation, common business practice for many firms is short-term oriented. On the contrary, a customer-focused firm begins by approaching sales as acquiring the right customer. The customer-focused firm also approaches the acquisition of customers as only the first step in managing the relationships with its customers. Once acquired, the customer must be retained. But, not always retained at any cost—a necessary condition is that the benefits outweigh the costs of acquiring *and* retaining that customer.

Customer-focused firms align all their activities and processes in acquiring and retaining the right customer. They see their value-creating assets as most profitably leveraged by focusing on the most valuable customers. In principle, the value of the customer is determined by contribution to the firm's objectives over the lifetime of the customer.

The right customer is that customer whose inclusion in the firm's target market helps maximize returns on the firm's assets.

A FIRM'S MOST PRECIOUS ASSET—CUSTOMER EQUITY

Ask a manager, "What is your firm's most valuable asset?" Chances are that you will not get the response, "my customers." You will find even fewer firms that actually make an assessment of this value in any real sense. The valuation of the customer is implicit in sales figures—essentially, the revenues generated by customers of the firm. What is the flaw in using sales as a proxy in valuing a firm's customers? Consider this. Two customers with the same cash value of purchases may not be of the same value to the firm. There may be differences in the cost of serving these two customers. The true value of the customer to the firm, or the equity that the firm has in that customer, must include all revenues and also all costs related to that customer, as in financial investments.

A recent framework by a team of researchers defines customer equity as the "total of the discounted lifetime value of all the firm's customers." They articulate three drivers of customer equity: value equity, brand equity, and relationship equity. They define value equity as the objective assessment of the utility of the brand, and value equity is driven by quality, price, and convenience; brand equity as the subjective assessment of the brand above and beyond the perceived value, and brand equity is driven by brand awareness, attitude towards the brand, and corporate ethics; and relationship equity as the tendency of the customer to stick with the brand, and relationship equity is driven by loyalty programmes, special recognition and treatment, affinity programmes, community-building programmes, and knowledge-building programmes. Their framework—the customer equity diagnostic—is offered as a way to determine which customers to acquire as well as what will enable their retention.

If we define customer value as the value of the firm or a product as perceived by the customer, customer equity is the converse and refers to the value of the customer to the firm. If the objective is to maximize the returns from your investments—the customer portfolio—you must maximize customer equity. This makes sense because you can maximize sustainable return on assets by maximising customer equity for the long term. To maximize customer equity, we must be able to measure it. If customer equity is simply the value of a customer to the firm, we can articulate that value in the same way that customers articulate our value to them. Just as customer value is the difference between benefits and costs to the customer, conversely, customer equity is the difference between the benefits and costs to the firm in serving a customer. One team of researchers describes their method of measuring customer equity as follows: "[we] first measure each customer's expected contributions towards offsetting the company's fixed costs over the expected life of that customer. Then we discount the expected contributions to a net present value at the company's target rate of return for marketing investments. Finally, we add together the discounted expected contributions of all current customers." Evident in their metric are the following important points about customer equity:

- It is the sum of the equity of all of a firm's customers.
- It summates the gross contribution of each customer, taking into account benefits as well as costs of serving a customer.
- It includes consideration of future revenues and variable costs from each customer.
- It is a time-discounted present value of future benefits to the firm.

It becomes evident that the customer equity concept when disaggregated to the individual customer level allows us to look at the revenues and costs of serving an individual customer. It helps answer the question, which customer should we serve? The ideal customer to the firm is the one that gives it the maximum long-term customer equity, which theoretically you want as a brand-loyal customer. However, as we will see in the next section, the converse is not true, because not all brandloyal customers provide maximum customer equity.

The concept of brand loyalty is a well-researched topic. The notion of a customer having a lifetime value and the prominence of database systems in managing customers have spawned a renewed interest in relationship marketing. Just making repurchases doesn't make a customer brand loyal. There must be some commitment by the customer to the firm for relational continuity reflecting a positive patronage bias. Not all brand-loyal customers have a positive disposition to the provider—some relationships may be forced because of a lack of choice. Brand loyalty reflects a financial, social, or structural bonding with the customer. Relationship marketing seeks to enhance the mutual benefits from the relationship with the right customer—seeking brand loyalty from the right customer. To determine who the right customer is, we need to understand what benefits the firm expects from an ideal customer.

At the outset, it is clear that the stream of purchases from the brandloyal customer is the primary benefit. In truth, the value of a brand-loyal customer to the firm must go beyond the purchases made over the lifetime of the relationship with that customer. As we know, revenues can be direct and indirect. Direct revenues are all of the customer's purchases, and indirect revenues are the cash value of all of the other benefits the customer accrues to the firm, in the form of direct revenues from referred customers. Costs to serve are drastically reduced, as brand-loyal customers are generally easier to serve. The argument is that as customers get familiar with the firm, its processes and products, customers will require less costly assistance from the firm in purchasing and using the product. Loyal customers may even be able to open up ways in which to reduce the costs of serving the customer. Other benefits of brand loyalty would include product improvement contributions, new product opportunities, ideal sources for market information, and favourable word of mouth. At an overall level, all these benefits add up to a degree of stability and potential growth for the firms. Those brand-loyal customers who are committed in their patronage recognize their benefits from the firm and show commitment in the provider firm.

To select the right customer, the firm must be able to measure the value of the loyal customer from all these benefits as well as the costs of acquiring and retaining that customer. It is not easy to quantify all of these benefits. But it is possible to calculate the direct and indirect revenues from each customer. It is also possible to calculate the acquisition costs and relationship maintenance costs. Information technology has allowed us to obtain that data and made it easy to calculate the lifetime value of a customer.

A commonly used practice inherited from the direct marketing industry experience is called RFM (referring to "recency, frequency, and monetary data")—a method to determine whom to send promotions from among your customers. It takes into account the value of a customer's purchases, how recent they were, and how often they were purchased. As with the danger of any one approach, RFM has been used without much consideration for other important dimensions of the most valuable customer, such as how profitable the customer really is. RFM is therefore not a proxy measure for the lifetime value of a customer. Indeed, if the costs of serving different customers show a variance, then the RFM method could attract the wrong customer. As we know, there are three main factors in calculating the lifetime value of a customer. It is not just a simple product of the value of each purchase and the number of times the customer will purchase the product over that customer's lifetime. The lifetime value of a customer should also include referral value. And, it should include the lifetime costs as well. CRM technology has made it possible to do this, but, how many firms actually use this understanding in how they design and implement their CRM solutions?

Lifetime revenues is the sum of all purchases that the customer will make. An assessment of the progression of purchases over the lifecycle of the customer is a key point to be made here. For instance, consider what a college student's financial lifecycle would mean to a bank. First, it is a savings or checking account with a debit card and perhaps even a credit card. The college student may also be a good candidate for an education loan. Once graduated, this ex-student is now in the market for a car loan, and quite soon a home mortgage. Once other life events such as marriage and children occur, there are more car loans, mortgages, home equity loans, trusts, custody accounts, education loans for children, and associated financial products that a typical family would need. USAA, the life insurance and financial services company, follows marriages, births, and other life events so that it can advise customers on changing needs. Every firm should attempt to develop such a long-term consumption profile for the typical customer in each segment, charting their potential purchases over a lifetime to take into account the life events of the customer—a customer lifecycle analysis. A similar case may be made for business customers based on an assessment of growth potential, so that any B2B firm has to project the growth of its customers and factor that into a lifetime value calculation.

Not all customers become brand loyal. We have seen that superior customer value is a prerequisite for brand loyalty. What percentage of new customers find the firm's customer value to be superior? The lifetime value of a customer must also factor the probability of the acquired customer becoming brand loyal. The probability consideration takes into account that a customer may not be a good fit, that a competitor may have been able to provide a better fit, or that the need situation changed for the customer, such as in the case of relocation of the consuming unit.

Lifetime Costs

An activity-based costing approach allows a firm to account for direct costs that the firm incurs in the relationship with a specific customer. Once again, with information technology it is possible, where it makes sense, to attribute marketing and operating costs to individual customers. To obtain the full benefit from CRM investments, it is important to track costs at the individual customer level as well. Costs include acquiring and remarketing to the customer over the lifetime of the customer. Costs also include value creation and delivery costs of serving the customer. Thus, the costs after acquisition include not only the costs of serving the customer, but also relationship maintenance and development costs such as the costs of cross-selling or upselling, called remarketing costs. Once again, as in Equation B, the costs related to the first purchase are separated from that of lifetime purchases so that the probability of repeat purchase is taken into account when calculating lifetime costs.

The indirect revenue of referrals from a loyal customer is an often overlooked aspect of customer equity. The typical CRM solution and database marketing approaches ignore the referral power of a customer in calculating the lifetime value of a customer. Most firms do not even capture this data, partly because it is difficult to obtain information when knowledge systems in a firm are not configured to obtain it. The other reason may be that firms are not proactively looking for referrals from their loyal customers in any systematic way.

How is the value of referrals from a customer calculated? To answer this question requires looking at the process and mechanics of how referrals work. Who provides a referral? Customers who are satisfied and who have a certain degree of loyalty are the ones who are likely to convey favourable messages about a firm and its products and services. A key piece of information needed here is what level of satisfaction a brand-loyal customer needs to have before being likely to refer a customer. The next obvious question is, who receives the referral? Customers are likely to convey this information to family, friends, and colleagues. However, not all who receive the referrals are appropriate customers for the firm. What proportion of the customers who received the referral are good candidates for the firm? Out of the ones that are appropriate for the firm, not all are likely to be suitably influenced by the referral to make the first purchase. Finally, if a purchase is actually made, what proportion of referred customers makes repeat purchases? Those that are moved to try the product may not all turn into loyal customers, but if they do, then their lifetime purchases add to the value of the customer making the initial referral. Equation C reflects these fractional outcomes in the mechanics of calculating referral value.

Maximising the collective lifetime value of its customers should be the goal in managing customer relations. By increasing the number of customers *and* by increasing the lifetime value of each customer, firms can maximize their long-term profitability. From earlier study it becomes clear that to maximize the lifetime value of customers, you need to:

- Maximize lifetime revenues
- Maximize lifetime referrals
- Minimize lifetime costs

Potential customers in a target market are by definition not yet customers. They may or may not be aware of or inclined to purchase from the firm. Firms have to nurture customers' dispositions to the firm through a number of stages before they can benefit from the loyalty of those customers. The acquisition process of customers could begin at any of the different stages on the road to loyalty. Customers may or not be aware or have an understanding of the features and benefits of the product. If the knowledge of the product is favourable, customers may have a liking or preference for the product. Some customers may even have purchased the product but may not be repeat purchasers, may not be loyal to the product, or may have switched to a competitor. The right customers from any stage need to be moved towards a state of loyalty to the firm and its products. Can CRM technology be configured to capture information about the customer's stage in this process?

Once the appropriate customers are acquired, firms must look for increased usage and frequency, cross-selling opportunities, and trading up to premium versions. Retaining customers requires proactive customer management. If not, as indicated earlier customers are likely to be indifferent to the firm, and a heavy user may become impatient and switch to the competition. Proactive customer management seeks to increase interest in the light user and treat the heavy user with appreciation and respect. Thus, in keeping with equation A the goal of maximising lifetime revenues is achieved by maximising the average purchase per year as well as the duration of the customer's relationship with the firm.

Referral customers have very low acquisition costs, since your brandloyal customers did the marketing for you. Following the mechanics of the process of word of mouth, it is clear from equation C that maximising lifetime referral value requires maximising the number of referrals from each customer and maximising the lifetime value of each referred customer. To maximize the number of referrals, one must maximize the drivers of referrals from a customer. In other words, firms must attempt to increase the probability of a customer making a referral of profitable customers. Firms must move loyal customers to become advocates of the firm.

When word of mouth is seen as a powerful customer acquisition tool, firms will find a way to stimulate referrals. Many firms are not proactive in stimulating referrals, assuming simply that "good word of mouth will happen if we do a good job." What must firms do to increase the value from referrals?

First, firms must identify the current and potential advocates of the firm. Firms must proactively look for individuals and organizations that are likely sources of referrals and stimulate and reward them for the right kind of referrals. Satisfied and loyal customers are not the only ones who can stimulate positive word of mouth. There are opinion leaders: such individuals and organizations as consumer reports, firms such as Gartner and Forrester, who might be considered experts in the field, and most important, the general and trade media. Other ambassadors for the firm include players in often overlooked sources such as suppliers, resellers, employees, and other stakeholders such as investors. Community chat rooms on the Web are rich sources of information for the firm about what word of mouth is transpiring among its stakeholders.

Second, firms must attempt to stimulate referrals. Any new customer acquisition activity should record information on how the customer was moved to deal with the firm. When the firm obtains and records this information in the consumption profile of any customer, it is able to use it to calculate the average number of customer referrals made by each current customer of the firm.

Customers and advocates with similar profiles need to be approached about playing a referral role. Since some customers may be amenable and others not, firms must explore what it would take to move suitable customers to play an advocate role.

Finally, from Equation C it is also clear that the better the fit between the referred customer and the firm's products, the greater the lifetime referral value. Research has also shown that the customers referred to by satisfied customers tend to be a particularly good fit with the firm and its products and services. The fit is better than with those customers attracted and acquired through marketing messages such as advertisements and coupon mailers. Brand-loyal advocates bring in like-minded customers. To get referrals to actually make a purchase or try the firm's offerings, it is necessary to get some incentives into the hands of the referred customers.

Reducing the costs of acquisition, costs of serving, and the cost of remarketing per customer can increase the lifetime value of a customer. Reducing costs to serve means that you need to be more efficient in the yield from your value-creating assets. We are drawn back to the discussion in Chapter 8 about yield management. Costs to serve per customer is reduced when you increase the cost efficiency or the capacity utilization efficiency. To reduce costs of acquisition and remarketing you need to be more effective in your marketing, both to new and to current customers. CRM technology can be used to continually learn from experience and utilize knowledge to reduce operating and marketing costs at the individual level.

DEMAND ANALYSIS

Demand analysis is a critical review of the profitability of customers being served at any given time so that demand management methods. Creative financing skills and practices by the firm can provide cost efficiencies in raising capital and purchase conveniences.

Demand analysis begins with detecting and identifying the demand patterns. Are there discernible nonrandom fluctuations in demand? Firms must first establish the cycles of demand in terms of the time frame across which demand fluctuations occur. Take the example of customer call centres. Utilization patterns may reveal that there are peaks and valleys during the day as well as across the days of the week, weeks of the month, and months of the year. By mapping customer interactions over a demand period, firms can identify all of these peaks and valleys in customer demand patterns. Since each time frame has a different pattern of fluctuation, firms must identify when they occur in each time frame. What is the extent of the fluctuation—how high are the peaks and how low are the valleys? Firms might want to focus on those peaks and valleys that display the highest variance from the desired levels of capacity utilization.

As the timing and patterns of the fluctuations are determined, it is also important to establish at which points in the firm customers interact and to identify the utilization patterns at each point of customer interaction. Managers must look at their blueprints and determine the demand patterns, particularly at the failpoints, for all of the appropriate time frames. The variation in significance of the failpoints makes it imperative to prioritize capacity allocation decisions according to their significance in affecting customer value.

It is necessary to identify the customers or the segments that interact at the different times and to determine their prospects for profitability. Different segment-mixes are likely to patronize the services at different times. Further, the proportion of each segment within the total number of customers served at any given time could be different. To enable prioritising capacity allocation, the size and profitability of each segment need to be examined. The size relates to the volume of revenues received from the customer, whereas profitability includes the revenues as well as the costs associated with serving that customer.

Yield management objectives cannot be met unless the firm understands customer behaviour in interaction patterns over the relevant time frames. Firms must use their understanding of customers to determine what causes the fluctuation in their demand patterns. Why do these patterns occur? What factors affect not just the customers' purchasing patterns but also their consumption patterns? When customers' consumption activities require interaction with the firm, it would require identifying the demand patterns in each interaction activity and its effect on the firm's capacity. This is where customer knowledge is critical. Without an understanding of the customer's purchasing and consumption decisions, it would be impossible to attempt effective demand management. Why do customers in each segment interact with the firm at the times that they do? Can that behaviour be changed and if so, what will change that behaviour? Once that is determined, it becomes apparent that the next question is: Are the costs of changing that behaviour worth the incremental effect it has on total profits? The answers to these questions lead to possible avenues for the firm to explore in its attempt to change customer behaviour.

Capacity analysis complements demand analysis and begins with identifying the processes in the blueprint that relate to each customer interaction. Very simply, the capacity in terms of servable customers for each value-creating process supporting each point of customer interaction needs to be calculated. The firm must identify what productive factors can be profitably adjusted to demand patterns by increasing or reducing capacity without affecting the quality of the customer experience. The alignment of the firm's assets and resources to demand fluctuations will require an analysis of the capacity of the productive factors of the firm.

The productive factors of employees, equipment, and facilities, allocated over a period of time, determine the capacity of a firm. The amount of time that the productive factors are available divided by the average time it takes to serve a customer gives the number of customers that could be served. Since the capacity for a service depends on the various steps in the process, the weakest link in the process, or the bottleneck, determines the capacity of the whole process. Capacity for a multistep process is said to be balanced if all the steps in the process are about equal in the number of customers they can serve in the same amount of time.

As we saw in the previous chapter, not all customer interactions with the firm are likely to be of critical importance in the customer experience. In order to prioritize the attention of capacity management practices, it is important to focus on those customer interactions that are likely to be critical incidents—the failpoints. Next, the cost of the productive factors for the value-creating processes for those critical incidents needs to be ascertained. The key question is: What is the feasibility of stretching or shrinking the productive factors? For each capacity-determining productive factor, an important input into capacity management decisions is how costs and customer value are affected by its shrinking or stretching.

There are several implementation considerations in determining which capacity management practice is appropriate in a situation. For example, what is the minimum capacity at which the firm must operate? The minimum capacity at which a firm must operate takes into account the volume of customers required to cover fixed costs (assuming variable costs are already covered in the pricing). The maximum capacity is, of course, the maximum number of customers that can be served. The optimum level of operation is not at the maximum capacity. Within this minimum-to-maximum range of capacity, there is an optimum capacity level at which both profits and customer satisfaction are maximized. Handling more customers than that could result in deteriorating quality. For example, there is a maximum tolerable waiting time at each interaction for most customers. When wait is inevitable, as we saw in the preceding chapter, there are considerations to be made. The main consideration is how these waits affect customer value. For example, in-process waiting is a less significant contributor to customer dissatisfaction than preprocess waiting. Adjusting capacity requires an analysis of wait time and its effect on customer experience.

Service firms must determine their optimum capacity based on frontline employee-customer ratio, such that quality is not compromised. For example, in airlines, the ratio of airport agents to passengers ranged from 15 to 1 at Continental to 68 to 1 at Southwest. Of course, the ratio should make sense based on the service design. As Southwest does not issue traditional boarding passes, they require fewer ticket agents at the airport. Similarly, frontline-to-customer ratios are commonly used as benchmarks in industries such as health care, education, and the hospitality among others. At every customer interaction point in the value creation and delivery process, firms must judge the desirable ratio of frontline capacity to customers.

Many operations optimization techniques seeking to minimize costs allow firms to ignore customer satisfaction unless specifically built into the algorithm. These yield management techniques ought to be designed and implemented with the primary

The objective for any firm is to maximize the return from its assets. To accomplish this, firms are naturally inclined to garner the most profitable segment of the market for which they are best suited. Firms need also to analyze the profitability of segments being served with the timing of their interactions with the firm. Which type of customer makes the interactions at what point in the demand period/cycle? The firm can then allocate its resources according to that profitability analysis.

It is possible to calculate a yield index to indicate how well a firm is doing in the realization of its profit potential—not revenues, but profits. The difference between the average price actually charged and the cost to serve the customer is the average profit per customer. Multiplying average profit per customer by number of customers should approximate the total profit of the service firm, which can also be seen as, simply, total revenues minus total costs. From an efficiency point of view, actual realized profits should be compared to the maximum potential profit. Equation A depicts this total profitability index as *revenue efficiency* (actual versus maximum possible revenues) minus *cost efficiency* (actual costs versus targeted costs). Since revenue is price times volume, Equation B translates the total revenue efficiency into price efficiency and volume efficiency. *Price efficiency* is the average price charged divided by the maximum price that could have been charged. *Volume efficiency* is the number of customers served compared to the number of customers that could have been served at full (optimum) capacity. The total cost efficiency can be similarly translated in the equation. Target costing, a technique used to determine the lifecycle cost at which a company must produce the product for a customer, would be very useful in ensuring that the profitability of the value produced by the assets is feasible.

If profit efficiency can be seen as price efficiency minus cost efficiency, Equation C reveals that the *yield index* for the firm is the profit efficiency multiplied by the volume efficiency. Equation D suggests that you could calculate these efficiencies for each segment to arrive at the yield index of each segment. Segments with the highest yield are served so that the total lifetime profitability of the segment mix is maximized.

Calculating the profitability efficiencies for different segments would reveal that not all customers cost the same to serve, just as not all customers bring the same revenues. Thus all segments are not equally profitable. Some cost less to serve and some bring more revenues than others. But, there maybe cyclical periods when you need the relatively less profitable customers to help generate revenue from idle capacity, as long as price charged can cover the variable costs and have some profit left over to help cover fixed costs. Firms need to examine the size and profitability of all of the customers/segments that are being served by the firm. Only then can firms pick the segment mix with maximum total profitability across a demand cycle.

They must also get the specific customers to interact with the firm at specific points in the demand cycle according to their profit contribution to the firm. In a hypothetical case: the proportion of the segments in the segment-mix must be such that the firm is maximising the sale of its most profitable value bundles as well as maximising serving the most profitable customers. The most profitable customers are gauged by their lifetime value.Thus, if value bundle I is the most profitable product for the firm, the firm should attempt to increase the percentage of this value bundle sold during any given time period. Further, assume that there are two segments A and B in this example. For each value bundle during a given demand period, the firm should maximize the proportion of the high-profitability segment being served.

Any yield management approach seeks to improve price efficiencies or cost efficiencies and at the same time attempts to maintain the demand at optimum levels. This is a challenge because of the inherent trade-off between price and quantity demanded. If you lower price, you could increase volume, but that does not automatically convert to profits because you may have sacrificed revenues and you could be spending more to attract and serve these customers. In other words, when you lower the price, you may improve volume efficiencies but lose price efficiencies and cost efficiencies as well. Therefore, a systematic approach to determine the most effective way to match demand and supply requires simultaneously measuring price, cost, and volume efficiencies.

Productive factors of the process are represented by capacity in the number of customers that can be served by the people, equipment, and facility. With activity-based costing methods, their costs can be assessed against their contribution to customer value.

Firms attempt to keep costs down based solely on financial criteria. Indeed, any adjustments to capacity that must be made to keep costs down must be based on their impact on customer value. Consider how some common practices to adjust capacity might effect customer value. Firms attempt to shrink capacity during low periods of demand. Practically speaking there is a limit to this—hotels cannot shrink or expand the number of rooms, for example. But it can close off rooms and other physical facilities and equipment for maintenance and reduce the staff during low periods. Customer-focused managers will consider the impact of these actions on customer value for patrons being served during that period.

During peak periods, firms increase staff and bring all equipment and physical facilities into the operation. When other opportunities to increase capacity are utilized, such as outsourcing, then quality control is the issue that has to be traded off with the cost and volume benefits. Firms may also investigate other customer value opportunities if it can put its value-creating assets to a different use. When the margins are attractive and the value-creating assets during low periods can be reconfigured to produce a different solution, firms might consider acquiring more capacity. In general, capacity management is about expanding capacity during peak times and decreasing it during periods of low demand so that cost and volume efficiencies can be maximized. Demand management involves smoothing the peaks and valleys so that revenue and volume efficiencies are maximized; the most common techniques are pricing and promotions tactics. An important question in this whole exercise is to determine whether the service lends itself to the various capacity management techniques. Ultimately, the customer-focused firm will maintain a caveat in adjusting capacity: how will it affect customer value?

When different segments must inevitably be handled at different times of the demand cycle, an important consideration to be made is availability of alternate segments. For example, Bermuda began targeting younger travellers, under the age of 49, to boost its offseason visitor revenues. With a resident population only one-tenth the size of the number of annual visitors, Bermuda's local economy depends on tourism. About a third of Bermuda's visitors are passengers on cruise ships. These cruise ship arrivals being seasonal, Bermuda is looking to attract younger vacationers year round instead of just the spring and summer high season. Bermuda used a guarantee to support perceptions of off-season weather—at least 68 degrees or a 10 percent discount in any hotel, dining, shopping, or ground transportation service! Segments can be mixed by their time of use or time of purchase. As a demand management tool, the timing of various consumption process activities such as purchase and use are levers that the firm can use to make its demand more predictable and to manage the utilization of its assets. For example, the time of purchase, use, and cancellation in travel, entertainment, hotels, and conferences, must all be considered in managing demand in service firms and in firms where assets are being used to produce services.

Group business is a savior for the hospitality business. It ensures a large volume of committed demand from one customer—but groups are usually booked far in advance and the price is discounted. The firm has to leave itself the appropriate amount of capacity for the anticipated "full-rated" customers for the same time period to be purchased closer to the time of use. When the anticipated demand is low, firms are forced to look for segments such as trade shows, business conferences, and executive seminars and the like. The Royal Caribbean Cruises positioned one of its new ships as "the first million dollar conference centre at sea." Segments to be served at any given time can be selected based on their lifetime value and their responsiveness or sensitivity to customer value changes.

Managing segments for maximum profitability by shifting demand involves understanding the sensitivity of the segments to the product bundle. Adjustments to the product can change customer value and shift demand. The productive factors can be aligned by the sensitivity of the segments to changes in customer value in such a way as to shift segments to other points in the demand cycle. But first, the firm must understand: What are the service preferences (value), sensitivity to price, and promotion specials? Will changing the customer value by changing either the benefits or costs of the value bundle change customer behaviour or shift demand to low-demand periods?

CONCLUSION

Firms create and deliver customer value as a bundle of benefits contained in a core and supplementary product. Since the core of any product is a commodity, the competitive advantage comes from the supplementary product. Designing and delivering superior customer value is all about adding value to the customer's value chain and doing it better than the competition. Paying careful attention to the details in each and every encounter with the customer ensures a customer-focused delivery of the value created by the firm. Since the customer-focused firm competes on service, it also faces the classic challenge of any service firm—matching demand and supply. In order to maximize the profitability from its value-creating assets, firms have to determine the most profitable mix of segments for its customer portfolio.

How do you design customer-focused solutions that compete on service? Let customer information drive the decision on how best to leverage the productive assets of the firm. Market-based as well as asset-based assessments are necessary to configure value-creating assets into core and supplementary product benefits that provide a sustainable competitive advantage.

How does a small startup bank beat the big boys of the banking industry in their own backyard? Commerce Bancorp in New Jersey is not your standard bank. You will find their branches open at 8:00 AM and at 8:00 PM, and for most of the day on weekends. Vernon Hill, founding CEO of the bank, who also owns Burger King franchises, has embraced retailing practices in successful firms such as Walmart, Home Depot, and Starbuck's. The core product at Commerce Bancorp is the business of banking, of course. But the total solution includes access and convenience benefits for the customer that most definitely distinguish it from other banks. There are even bathrooms for patrons in each branch at Commerce Bancorp. The total solution for any product includes a core product with supplementary features that in combination present a resultant value to the customer. Product differentiation and superior customer value is not in its core product, but in that total solution. The total solution for Commerce Bancorp is not just banking delivered by human or automated tellers in physical branches, it is banking at the customer's convenience when, where, and how the customer wants it.

Indeed, the difference in a customer-oriented firm is very evident at any Commerce Bancorp branch. Commerce bank has found powerful ways of differentiating itself by being customer focused and then it has been able to execute its customer-focused value creation and delivery.

Firms create and deliver value from their assets. Firms must determine how they might be able to create customer value that is superior to the alternatives available to the customer. With a customer focus, the firm seeks to design a superior solution that will provide the firm with sustainable profits. This chapter covers issues and decisions involved in conceiving, designing, and delivering the customer-focused product offering. What must happen to ensure that the productive assets of the firm, facilities, processes, and people, are set up to create and deliver customer-focused value?

5

Risk Management

FUNDAMENTALS

Risk management is attempting to identify and then manage threats that could severely impact or bring down the organization. Generally, this involves reviewing operations of the organization, identifying potential threats to the organization and the likelihood of their occurrence, and then taking appropriate actions to address the most likely threats.

Traditionally, risk management was thought of as mostly a matter of getting the right insurance. Insurance coverage usually came in rather standard packages, so people tended to not take risk management seriously. However, this impression of risk management has changed dramatically. With the recent increase in rules and regulations, employee-related lawsuits and reliance on key resources, risk management is becoming a management practice that is every bit as important as financial or facilities management.

There are several basic activities which a nonprofit organization can conduct to dramatically reduce its chances of experiencing a catastrophic event that ruins or severely impairs the organization.

Organizations should regularly undertake comprehensive, focused assessment of potential risks to the organization. This focused assessment should occur at least twice a year by a team of staff members representing all the major functions of the organization. The assessment should be carefully planned, documented and methodically carried out.

Comprehensive checklists help a great deal to quickly review a wide range of organizational aspects. Other aspects require more careful review.

Checklists in the following sections cover almost 140 considerations to ensure a well run and highly protected organization.

GOOD MANAGEMENT

Efforts undertaken to manage an organization well also contributes to sound risk management. For example, a fully attentive board with a wide range of skills may be the most important guard against major threats to an organization.

Careful strategic planning and effective supervision helps ensure organizational resources are closely aligned to accomplishing the organization's mission, and that staff and volunteers are treated fairly and comply with rules and regulations.

Every organization must have up-to-date policies which guide the relationships between staff and management. There has been a noticeable increase in lawsuits regarding wrongful termination, harassment and discrimination, disagreements about promotions or salary actions, etc. Parties to lawsuits include the organization, management and/or board members. Therefore, personnel policies must be reviewed at least once a year by an outside advisor who is an expert about all of the employee-related laws and regulations.

Be sure that management is well versed about the policies. Typically, courts will interpret actions by organizational personnel as representative of the organization's preferred course of action and superseding related, documented policies.

You might first review this information and then invite an insurance agent (or better yet, an insurance broker) to visit your organization to provide you an overview of the types of insurance typically sold to nonprofits. Note that many insurance professionals might not understand the nature of nonprofits. Therefore, you might first ask a few people from fellow nonprofits for references.

As dreadful as it may sound, you must schedule two hours sometime during the year to close your door and study your insurance policies.

Note any questions and pose them to your insurance professional. Ask him or her to provide you a written, clear description regarding any ambiguities and to do so on company letterhead with his or her signature.

Note that Directors and Officers Insurance (D and O, and covered in the above "Insurance Against Liabilities" section) is increasingly considered because of the increasing number of lawsuits. In addition, D and O insurance helps attract highly experienced board members. Be sure your D and O insurance covers "insured vs. insured" which covers employee-related lawsuits and also covers ongoing costs to address a lawsuit (rather than paying only when the outcome of a lawsuit has been decided).

RESOURCE MANAGEMENT

People

This aspect of risk management is often overlooked. Each key role in an organization should have some type of resource to back up performance of that role.

For example, another person in the organization should have general understanding of another person's role in case that other person for some reason is not able to perform the role. The use of up-to-date job descriptions, todo lists and receiving regular status reports both help to ensure understanding of how others carry out their roles. Have a staff member back up another member who is on vacation.

During staff meetings, have a staff member give a presentation about their role and how they carry it out.

Ensure that each critical role has at least one backup person who can step in to conduct the role.

The backup assignment should be part of the person's job description to help the person take the assignment seriously.

General Facilities

- Always lock your doors. This seems obvious, but too many organizations fail to do so.
- Ensure your fire protection systems are fully functional by scheduing to test fire alarms twice a year or demanding that your facility's owner test alarms twice a year. Note that certain electrical equipment can be severely damaged from water sprinklers. Arrange adequate covering or arrangement to minimize water seepage if overhead sprinklers open up.
- Conduct inspections twice a year, including to:
  - Inspect floors for ripped carpets
  - Look for cables or wires laying on the floor (tape over them if you have to)
  - Notice any electical outlets with black soot hear outlets (this indicates electrical shortages)
  - Ask all staff if their office accommodations are sufficient, *e.g.*, their chairs are entirely comfortable (tilted correctly for their backs and at the right heights), is lighting sufficient for desk and computer work, etc.
  - Notice any heavy items on or near the floor which staff must continually stoop to lift, *e.g.*, boxes of paper for the copier or printers; open boxes before they're set on the floor or stack heavy items in a storage room on a shelf
  - Ensure all doors have fully functional door knobs (it's amasing how long people can tolerate something as small as a knob that continually jams so the door is difficult to open)
  - Ensure there is a well-stocked first-aid kit available to all staff
  - Post emergency numbers on the wall near the central phone
  - During the winter, ensure adequate ice removal, e.g., spread sand over ice or use salt to melt ice
  - Schedule ten minutes in a staff meeting once a year for the entire staff to reflect on the quality of the facilities

Preventing Employee Theft

Many people consider accounting a tedious job, but not John Lewis. Throughout his three-year tenure with Unified Trucking he had ostensibly been a model employee, missing only a few days of work and conquering the Herculean task of bookkeeping single-handedly. The companyÕs continued growth and profitability were the only indications management had ever needed to determine that John performed his job well. His professionalism and dedication made supervision unnecessary. John insisted on handling any problems or discrepancies personally, and made it clear that the buck stopped with him.

In fact, many bucks did stop with him, followed him home and neatly deposited themselves into his bank account. In three short years John managed to use his authority and exclusive bookkeeping access to bilk the company of nearly $100,000. As often happens, JohnÕs illicit activities were only revealed by accident. If janitorial workers had not discovered a suspicious amount of discarded receipts, the theft would have continued undetected.

Specialists say the cost of employee theft and embezzlement adds up to billions of dollars annually. For most companies, employee theft is a much more serious concern than burglars or shoplifters. In the retail industry, where theft of all types is a recurring problem, businesses recover an average of $1,350 from each employee apprehended for stealing, compared to $196 recovered from shoplifters. With dramatic figures like these, taking steps to eliminate theft and graft within a firm are sure to yield returns.

Should you consider your business immune to employee theft, think again. Security experts estimate that as many as 30 percent of all employees do steal, and that another 60 percent will steal if given sufficient motive and opportunity. The current economic hard times only add to the temptation of personnel to take what does not belong to them.

Yet protecting yourself from pilfering may be easier than you think. A comprehensive programme to eliminate employee theft can be simple and inexpensive, while at the same time increasing productivity and providing avenues for improved management-worker relations.

Know the Frequently Used Schemes having an elementary understanding of the more common forms of employee theft will help you formulate a strategy for subverting them. Here are just a few:

- Forging Receipts: Salespersons can charge a customer one sum, ring up a receipt for less, and pocket the difference.
- Hiding Receipts: When bookkeeping is sloppy and little supervision exists, employees can keep cash and receipts without raising an eyebrow.
- Pocketing Loose Change: Small sums of money, such as fees or petty cash, may not be missed at all.

- Pilfering Merchandise: Goods your firm purchases may never even make it to the shelves.
- Fictitious Payroll: Occasionally personnel managers will authorize salary for fictitious workers, then keep it for themselves.
- Overbilling Expenses: Managers with expense accounts may submit receipts twice and be reimbursed twice, or inflate actual expenses incurred.
- Purchasing Fraud: Employees sometimes declare themselves suppliers of nonexistent goods, and subsequently reimburse themselves handsomely.

Watch for the tell-tale signs of internal theft. One subtle but noticeable indication of dishonest employees may be an unexplained rise in their living standards. Be careful, however, as newfound wealth or sudden success may occur for a number of reasons of which you might not be aware. Be absolutely certain about a staff memberOs misconduct before making accusations that can strain worker relations, or even elicit a lawsuit.

Pay close attention to management-level personnel who insist on handling routine clerical tasks themselves. And be on guard for clients complaining about overcharging or inconsistencies in shipping and billing practices. Following up on customer grievances often reveals clandestine theft.

Some employees have theft in mind from the start. You should be able to weed out these people by performing thorough background checks on all new hire prospects, particularly for sensitive positions involving the flow of money. Call previous employers to verify resume and application information. Invest sufficient time to make sure applicants do not have a history of stealing from previous employers, and that all credentials and references are valid. Do not be overly zealous, however. Some good workers have made mistakes they genuinely regret and have never repeated them.

Many businesses conduct honesty testing in their hiring procedures and evaluations of current staff members. Honesty tests are standardized, commercially available written examinations that provide psychological evaluations of a candidateOs ethical dispositions and attitudes towards work. These tests can purportedly identify problem employees who have either stolen in the past or who will be unproductive workers. Honesty testing has been hailed by some for helping to eliminate pilfering, reduce employee turnover and increase productivity. It has also been criticized and challenged by those who feel the tests are either inaccurate or a violation of rights to privacy and other civil rights.

While the majority of workers will not go out of their way to steal, the best defence is careful supervision that removes any easy opportunities. Even though delegation of tasks is unavoidable, try to have a management-level supervisor oversee inventory and bookkeeping. If this is not possible, consider dividing these tasks among several staff members so no single employee has too much authority. Shifting responsibilities from one person to another allows them to check each otherOs work for accuracy and suspicious activities. It also makes collusion between employees, or between an employee and an outside source, such as a distributor, considerably less likely.

Occasional inspections or audits of inventory and bookkeeping help in preventing fraud and theft. Have an outside auditor or top manager perform the inspection on a periodic but unscheduled basis, thereby keeping records current and reducing theft opportunities. Requiring accounting employees to take vacations can also help the monitoring of bookkeeping records. Those who cover during vacation absences serve as an additional check on accounting discrepancies.

Most successful embezzlement schemes would have failed if inventory and accounting records were organized and up to date. If records are always behind and the work is sloppy, theft will be much harder to detect. You should regularly reconcile invoices and payments, as well as shipping and receiving bills. At least one software package is available that automatically examines your records and checks them for suspicious activities. Even without the sophistication of specialized software, your current accounting system may be able to give you useful information, such as revealing accounts that consistently show discrepancies.

It is possible to install physical obstacles to theft, such as alarm systems and secured, restricted areas. However, be aware that such obvious measures can have a negative effect on morale. While overt tactics to deter theft help prevent losses, they also convey very clearly to employees that they are not trusted.

Workers will be less likely to steal if you create an environment in which they think there is a good chance of being caught. Training and "employee awareness" programmes can inform workers about stealing problems and keep them on the lookout for theft of any kind. A good programme can be motivational and enjoyable — highlighted, for example, by group rewards for departments that show decreased rates of theft. When management and labour work together to solve the problem, an additional result can be improved relations and higher morale.

To make a security programme such as this effective, it is crucial employees know they can turn over incriminating information on anyone in the firm without fearing job loss or other repercussions. Stress that management and supervisors are not above suspicion and that employee complaints will be taken seriously. Some programmes feature special phone numbers or other means for workers to leave anonymous tips. Others offer rewards for informants while still guaranteeing their anonymity. A more positive approach may be to institute a profit-sharing plan which fosters loyalty, encourages personnel to monitor one another, and brings each employeeOs interests closer in line with those of the company.

The most troubling cases of employee theft occur when workers are in desperate financial straits. Common problems, such as heavy medical expenses, can temporarily put people into situations where stealing seems necessary for survival. Let employees know in advance that they can come to management for assistance rather than resorting to theft. Although no company is a charitable organization, consider helping distressed staff members find financial counseling. Some businesses even go so far as to provide short-term loans for reliable personnel.

Intimately linked with financial problems and theft is employee substance abuse. If your firm does not already have a procedure for screening workers for drugs or alcohol, it may benefit from one. Even if the company doesnOt actually test, the mere threat has an effect and may weed out some people who might otherwise steal to support their drug or alcohol habit. A programme that assists with counseling for personnel who admit to problems could help ameliorate the stranglehold these substances put on employees lives, including their finances.

To reinforce these other measures, a company should distribute clear, written policies on ethical behaviour to be signed by each employee —including the owner. It should be emphasized that there is no such thing as an "acceptable amount" of employee crime, and that, in fact, none at all will be tolerated. There should also be no double standard at work: all infractions should be punished regardless of how important the person or how small the infraction.

When formulating policies for theft and graft, some difficult decisions are involved. For example, should every employee found stealing be dismissed, or worse yet prosecuted? Or should the punishment fit the nature of the crime and be sensitive to extenuating circumstances, such as financial troubles? Be aware that severe punishments can sometimes do more harm than good, straining relations with employees and causing those who do steal to be extra careful in covering their tracks.

Employees need to know that one uniform ethical standard applies to everyone in the firm. Executives and managers should be positive role models for workers. If management is found dipping into petty cash, fudging on expense accounts or taking home equipment, personnel will feel justified in doing the same. As is always ideally the case, leadership and direction begin at the highest level.

When an envelope containing an entire dayOs worth of transactions disappeared, Dianne Oliver — owner of an eight-employee Merle Norman cosmetic franchise in Concord, California — immediately decided to institute a more formal system of storing money. "It's now put into a locked cash drawer under the computer after each transaction, with the employee entering the stock number if a product was sold, the method of payment, and how much was paid. The computer indicates the amount of change to be given. Each night, We tabulate to see that everything matches up." Oliver, who finds this method also helps her "keep control of inventory," does frequent checks on popular items to ensure no stock is missing. "And employees can buy all beauty products at wholesale, which helps eliminate temptation." "High ticket" items are placed at the back of the 1,000-foot store, with only a few display products kept up front near the door. In addition to a wide range of beauty supplies, Oliver also sells watches and jewelry, which are kept in locked cases. "The watch case is even chained to the countertop," she explains. "And whenever an employee permanently departs, every lock is changed."

PROJECT MANAGEMENT

Project management is a carefully planned and organized effort to accomplish a specific (and usually) one-time effort, for example, construct a building or implement a new computer system. Project management includes developing a project plan, which includes defining project goals and objectives, specifying tasks or how goals will be achieved, what resources are need, and associating budgets and timelines for completion.

It also includes implementing the project plan, along with careful controls to stay on the "critical path", that is, to ensure the plan is being managed according to plan.

Project management usually follows major phases (with various titles for these phases), including feasibility study, project planning, implementation, evaluation and support/maintenance. (Programme planning is usually of a broader scope than project planning, but not always.)

Almost any human activity that involves carrying out a non-repetitive task can be a project. So we are all project managers! We all practise project management (PM).

But there is a big difference between carrying out a very simple project involving one or two people and one involving a complex mix of people, organisations and tasks.

This has been true for millennia, but large-scale projects like the Pyramids often used rather simple control and resource techniques including brute force to 'motivate' the workforce!

The art of planning for the future has always been a human trait. In essence a project can be captured on paper with a few simple elements: a start date, an end date, the tasks that have to be carried out and when they should be finished, and some idea of the resources (people, machines etc) that will be needed during the course of the project.

When the plan starts to involve different things happening at different times, some of which are dependent on each other, plus resources required at different times and in different quantities and perhaps working at different rates, the paper plan could start to cover a vast area and be unreadable.

This was a problem facing the US Navy in the development of the Polaris missile system. There were so many aspects to the project that a new technique had to be invented to cope with it: the PERT technique. This and later developments led to mathematical techniques that can be used to find the critical path through a series of planned tasks that interconnect during the life of a project.

You could begin the story of modern project management from this time. But that would be unfair as project management is not only about planning but also about human attributes like leadership and motivation.

Nevertheless, the idea that complex plans could be analysed by a computer to allow someone to control a project is the basis of much of the development in technology that now allow projects of any size and complexity not only to be planned but also modelled to answer 'what if?' questions.

The original programmes and computers tended to produce answers long after an event had taken place. Now, there are many project planning and scheduling programmes that can provide real time information, as well as linking to risk analysis, time recording, costing, estimating and other aspects of project control.

But computer programmes are not project management: they are tools for project managers to use. Project management is all that mix of components of control, leadership, teamwork, resource management etc, that goes into a successful project.

Project managers can be found in all industries. Their numbers have grown rapidly as industry and commerce has realised that much of what it does is project work. And as project-based organisations have started to emerge, project management is becoming established as both a professional career path and a way of controlling business.

So opportunities in project management now exist not only in being a project manager, but also as part of the support team in a project or programme office or as a team leader for part of a project. There are also qualifications that can be attained through the professional associations.

One reason for the rapid growth is the need to understand how to look after complex projects, often in high tech areas, which are critical to business success but also have to use scarce resources efficiently.

Most people still want their projects to be on time, meet quality objectives, and not cost more than the budget. These form the classic time, quality, cost triangle.

In fact if you have an unlimited budget and unlimited time, project management becomes rather easy. For most people, however, time and money are critical and that is what makes project management so important today.

ORGANIZATIONAL CHANGE AND DEVELOPMENT

The field of Organization Development is focused on improving the effectiveness of organizations and the people in those organizations. OD has a rich history of research and practice regarding change in organizations.

Your nature and the way you choose to work has significant impact on your client's organization, whether you know it or not. You cannot separate yourself from your client's organization, as if you are some kind of detached observer. You quickly become part of your client's system — the way the people and processes in the organization work with each other on a recurring basis. Thus, it is critical that you have a good understanding of yourself, including your biases (we all have them), how you manage feedback and conflict, how you like to make decisions and solve problems, how you naturally view organizations, your skills as a consultant, etc.

Nowadays, with the complex challenges faced by organizations and the broad diversity of values, perspectives and opinions among the members of those organizations, it's vital that change agents work from a strong set of principles to ensure they operate in a highly effective and ethical manner.

There are several phrases regarding organizational change and development that look and sound a lot alike, but have different meanings. As a result of the prominence of the topic, there seems to be increasingly different interpretations of some of these phrases, while others are used interchangeably. Without at least some sense of the differences between these phrases, communications about organizational change and development can be increasingly vague, confusing and frustrating.

There are different overall types of organizational change, including planned versus unplanned, organization-wide versus change primarily to one part of the organization, incremental (slow, gradual change) versus transformational (radical, fundamental), etc.. Knowing which types of change you are doing helps all participants to retain scope and perspective during the many complexities and frequent frustrations during.

Successful change efforts often include several key roles, including the initiator, champion, change agent, sponsor and leaders. The following article describes each of these roles.

Organization-wide change in corporations should involve the Board of Directors. Whether their members are closely involved in the change or not, they should at least be aware of the change project and monitor if the results are being achieved or not. How to Make Sure the Board of Directors Participates in the Project for Change.

As the change agent, you might be performing different roles during the project. The following article might help you decide which role to perform.

Appreciative Inquiry is a recent and powerful breakthrough in organizational change and development. It's based on the philosophy that "problems" are often caused as much by our perception of them as problems as by other influencing factors. The philosophy has spawned a strong movement that, in turn, has generated an increasing number of models, tools and tips, most of which seem to build from the positive perceptions (visions, fantasies, wishes and stories) of those involved in the change effort.

VARIOUS MODELS FOR CHANGE MANAGEMENT

Many people would agree that traditional models of organizational performance management are also models for managing change.

A typical planned, systemic (and systematic) organizational development process often follows an overall action research approach. There are many variations of the action research approach, including by combining its various phases and/or splitting some into more phases. This section provides resources that are organized into one variation of the action research approach. Note that the more collaborative you are in working with members of the organization during the following process, the more likely the success of your overall change effort.

Phase 1

This phase is sometimes called the "Contracting" and/or "Entry" phase. This phase is usually where the relationship between you (the initial change agent) and your client starts, whether you are an external or internal consultant. Experts assert that this phase is one of the most - if not the most - important phases in the organizational change process. Activities during this stage form the foundation for successful organizational change. The quality of how this phase is carried out usually is a strong indicator of how the project will go.

Phase 2

The more collaborative the change agent is in working with members of the client's organization, the more likely that the change effort will be successful. Your client might not have the resources to fully participate in all aspects of this discovery activity — the more participation they can muster, the better off your project will be.

Whether you are an external or internal change agent in this project, you and your client will work together during this phase to understand more about the overall priority of the change effort and how you all can effectively address it. It might be a major problem in the organization or an exciting vision to achieve. Together, you will collect information, analyze it to identify findings and conclusions, and then make recommendations from that information. Sometimes the data-collection effort is very quick, for example, facilitating a large planning meeting. Other times, the effort is more extensive, for example, evaluating an entire organization and developing a complete plan for change.

The nature of discovery also depends on the philosophy of the change agent and client. For example, subscribers to the philosophy of Appreciative Inquiry (referenced above) might conduct discovery, not by digging into the number and causes of problems in the organization, but by conducting interviews to disover the visions and wishes of people in the organization.

Sometimes, people minimize the importance of - or altogether skip - this critical discovery phase, and start change management by articulating an ambitious and comprehensive vision for change. Many would argue that it is unethical to initiate a project for organizational change without fully examining (or discovering) the current situation in the client's organization. Focusing most of the change efforts on achieving a robust vision, without at least some careful discovery, often can be harmful to your client's organization because your project can end up dealing with symptoms of any current issues, rather than the root causes. Also, the project could end up pushing an exciting vision that, while initially inspiring and motivating to many, could be completely unrealistic to achieve — especially if the organization already has many current, major issues to address. Therefore, when working to guide change in an organization that already is facing several significant issues, you are usually better off to start from where your client is at — that usually means conducting an effective discovery to identify priorities for change.

One of the most powerful means to cultivate collaboration is by working with a project team. Besides, no change agent sees all aspects of the situation in the organization — team members help to see more of those various aspects.

Phase 3

In the previous phase about discovery, you and your client conducted research, discovered various priorities that needed attention, generated recommendations to address those priorities, and shared your information with others, for example, in a feedback meeting. Part of that meeting included discussions - and, hopefully, decisions - about the overall mutual recommendations that your client should follow to in order address the priorities that were identified by you and your client during your discovery. This phase is focused on further clarifying those recommendations, along with developing them into various action plans. The various plans are sometimes integrated into an overall change management plan. Thus, the early activities in this phase often overlap with, and are a continuation of, the activities near the end of the earlier discovery phase. This is true whether you are an external or internal consultant. Action plans together can now provide a clear and realistic vision for change. They provide the "roadmap" for managing the transition from the present state to the desired future state.

Development of the various action plans is often an enlightening experience for your client as members of their organization begin to realize a more systematic approach to their planning and day-to-day activities. As with other activities during change management, plans can vary widely in how they are developed. Some plans are very comprehensive and systematic (often the best form used for successful change). Others are comprised of diverse sections that are expected to somehow integrate with each other. Subscribers to the philosophy of Appreciative Inquiry (referenced above) might do planning by building on past positive outcomes and on the strengths of members of the organization.

Phase 4

During this phase, emphasis is on sustaining and evaluating the change effort, including by addressing resistance that arises from members of the organization — and sometimes in the change agent, as well.

Evaluation occurs both to the quality of implementation of plans so far during the project and also regarding the extent of achievement of desired results from the project. Results might be whether certain indicators of success have been achieved, all issues have been addressed, a vision of success has been achieved, action plans have been implemented and/or leaders in the organization agree the project has been successful.

As part of the final evaluation, you might redo some of the assessments that you used during the discovery phase in order to measure the difference made by the project.

If the Project Gets Stuck

During this phase, if the implementation of the plans gets stalled for a long time, for example, many months, then you might cycle back to an earlier phase in the process in order to update and restart the change management project. Projects can get stuck for a variety of reasons, *e.g.*, if the overall situation changes (there suddenly are new and other priorities in the client's organization), people succumb to burnout, key people leave the organization, the relationship between the consultant and client changes, or people refuse to implement action plans.

Project Termination

These activities are very important to address, even if all participants agree that the project has been successful and no further activities are needed. Project termination activities recognize key learnings from the project, acknowledge the client's development, and identify next steps for you and your client. They also help to avoid "project creep" where the project never ends because the requirements for success keep expanding.

The field of Organization Development uses a variety of processes, approaches, methods, techniques, applications, etc., (these are often termed "interventions") to address organizational issues and goals in order to increase performance. The following partial list of interventions is organized generally in the order presented by Cummings and Worley in their "Organization Development and Change". The following types of interventions are often highly integrated with each other during a project for change.

There are no standard activities that always successfully address certain types of issues in organizations. Many times, the success of a project lies not with having selected the perfect choice of activities, but rather with how honest and participative people were during the project, how much they learned and how open they were to changing their plans for change.

However, there are some basic considerations that most people make when selecting from among the many choices for organizational development, or capacity building, activities. Considerations include:

- First, does the change-management method (if one was used) suggest what organizational development activities to use now, for example, the method of strategic management might suggest that a SWOT analysis be done, strategic goals be established along with action plans for each goal, and then implementation of the action plans be closely monitored.
- Is the activity most likely to address the findings from the discovery, that is, to solve the problems or achieve the goals? To find out, review any research about use of the activity, discuss the potential outcomes with experts and also with members of the organization. Consider posing your questions in online groups of experts about change.
- Does the nature of the activity match the culture of the organization? The best way to find out is to discuss the activity with members of the organization.
- Does the change agent and key members of the organization have the ability to conduct the activity? For example, technostructural and strategic interventions sometimes require technical skills that are not common to many people.
- Does the activity require more time to conduct than the time available in which to address the problem or goal? For example, a cash crisis requires immediate attention, so while a comprehensive strategic planning process might ultimately be useful, the four to five months to do that planning is impractical.
- Does the client's organization have the resources that are necessary to conduct the activity, considering resources such as funding, attention and time from people and facilities.

Before you and your client select types of interventions for the project, be aware of your strong biases about how you view organizations. Without recognising those biases, you might favour certain types of interventions primarily because those are the only ones you can readily see and understand, even if other types of interventions might be much more effective in your project.

With today's strong emphasis on humanistic values, the following interventions are getting a great deal of attention and emphasis during efforts for change. They focus on helping members of the organization to enhance themselves, each other and the ways in which they work together in order to enhance their overall organization. Although the types of interventions selected for a project depend on a variety of considerations and the interventions in a project often are highly integrated with each other, the following human process interventions might be particularly helpful during change projects in organizations where there is some combination of the following: many new employees, different cultures working together, many complaints among organizational members, many conflicts, low morale, high turnover, ineffective teams, etc.

Human Resource Management Interventions

Performance is in regard to setting goals, monitoring progress to the goals, sharing feedback, reinforcing activities to achieve goals and dissuading those that don't. Performance also is in regard to developing employees, including by enhancing their overall sense of well-being. Although the types of interventions selected for a project depend on a variety of considerations and the interventions in a project often are highly integrated, the following human resource interventions might be particularly helpful in the following kinds of situations: new organizational goals have been established, a major new system or technology must be implemented in a timely fashion, many new employees, plans don't seem to get implemented, productivity is low, ineffective teams, etc.

The following activities focus especially on the organization and its interactions with its external environment, and often involve changes to many aspects of the organization, including employees, groups, technologies, products and services, etc. Although the types of interventions selected for a project depend on a variety of considerations and the interventions in a project often are highly integrated, the following strategic interventions might be particularly helpful in the following kinds of situations: rapid changes in the external environment, rapid or stagnant sales, significantly increased competition, rapid expansion of markets, mergers and acquisitions, the need for quick and comprehensive change throughout the organization, etc.

Significant organizational change occurs, for example, when an organization changes its overall strategy for success, adds or removes a major section or practice, and/or wants to change the very nature by which it operates. It also occurs when an organization evolves through various life cycles, just like people must successfully evolve through life cycles. For organizations to develop, they often must undergo significant change at various points in their development. That's why the topic of organizational change and development has become widespread in communications about business, organizations, leadership and management.

Leaders and managers continually make efforts to accomplish successful and significant change — it's inherent in their jobs. Some are very good at this effort (probably more than we realize), while others continually struggle and fail. That's often the difference between people who thrive in their roles and those that get shuttled around from job to job, ultimately settling into a role where they're frustrated and ineffective.

There are many schools with educational programmes about organizations, business, leadership and management. Unfortunately, there still are not enough schools with programmes about how to analyze organizations, identify critically important priorities to address (such as systemic problems or exciting visions for change) and then undertake successful and significant change to address those priorities. This Library topic aims to improve that situation.

Successful organizational change can be quite difficult to accomplish — it can be like trying to change a person's habits. Fortunately, there is an increasing body of research, practice and tools from which we all can learn.

A major goal of this Library topic is to make this body of information much more accessible to many — to give the reader more clear perspective on overall organizational change and development, along with sufficient understanding to begin applying principles and practices for successful change in their roles and organizations. The following resources are not sufficient to guide a large, comprehensive and detailed organizational change effort — that amount of resources comprises a significantly sized book — and besides, there is no standard procedure for guiding change.

However, the following resources might be sufficient to provide the reader at least a framework that takes him or her from which to begin guiding change in smaller efforts for organizational change — and then to begin to learn more.

There are many approaches to guiding change — some planned, structured and explicit, while others are more organic, unfolding and implicit. Some approaches work from the future to the present, for example, involving visioning and then action planning about how to achieve that vision. Other approaches work from the present to the future, for example, identifying current priorities (issues and/or goals) and then action planning about to address those priorities (the action research approach is one example).

Different people often have very different — and strong — opinions about how change should be conducted. Thus, it is likely that some will disagree with some of the content in this topic. That's what makes this topic so diverse, robust and vital for us all.

Understanding Organizations, Leadership and Management

To really understand organizational change and begin guiding successful change efforts, the change agent should have at least a broad understanding of the context of the change effort. This includes understanding the basic systems and structures in organizations, including their typical terms and roles. This requirement applies to the understanding of leadership and management of the organizations, as well. That is why graduate courses in business often initially include a course or some discussion on organizational theory. Organizational change should not be conducted for the sake of change. Organizational change efforts should be geared to improve the performance of organizations and the people in those organizations. Therefore, it's useful to have some understanding of what is meant by "performance" and the various methods to manage performance in organizations.

Systems Thinking

The past few decades have seen an explosion in the number of very useful tools to help change agents to effectively explore, understand and communicate about organizations, as well as to guide successful change in those organizations. Tools from systems theory and systems thinking especially are a major breakthrough. Even if the change agent is not an expert about systems theory and thinking, even a basic understanding can cultivate an entire new way of working.

There are numerous, major methods and movements to regularly increase the performance of organizations. Each includes regular recurring activities to establish organizational goals, monitor progress towards the goals, and make adjustments to achieve those goals more effectively and efficiently.

Any or all of the following approaches will improve organizational performance depending on if they are implemented comprehensively and remain focused on organizational results. Some of the following, *e.g.*, organizational learning and knowledge management, might be interpreted more as movements than organization performance strategies because there are wide interpretations of the concepts, not all of which include focusing on achieving top-level organizational results. However, if these two concepts are instilled across the organization and focus on organizational results, they contribute strongly to organizational performance. On the other hand, the Balanced Scorecard, which is deliberately designed to be comprehensive and focused on organizational results, will not improve performance if not implemented from a strong design.

PLANNING A PROJECT

Before describing the role and creation of a specification, we need to introduce and explain a fairly technical term: a numbty is a person whose brain is totally numb. In this context, numb means "deprived of feeling or the power of unassisted activity"; in general, a numbty needs the stimulation of an electric cattle prod to even get to the right office in the morning.

Communication with numbties is severely hampered by the fact that although they think they know what they mean (which they do not), they seldom actually say it, and they never write it down. And the main employment of numbties world-wide is in creating project specifications. You must know this - and protect your team accordingly.

A specification is the definition of your project: a statement of the problem, not the solution. Normally, the specification contains errors, ambiguities, misunderstandings and enough rope to hang you and your entire team. Thus before you embark upon the the next six months of activity working on the wrong project, you must assume that a numbty was the chief author of the specification you received and you must read, worry, revise and ensure that everyone concerned with the project (from originator, through the workers, to the end-customer) is working with the same understanding.

The outcome of this deliberation should be a written definition of what is required, by when; and this must be agreed by all involved. There are no short-cuts to this; if you fail to spend the time initially, it will cost you far more later on. The agreement upon a written specification has several benefits:

- The clarity will reveal misunderstandings
- The completeness will remove contradictory assumptions
- The rigour of the analysis will expose technical and practical details which numbties normally gloss over through ignorance or fear
- The agreement forces all concerned to actually read and think about the details

The work on the specification can seen as the first stage of Quality Assurance since you are looking for and countering problems in the very foundation of the project - from this perspective the creation of the specification clearly merits a large investment of time.

From a purely defensive point of view, the agreed specification also affords you protection against the numbties who have second thoughts, or new ideas, half way through the project. Once the project is underway, changes cost time (and money).

The existence of a demonstrably-agreed specification enables you to resist or to charge for (possibly in terms of extra time) such changes. Further, people tend to forget what they originally thought; you may need proof that you have been working as instructed. The places to look for errors in a specification are:

- The global context: numbties often focus too narrowly on the work of one team and fail to consider how it fits into the larger picture. Some of the work given to you may actually be undone or duplicated by others. Some of the proposed work may be incompatible with that of others; it might be just plain barmy in the larger context.

- The interfaces: between your team and both its customers and suppliers, there are interfaces. At these points something gets transferred. Exactly what, how and when should be discussed and agreed from the very beginning. Never assume a common understanding, because you will be wrong. All it takes for your habitual understandings to evaporate is the arrival of one new member, in either of the teams. Define and agree your interfaces and maintain a friendly contact throughout the project.
- Time-scales: numbties always underestimate the time involved for work. If there are no time-scales in the specification, you can assume that one will be imposed upon you (which will be impossible). You must add realistic dates. The detail should include a precise understanding of the extent of any intermediate stages of the task, particularly those which have to be delivered.
- External dependencies: your work may depend upon that of others. Make this very clear so that these people too will receive warning of your needs. Highlight the effect that problems with these would have upon your project so that everyone is quite clear about their importance. To be sure, contact these people yourself and ask if they are able to fulfil the assumptions in your specification.
- Resources: the numbty tends to ignore resources. The specification should identify the materials, equipment and manpower which are needed for the project. The agreement should include a commitment by your managers to allocate or to fund them. You should check that the actual numbers are practical and/or correct. If they are omitted, add them - there is bound to be differences in their assumed values.

This seems to make the specification sound like a long document. It should not be. Each of the above could be a simple sub-heading followed by either bullet points or a table - you are not writing a brochure, you are stating the definition of the project in clear, concise and unambiguous glory.

Of course, the specification may change. If circumstances, or simply your knowledge, change then the specification will be out of date. You should not regard it as cast in stone but rather as a display board where everyone involved can see the current, common understanding of the project. If you change the content everyone must know, but do not hesitate to change it as necessary.

Having decide what the specification intends, your next problem is to decide what you and your team actually need to do, and how to do it. As a manager, you have to provide some form of framework both to plan and to communicate what needs doing. Without a structure, the work is a series of unrelated tasks which provides little sense of achievement and no feeling of advancement. If the team has no grasp of how individual tasks fit together towards an understood goal, then the work will seem pointless and they will feel only frustration.

To take the planning forward, therefore, you need to turn the specification into a complete set of tasks with a linking structure. Fortunately, these two requirements are met at the same time since the derivation of such a structure is the simplest method of arriving at a list of tasks.

WORK BREAKDOWN STRUCTURE

Once you have a clear understanding of the project, and have eliminated the vagaries of the numbties, you then describe it as a set of simpler separate activities. If any of these are still too complex for you to easily organise, you break them down also into another level of simpler descriptions, and so on until you can manage everything. Thus your one complex project is organised as a set of simple tasks which together achieve the desired result.

The reasoning behind this is that the human brain (even yours) can only take in and process so much information at one time. To get a real grasp of the project, you have to think about it in pieces rather than trying to process the complexity of its entire details all at once.

Thus each level of the project can be understood as the amalgamation of a few simply described smaller units.

In planning any project, you follow the same simple steps: if an item is too complicated to manage, it becomes a list of simpler items. People call this producing a work breakdown structure to make it sound more formal and impressive. Without following this formal approach you are unlikely to remember all the niggling little details; with this procedure, the details are simply displayed on the final lists.

One common fault is to produce too much detail at the initial planning stage. You should be stop when you have a sufficient description of the activity to provide a clear instruction for the person who will actually do the work, and to have a reasonable estimate for the total time/effort involved. You need the former to allocate (or delegate) the task; you need the latter to finish the planning.

TASK ALLOCATION

The next stage is a little complicated. You now have to allocate the tasks to different people in the team and, at the same time, order these tasks so that they are performed in a sensible sequence.

Task allocation is not simply a case of handing out the various tasks on your final lists to the people you have available; it is far more subtle (and powerful) than that. As a manager you have to look far beyond the single project; indeed any individual project can be seen as merely a single step in your team's development. The allocation of tasks should thus be seen as a means of increasing the skills and experience of your team - when the project is done, the team should have gained.

In simple terms, consider what each member of your team is capable of and allocate sufficient complexity of tasks to match that (and to slightly stretch). The tasks you allocate are not the ones on your finals lists, they are adapted to better suit the needs of your team's development; tasks are moulded to fit people, which is far more effective than the other way around. For example, if Arthur is to learn something new, the task may be simplified with responsibility given to another to guide and check the work; if Brenda is to develop, sufficient tasks are combined so that her responsibility increases beyond what she has held before; if Colin lacks confidence, the tasks are broken into smaller units which can be completed (and commended) frequently.

Sometimes tasks can be grouped and allocated together. For instance, some tasks which are seemingly independent may benefit from being done together since they use common ideas, information, talents. One person doing them both removes the start-up time for one of them; two people (one on each) will be able to help each other.

The ordering of the tasks is really quite simple, although you may find that sketching a sequence diagram helps you to think it through (and to communicate the result). Pert charts are the accepted outcome, but sketches will suffice. Getting the details exactly right, however, can be a long and painful process, and often it can be futile. The degree to which you can predict the future is limited, so too should be the detail of your planning. You must have the broad outlines by which to monitor progress, and sufficient detail to assign each task when it needs to be started, but beyond that - stop and do something useful instead.

At the initial planning stage the main objective is to get a realistic estimate of the time involved in the project. You must establish this not only to assist higher management with their planning, but also to protect your team from being expected to do the impossible. The most important technique for achieving this is known as: guesstimation.

Guesstimating schedules is notoriously difficult but it is helped by two approaches:

- Make your guesstimates of the simple tasks at the bottom of the work break down structure and look for the longest path through the sequence diagram
- Use the experience from previous projects to improve your guesstimating skills

The corollary to this is that you should keep records in an easily accessible form of all projects as you do them. Part of your final project review should be to update your personal data base of how long various activities take. Managing this planning phase is vital to your success as a manager.

Some people find guesstimating a difficult concept in that if you have no experience of an activity, how can you make a worthwhile estimate? Let us consider such a problem: how long would it take you to walk all the way to the top of the Eiffel Tower or the Statue of Liberty? Presuming you have never actually tried this (most people take the elevator part of the way), you really have very little to go on. Indeed if you have actually seen one (and only one) of these buildings, think about the other. Your job depends upon this, so think carefully.

One idea is to start with the number of steps - guess that if you can. Notice, you do not have to be right, merely reasonable. Next, consider the sort of pace you could maintain while climbing a flight of steps for a long time. Now imagine yourself at the base of a flight of steps you do know, and estimate a) how many steps there are, and b) how long it takes you to climb them (at that steady pace). To complete, apply a little mathematics.

Now examine how confident you are with this estimate. If you won a free flight to Paris or New York and tried it, you would probably (need your head examined) be mildly surprised if you climbed to the top in less than half the estimated time and if it took you more than double you would be mildly annoyed. If it took you less than a tenth the time, or ten times as long, you would extremely surprised/annoyed. In fact, you do not currently believe that that would happen (no really, do you?). The point is that from very little experience of the given problem, you can actually come up with a working estimate - and one which is far better than no estimate at all when it comes to deriving a schedule. Guesstimating does take a little practice, but it is a very useful skill to develop.

There are two practical problems in guesstimation. First, you are simply too optimistic. It is human nature at the beginning of a new project to ignore the difficulties and assume best case scenarii - in producing your estimates (and using those of others) you must inject a little realism. In practice, you should also build-in a little slack to allow yourself some tolerance against mistakes. This is known as defensive scheduling. Also, if you eventually deliver ahead of the agreed schedule, you will be loved.

Second, you will be under pressure from senior management to deliver quickly, especially if the project is being sold competitively. Resist the temptation to rely upon speed as the only selling point. You might, for instance, suggest the criteria of: fewer errors, history of adherence to initial schedules, previous customer satisfaction, "this is how long it takes, so how can you trust the other quotes".

ESTABLISHING CONTROLS

When the planning phase is over (and agreed), the "doing" phase begins. Once it is in motion, a project acquires a direction and momentum which is totally independent of anything you predicted. If you come to terms with that from the start, you can then enjoy the roller-coaster which follows. To gain some hope, however, you need to establish at the start (within the plan) the means to monitor and to influence the project's progress. There are two key elements to the control of a project

- Milestones (clear, unambiguous targets of what, by when)
- Established means of communication

For you, the milestones are a mechanism to monitor progress; for your team, they are short-term goals which are far more tangible than the foggy, distant completion of the entire project. The milestones maintain the momentum and encourage effort; they allow the team to judge their own progress and to celebrate achievement throughout the project rather than just at its end.

The simplest way to construct milestones is to take the timing information from the work breakdown structure and sequence diagram. When you have guesstimated how long each sub-task will take and have strung them together, you can identify by when each of these tasks will actually be completed. This is simple and effective; however, it lacks creativity.

A second method is to construct more significant milestones. These can be found by identify stages in the development of a project which are recognisable as steps towards the final product.

Sometimes these are simply the higher levels of your structure; for instance, the completion of a market-evaluation phase. Sometimes, they cut across many parallel activities; for instance, a prototype of the eventual product or a mock-up of the new brochure format. If you are running parallel activities, this type of milestone is particularly useful since it provides a means of pulling together the people on disparate activities, and so:

- They all have a shared goal (the common milestone)
- Their responsibility to (and dependence upon) each other is emphasised
- Each can provide a new (but informed) viewpoint on the others' work
- The problems to do with combining the different activities are highlighted and discussed early in the implementation phase
- You have something tangible which senior management (and numbties) can recognise as progress
- You have something tangible which your team can celebrate and which constitutes a short-term goal in a possibly long-term project
- It provides an excellent opportunity for quality checking and for review

Of course, there are milestones and there are mill-stones. You will have to be sensitive to any belief that working for some specific milestone is hindering rather than helping the work forward.

If this arises then either you have chosen the wrong milestone, or you have failed to communicate how it fits into the broader structure.

Communication is your everything. To monitor progress, to receive early warning of danger, to promote cooperation, to motivate through team involvement, all of these rely upon communication. Regular reports are invaluable - if you clearly define what information is needed and if teach your team how to provided it in a rapidly accessible form. Often these reports merely say "progressing according to schedule".

These you send back, for while the message is desired the evidence is missing: you need to insist that your team monitor their own progress with concrete, tangible, measurements and if this is done, the figures should be included in the report. However, the real value of this practice comes when progress is not according to schedule - then your communication system is worth all the effort you invested in its planning.

At the planning stage, you can deal with far more than the mere project at hand. You can also shape the overall pattern of your team's working using the division and type of activities you assign.

Ask your team. They too must be involved in the planning of projects, especially in the lower levels of the work breakdown structure. Not only will they provide information and ideas, but also they will feel ownership in the final plan.

This does not mean that your projects should be planned by committee - rather that you, as manager, plan the project based upon all the available experience and creative ideas. As an initial approach, you could attempt the first level(s) of the work breakdown structure to help you communicate the project to the team and then ask for comments. Then, using these, the final levels could be refined by the people to whom the tasks will be allocated. However, since the specification is so vital, all the team should vet the penultimate draft.

There are two pitfalls to avoid in project reviews:

- They can be too frequent
- They can be too drastic

The constant trickle of new information can lead to a vicious cycle of planning and revising which shakes the team's confidence in any particular version of the plan and which destroys the very stability which the structure was designed to provide.You must decide the balance. Pick a point on the horizon and walk confide ntly towards it. Decide objectively, and explain beforehand, when the review phases will occur and make this a scheduled milestone in itself.

Even though the situation may have changed since the last review, it is important to recognise the work which has been accomplished during the interim. Firstly, you do not want to abandon it since the team will be demotivated feeling that they have achieved nothing. Secondly, this work itself is part of the new situation: it has been done, it should provide a foundation for the next step or at least the basis of a lesson well learnt. Always try to build upon the existing achievements of your team.

No plan is complete without explicit provision for testing and quality. As a wise manager, you will know that this should be part of each individual phase of the project. This means that no activity is completed until it has passed the (objectively) defined criteria which establishes its quality, and these are best defined (objectively) at the beginning as part of the planning.

When devising the schedule therefore you must include allocated time for this part of each activity. Thus your question is not only: "how long will it take", but also: "how long will the testing take". By asking both questions together you raise the issue of "how do we know we have done it right" at the very beginning and so the testing is more likely to be done in parallel with the implementation. You establish this philosophy for your team by include testing as a justified (required) cost.

Another reason for stating the testing criteria at the beginning is that you can avoid futile quests for perfection. If you have motivated your team well, they will each take pride in their work and want to do the best job possible. Often this means polishing their work until is shines; often this wastes time. If it clear at the onset exactly what is needed, then they are more likely to stop when that has been achieved. You need to avoid generalities and to stipulate boundaries; not easy, but essential.

The same is also true when choosing the tools or building-blocks of your project. While it might be nice to have use of the most modern versions, or to develop an exact match to your needs; often there is an old/existing version which will serve almost as well (sufficient for the purpose), and the difference is not worth the time you would need to invest in obtaining or developing the new one. Use what is available whenever possible unless the difference in the new version is worth the time, money and the initial, teething pains.

A related idea is that you should discourage too much effort on aspects of the project which are idiosyncratic to that one job. In the specification phase, you might try to eliminate these through negotiation with the customer; in the implementation phase you might leave these parts until last. The reason for this advice is that a general piece of work can be tailored to many specific instances; thus, if the work is in a general form, you will be able to rapidly re-use it for other projects. On the other hand, if you produce something which is cut to fit exactly one specific case, you may have to repeat the work entirely even though the next project is fairly similar. At the planning phase, a manager should bare in mind the future and the long-term development of the team as well as the requirements of the current project.

As a manager, you have to regulate the pressure and work load which is imposed upon your team; you must protect them from the unreasonable demands of the rest of the company. Once you have arrived at what you consider to be a realistic schedule, fight for it. Never let the outside world deflect you from what you know to be practical. If they impose a deadline upon you which is impossible, clearly state this and give your reasons. You will need to give some room for compromise, however, since a flat NO will be seen as obstructive. Since you want to help the company, you should look for alternative positions.

You could offer a prototype service or product at an earlier date. This might, in some cases, be sufficient for the customer to start the next stage of his/her own project on the understanding that your project would be completed at a later date and the final version would then replace the prototype.

The complexity of the product, or the total number of units, might be reduced. This might, in some cases, be sufficient for the customer's immediate needs. Future enhancements or more units would then be the subject of a subsequent negotiation which, you feel, would be likely to succeed since you will have already demonstrate your ability to deliver on time.

You can show on an alternative schedule that the project could be delivered by the deadline if certain (specified) resources are given to you or if other projects are rescheduled. Thus, you provide a clear picture of the situation and a possible solution; it is up to your manager then how he/she proceeds.

The most common error in planning is to assume that there will be no errors in the implementation: in effect, the schedule is derived on the basis of "if nothing goes wrong, this will take...". Of course, recognising that errors will occur is the reason for implementing a monitoring strategy on the project. Thus when the inevitable does happen, you can react and adapt the plan to compensate. However, by carefully considering errors in advance you can make changes to the original plan to enhance its tolerance. Quite simply, your planning should include time where you stand back from the design and ask: "what can go wrong?"; indeed, this is an excellent way of asking your team for their analysis of your plan.

You can try to predict where the errors will occur. By examining the activities' list you can usually pinpoint some activities which are risky (for instance, those involving new equipment) and those which are quite secure (for instance, those your team has done often before). The risky areas might then be given a less stringent time-scale - actually planning-in time for the mistakes. Another possibility is to apply a different strategy, or more resources, to such activities to minimise the disruption. For instance, you could include training or consultancy for new equipment, or you might parallel the work with the foundation of a fall-back position.

At the end of any project, you should allocate time to reviewing the lessons and information on both the work itself and the management of that work: an open meeting, with open discussion, with the whole team and all customers and suppliers. If you think that this might be thought a waste of time by your own manager, think of the effect it will have on future communications with your customers and suppliers.

PLANNING FOR THE FUTURE

With all these considerations in merely the "planning" stage of a project, it is perhaps surprising that projects get done at all. In fact projects do get done, but seldom in the predicted manner and often as much by brute force as by careful planning. The point, however, is that this method is non-optimal. Customers feel let down by late delivery, staff are demotivated by constant pressure for impossible goals, corners get cut which harm your reputation, and each project has to overcome the same problems as the last.

With planning, projects can run on time and interact effectively with both customers and suppliers. Everyone involved understands what is wanted and emerging problems are seen (and dealt with) long before they cause damage. If you want your projects to run this way - then you must invest time in planning.

Significant organizational change occurs, for example, when an organization changes its overall strategy for success, adds or removes a major section or practice, and/or wants to change the very nature by which it operates. It also occurs when an organization evolves through various life cycles, just like people must successfully evolve through life cycles. For organizations to develop, they often must undergo significant change at various points in their development. That's why the topic of organizational change and development has become widespread in communications about business, organizations, leadership and management.

Leaders and managers continually make efforts to accomplish successful and significant change — it's inherent in their jobs. Some are very good at this effort (probably more than we realize), while others continually struggle and fail. That's often the difference between people who thrive in their roles and those that get shuttled around from job to job, ultimately settling into a role where they're frustrated and ineffective. There are many schools with educational programmes about organizations, business, leadership and management. Unfortunately, there still are not enough schools with programmes about how to analyze organizations, identify critically important priorities to address (such as systemic problems or exciting visions for change) and then undertake successful and significant change to address those priorities.

There are many approaches to guiding change — some planned, structured and explicit, while others are more organic, unfolding and implicit. Some approaches work from the future to the present, for example, involving visioning and then action planning about how to achieve that vision. Other approaches work from the present to the future, for example, identifying current priorities (issues and/or goals) and then action planning about to address those priorities (the action research approach is one example). Different people often have very different — and strong — opinions about how change should be conducted. Thus, it is likely that some will disagree with some of the content in this topic. That's what makes this topic so diverse, robust and vital for us all.

To really understand organizational change and begin guiding successful change efforts, the change agent should have at least a broad understanding of the context of the change effort. This includes understanding the basic systems and structures in organizations, including their typical terms and roles. This requirement applies to the understanding of leadership and management of the organizations, as well. That is why graduate courses in business often initially include a course or some discussion on organizational theory. This topic includes several links to help you gain this broad understanding. Organizational change should not be conducted for the sake of change. Organizational change efforts should be geared to improve the performance of organizations and the people in those organizations. Therefore, it's useful to have some understanding of what is meant by "performance" and the various methods to manage performance in organizations.

The past few decades have seen an explosion in the number of very useful tools to help change agents to effectively explore, understand and communicate about organizations, as well as to guide successful change in those organizations. Tools from systems theory and systems thinking especially are a major breakthrough. Even if the change agent is not an expert about systems theory and thinking, even a basic understanding can cultivate an entire new way of working.

IN THE END OF THIS STAGE, WE CAN SAY

The owner of a fast food franchise in East Los Angeles panicked when his drive-through cashier was robbed at gunpoint. While the criminals escaped with all the day's receipts, an even greater loss was the owner's peace of mind. Since his wife and daughter both worked at the restaurant, he stood to lose a lot more than money if the robbers returned. What could the owner have done to make his business and his family safe?

In this case, a simple bulletproof one-way drive-through window would have made the robbery impossible. More importantly, such a deterrent might make criminals think twice about their chosen target.

American businesses lose billions of dollars each year as a result of crime. Small operations are especially likely to be victims, losing at least 20 times more money than do large corporations. In fact, shoplifting, robbery and burglary put such a disproportionate strain on small firms that many disintegrate as a result. Business owners can even be held liable for crimes against people that are committed on their property, meaning their livelihood can be threatened by random acts of violence as well.

Employees of a sportswear manufacturing facility in Los Angeles were devastated when a man came in during working hours and murdered two of their coworkers before killing himself. The company's owner was shocked to learn that he could be held financially responsible for the trauma his staff experienced because access to the work area was not controlled effectively.

However, if the sportswear manufacturer had been able to prove to a judge that he had taken precautions — even minimal ones — to safeguard his building and his employees, he would have been absolved of liability.

No matter what kind of venture you own, you have assets and employees that require protection. Many entrepreneurs fail to realize the amount of damage crime can cause. They are also unaware that the most important security measures are inexpensive and simple to implement. As a business owner, you need to step back occasionally and conduct a security review, keeping in mind the three Ds of crime prevention: deter, delay and detect.

Deterring criminals is the key to making sure your business is not an easy target. Simple and inexpensive measures such as replacing old locks, hiding expensive equipment from passers-by, and putting bars on windows can cause would-be criminals to seek more vulnerable prey. Anything that tells potential thieves you have paid attention to the security of your building can be an effective deterrent.

Delaying a crime, or preventing quick access to valuable merchandise or equipment, is the second crucial step in protecting your business. The owner of a California office supply store learned the importance of delaying criminals after experiencing repeated burglaries, each of which resulted in losses of almost $10,000 in merchandise. Although the store had a locked accordion gate behind glass entrance doors, the gate was secured with a cheap lock. A sturdier, slightly more expensive lock could have occupied the burglars long enough for the police to reach the scene after the alarm was activated.

The last of the three Ds, detection, is accomplished by more complex technology like alarms or surveillance equipment. However, these products — such as window glass bugs or motion detectors — can actually give a false sense of security. For experienced criminals know that alarm companies and police communications centers must go through a number of steps before reaching the location of a break-in. This gives them ample opportunity to escape with valuable equipment or merchandise. For this reason, law enforcement officials maintain that alarms and surveillance should only be used as back-up security devices.

Although detection is generally not effective at preventing a crime, it can decrease the amount of time a burglar has inside the building and is therefore an important component of building security. However, don't spend disproportionate amounts of money on high-tech equipment. Focus instead on inexpensive, low-tech tools for deterring or delaying criminals.

After you install new security precautions, the job is not finished until you have also made adjustments to your daily operations and employee training. "Not enough people are looking at the big picture," asserts Michael Harding, a Southern California law enforcement officer. "Your physical security will not be effective without operational security and good employee training. The three are tied together."

In the case of the Los Angeles fast-food franchise that was robbed at gunpoint, Harding found simple solutions to the many security problems existing there. The restaurant's back door and a storage room door were left unlocked during business hours, for example, and employees tended to leave them wide open for the sake of fast movement between areas of the building. "All I had to do was tell them to close and lock their doors," says Harding. "It sounds obvious, but it could really save a lot of worry."

With careful thought, you can probably identify most of your own security weaknesses. First, determine exactly what requires protection in your office, store or factory. Use common sense. For instance, don't spend a lot of money on alarms and access control for a storage area that only houses basic supplies such as boxes or business forms. For areas such as this, good locks should be sufficient.

In addition, step back and look realistically at your neighbourhood and personnel. Don't go overboard by surrounding your building with Dobermans, or conversely, take unnecessary risks with valuable resources by depending only on trust for security.

Also evaluate how well your existing security arrangements address likely threats to your business. Be sure to go over every detail from the types of locks you install and your system of key distribution to employee identification and after-hours use of the facility. Even simple things like lighting can be extremely important.

If you are uncertain about the vulnerable points in your building and how to protect them, consider calling in a security professional to conduct a comprehensive evaluation of your premises and daily operations.

The best analysis will only be possible after the consultant observes typical personnel activity and thoroughly examines the various access points at all sides of the building and on the roof. Ask for a complete report of the evaluations and recommendations after the professional has explained them to you in a face-to-face consultation.

Keep in mind as you look for a consultant that the person you hire may have a product to sell other than knowledge about security. Although the professional often provides excellent advice, use common sense about any product recommendations the consultant makes.

Officer Harding recommends consultants who are currently in law enforcement because they have the greatest expertise in crime prevention and nothing to sell but the most up-to-date information. Just as fashion and food trends change with the times, so do crimes. "We get to interview the bad guys when we arrest them for a break-in," Harding says, "so we know all their latest secrets."

Aside from carefully controlling traffic through your premises, access control keypads and card readers provide many benefits that will save you money and worry in the long run.

To keep track of who goes in and out of the various doors in their four buildings, Insignia Commercial Group in Austin, Texas has used access control keypads for years. Michael Osborne, chief engineer, says he utilizes the system for much more than security purposes, however. "We've got the access system tied into energy control too," he says. "That way, only designated people can turn on the air conditioning and lights after hours by using their codes."

The system, designed by Hirsch Electronics in Irvine, California, has appeared in films like "Jurassic Park." "The keypads have a high-tech look that many business owners really like. Employees feel safer, and visitors know they're dealing with the latest in security," reports Rob Zivney of Hirsch Electronics. Osborne agrees that appearance is one of the added benefits of electronic access control.

Just as with other building security measures, access control systems require thorough user training to work well. Osborne says all the companies located in Insignia's buildings have a tenant manual that describes exactly how to operate the system. As he explains, "The manual reminds people not to let anyone in behind them as they enter, for example, and never to punch in a code while someone is watching."

When looking around the inside of your building, do you see valuable equipment or merchandise that a thief could collect in five minutes or less? Then maybe your alarm system just isn't enough. Consider the steps and time involved between the alarm being triggered and the arrival of a police officer at your site.

- The alarm goes off when someone breaks in or trespasses.
- The security company must identify the location of the alarm.
- The security company calls the location to make sure the alarm was not set off accidentally by someone authorized with a special code.
- The security company contacts the local sheriff or other police communication center.
- The police enter the location into a computer and look for an on-duty officer in the area.
- The police communication center sends an officer to the location.
- The officer arrives on the scene of the break-in, often five minutes or more after the alarm originally sounded.

Whether a business operates out of a factory, garage, store or office suite, good key control can protect the people, property and information inside.

The little words "Do Not Duplicate" on all of your office keys sound like good insurance against unauthorized entry. Unfortunately, they mean almost nothing in most cases, says Alan Stelzer of Antrim's Security Co. in Pasadena, California. Stelzer strongly recommends keys that can only be duplicated by the manufacturers or their agents when you present a registration card and positive identification. All of the copies should then be listed by their consecutive serial numbers and the employees who use them.

One of the best features of the latest locks is that they can be installed into existing door hardware. A locksmith inserts or removes a columnar unit rather than installing expensive new materials. "This system, including a master key which only you use to unlock all of the doors, is a must for security, especially since it requires little time and investment," says Stelzer.

In today's high-tech world, a decidedly low-tech solution can still be effective. For many types of businesses like automobile dealerships, construction sites or warehouses, guard dogs can be an excellent crime deterrent.

Unlike security systems or alarms, guard dogs can cover large outdoor areas, and they continue to work during a power outage. Unlike a human guard, a well-trained dog stays alert throughout the night, and a dog's heightened senses of smell and hearing can detect intruders long before humans can. Dogs are also the least expensive guards, costing about $500 a month for full service.

At the minimum, a good guard dog service should provide nightly delivery and pick-up, in which case you and your employees do not have to come into actual contact with the animal. Your guard dog service must also must carry liability insurance, which protects you from responsibility for injuries the dog might inflict on passers-by or trespassers.

If you are thinking about using a guard dog to protect your premises, consider several issues. First, a good guard dog is an effective deterrent, but should only be used for that purpose. "If people want to steal, they're going to steal," claims J.R. Ewing of Century Dogs in Los Angeles, California.

The second thing to remember is that a determined criminal can find ways around almost any defence, including guard dogs. For example, mace, sedatives or other weapons can effectively disable even the most vigilant of animals. However, the presence of a guard dog does make your business far less appealing to would-be thieves who might decide to move on to more poorly protected premises.

To thoroughly safeguard your business, combine guard dog service — if appropriate — with other measures like good fences, locks and an alarm system.

The following is a simplified list of building features a security consultant would examine. Assess whether your security provisions are good, satisfactory, unsatisfactory or nonexistent. Fixing a few simple problems can go a long way in preventing crime.

PERIMETER

- *Lighting:* Do you have lights at all entrances? Are they protected from vandals and thieves?
- *Fences/Walls:* Is it possible to get over or under them? What are they made of? Are they in good condition?
- *Gates:* Are any left unsecured? Are they in good condition?

- *Storage Yard*: Do you have materials next to the fence or entrance? Are the materials hidden from passers-by?
- *Parking Lots*: Is employee parking separate from parking for the general public? How close to the building is it? Is there enough lighting?
- *Address Numbers*: Are they legible and visible from the street?
- *Pedestrian/Vehicle Access*: How well is it monitored? Is it in front of the building?

DOORS

Can they be pried open? Are they solid in construction? Do they have reliable dead bolts? What kind of strike plates do they have? Are your closing procedures listed and uniform?

WINDOWS

Are they secured with screw locks, pins or sturdy cranks? Are louvers glued shut or otherwise secured? Are there drapes or blinds that prevent would-be thieves from seeing inside your property?

ROOF

Are all skylights, vents and hatchways secured or covered? Do trees, drain pipes or walls allow easy access to the roof?

INTERIOR

- *Lighting*: Do you have lights on after hours? Is there an emergency back-up system?
- *Valuables*: Are they out of view of any passers-by?
- *Storage/Offices/Saferoom*: Are they secured with high-quality locks? Are there phones in each room to allow emergency calls?

SPECIAL AREAS

- *Loading Docks*: Are they well-marked and secure?
- *Employee Training*: Have your employees been trained in crime awareness and prevention?
- *Key Control*: Do you have a foolproof system to keep track of key distribution? Do you know many copies have been made? Trash Areas: Are your trash bins enclosed and locked?

SECURITY SYSTEMS

- *Alarm System*: Is it monitored? Does it include a panic device? Do you have prominent signs announcing its presence?
- *Closed-Circuit TV*: How is it monitored? Is there a time delay?

- *Guards*: What kind of training do they have? Are they bonded? How thorough a background check have you conducted on them?
- *Guard Dogs*: How many do you have? During what hours are they present? Have you posted warnings prominently? Are you aware of your liability in case of attack?

If you are unable to answer many of these questions, a professional security consultation is in order. Remember that by investing a few hundred dollars now, you may be saving thousands of dollars in the long term.

Excerpted with permission from "Small Business Success" magazine, Volume X, produced by Pacific Bell Directory in partnership with the U.S. Small Business Administration and the Partners for Small Business Excellence.

6

Customer Measurement in Hotel Management System

Every company must be able to satisfy and retain customers. That is the key to its business performance. Your job—as an executive in charge of improving quality, customer satisfaction, or loyalty—may be to enable others to act through training and support. Alternatively, if you're in the quality, customer assessment, or development areas of your company, your job may be to do the work directly—to collect, analyze, or use customer data to improve quality, satisfaction, and retention. Whether you are an enabler or a doer, customer satisfaction and retention are your responsibility. Providing high-quality products and services builds strong relationships with customers and ensures future revenue streams.

Even though you may agree about the importance of customers in driving performance, an important question remains. Does your company align its activities to satisfy and retain customers? Too often the answer is either "no" or "not so well." To help understand the problem, consider how a customer focus has evolved in recent decades.

In the 1970s, quality gurus argued that "quality is free." That is, a tireless pursuit of improvement should not only increase efficiency but also increase customer satisfaction in the process, saving enough on costs and bringing in enough new and repeat business to more than cover any expenditures on quality. This was an underlying concept in the success of many Japanese companies. In the 1980s the experts began to focus more directly on increasing customer satisfaction as an explicit goal.

Satisfying and keeping customers, it was argued, is simply less expensive than constantly replacing them. More recently, quality and satisfaction have been viewed as not sufficient by themselves. Companies boast of moving "beyond" quality and satisfaction to focus directly on customer loyalty as the key to profitability.

Yet to argue that quality, or satisfaction, or loyalty is what matters misses the point. These factors form a chain of cause and effect, building on each other so that they cannot be treated separately. They represent a system that must be measured and managed as a whole if you want to maximize results.

An example from our teaching experiences underscores the nature of the problem and why companies need to take a systems approach to customer measurement and management. Back in 1993 an executive seminar participant from a Fortune 100 company introduced himself as the "customer satisfaction manager" for his organization. This prompted one of the authors to ask, "What happened to the quality manager?" The participant replied that quality was passé, and that customer satisfaction had become the hot topic in his organization. In fact, being the quality manager had become the "kiss of death" from a career standpoint—a dead-end job! Five years later, a seminar participant from the same company introduced himself as the "customer loyalty manager" for the organization. Again the natural question arose, "What happened to the customer satisfaction manager?" "Oh, him?" It turned out that the satisfaction manager was now the one with the dead-end job.

Many business organizations are beginning to recognize the need to avoid this "Book of the Month Club" mentality and to view customers from a systems perspective. They want explicit linkages that extend from internal processes to customer perceptions to customer satisfaction to loyalty—and ultimately to bottom-line performance. The framework in this book will give executives hard numbers and not just persuasive theories to show that the connection is real and that improving satisfaction and loyalty really does improve profits. And those on the front lines—the quality engineers and service providers—will get specific guidance on what to improve and how to improve it to get the optimal response from customers.

This book will show you how to create an integrated customer measurement and management system that will help you allocate resources and increase profits. To create such a system, you must first understand your company's entire system for generating profit, from internal quality through to business performance. A systems approach acts on the basis of collected and interpreted customer data—but then you have to use the data to allocate resources and create change in the system or else you merely waste time and money.

With an effective customer measurement and management system, you can build organizational value. To do so, you will continually pursue three key activities that underlie a customer orientation: (1) gather customer information, (2) spread that information throughout the organization, and (3) use the information to maintain, improve, or innovate in products and processes.

You need solid information about the concrete product and service attributes or features that customers value, the more abstract consequences and benefits these attributes provide, and ultimately the personal values they serve. The purpose is to understand what your customers want not only in today's products and services but in tomorrow's as well. When you understand your customers at the various levels that motivate their behaviour, you can see their present needs and predict their future needs as well.

To maintain a customer orientation throughout your organization, you need to make sure that customer information gets to everyone who is involved— either directly or indirectly— in improving quality and value and satisfying customers. This both prepares the entire organization for change and provides benchmarks by which to monitor its performance. Finally, you need to prime the organization to act on the customer information to improve product and service offerings so as to increase satisfaction, loyalty, and profitability. This makes it essential to clarify the links among these three factors and understand how your company delivers a compelling product to its customers.

Creating a customer measurement and management system is central to the pursuit of all three of these activities. With such a system in place, you have your customer information in a form that can serve as a basis for both incremental and more revolutionary product and service improvements. The system also makes it easier to share customer information throughout an organization, enhancing its ability to follow through on that information to make product and process changes. It is essential to view customer measurement from a systems perspective that encompasses multiple areas of measurement and expertise (from engineering and design through market research and strategy to finance and accounting) so that you pick up both concrete and abstract details— both what the customers like and dislike and why they react that way—and develop information that will be genuinely useful.

Now you may well be saying, "But we already do a good job of gathering customer information, spreading it, and acting on the voice of the customer." The question is whether you really adopt the "lens of the customer" in this process or fall into the trap of relying on the "lens of the organization."

The lens of the customer shows you your products and services—and the benefits they provide—from your customers' perspective. You see them as they really are in the marketplace, rather than the different and potentially misleading picture you're likely to get from the lens of your own organization. For example, if you run a convenience store chain you may be inclined to view the chain's stores as providing customers with people (service), products (from soft drinks to gasoline), and operations (such as opening hours), each under the management of a different department or business function. The problem is that customers may not share this perspective. Customers view products and services from the standpoint of the benefits they provide and problems they solve, which may not align well with individual business process areas. In this case, customers are looking for safety, convenience, and cleanliness, which are benefits that are not uniquely provided by specific business process areas. Rather, they cut across the people, products, and operating policies of the stores.

Aside from providing a more accurate picture of the drivers of satisfaction and loyalty, adopting the lens of the customer has other advantages. It blurs functional boundaries and provides a common basis and language for communication. The forging of concrete links from area to area within a company is also a key to effective implementation. When an organization reaches a consensus on the importance of customer benefits that are not defined along functional or business process lines, it finds it much easier to engage in the cross-functional activities required to truly innovate and implement change.

We emphasize the word *framework* here. Our aim is to show just what links and models are possible.The actual elements and links in any model vary tremendously from company to company and context to context. After describing the framework, we will illustrate this point using two very different cases in which companies (Volvo and Sears) have developed models to become more customer focused.

The framework includes four general areas: internal quality, external quality and satisfaction, customer loyalty and retention, and financial performance. *Internal quality* encompasses various production and maintenance processes. In the case of a manufactured product, it includes everything from manufacturing processes to the physical characteristics and attributes that describe the product. In a service and retailing context, it includes the service offer, the physical surroundings, and the satisfaction of employees and the resulting service quality they provide.

External quality and satisfaction encompasses what customers see in the purchase and consumption experience: the attributes and benefits that products and services provide and the costs they impose, and the conclusions the customers draw about the company. In the area of customer loyalty and retention, *loyalty* is a customer's intention or predisposition to buy, while *retention* is the behaviour itself (as when a customer returns to a restaurant, comes back to buy the same brand of car, or purchases another financial instrument from the same institution). Although we will use the term *loyalty* at times to encompass both intended loyalty and actual retention, it is important to understand the distinction. When actual retention information is available, it proves extremely valuable in sorting out the drivers of financial performance. When it is unavailable, as it often is, you can use loyalty measures as a proxy for retention.

Quality, satisfaction, and loyalty ultimately affect financial performance, both directly and indirectly. The framework illustrates this point and highlights the possibility that there may be a tension between direct and indirect effects. Consider first the impact of internal quality. Producing a high-quality product or service at an attractive price indirectly affects financial performance through its effect on external customer perceptions of the purchase-consumption experience. But internal quality may also have a direct effect on costs and revenues. According to the "quality is free" argument, improvements in internal quality can increase productivity and lower internal costs and thus directly increase profitability. Recent research suggests, however, that this link is likely to be more positive for products and less positive or even negative for services. Why the difference? Services are produced and delivered at a time and place that is typically dictated by the customer. Thus improving service quality often requires an increase in personnel and operating or contact hours, which raises operating costs.

The external quality, value, and customer satisfaction component of the framework also has both direct and indirect effects on costs and revenues. Indirectly, a positive overall experience predisposes customers to stay loyal towards a product, service, or provider, which generates future sales. Satisfaction thus contributes to financial performance through its effect on loyalty and retention. But satisfaction also has direct effects, independent of loyalty. The cost of maintaining a customer account—or fixing a product—is a direct function of how happy the customer is. Satisfied customers are less likely to demand expensive product repairs or replacements or to invoke service guarantees. Also—even outside the world of TV commercials—people do talk about the products and services they buy, and your company's entry into that stream of word-of-mouth publicity is through perceived quality and satisfaction rather than through loyalty. Satisfaction is *news*—something to talk about—while loyalty is a background state that goes without saying unless something happens to damage it.

The direct effects of loyalty and retention on performance include revenues from repeat purchases, reduction in costs of finding new customers (to replace lost customers), and revenues generated through cross-selling. Another direct effect is the price premium that loyal customers often pay. Because loyal customers are not actively shopping for alternatives, they tend to be insulated from price incentives and offers such as coupons, price cuts, and free merchandise.

The recent turnaround at Volvo Car Company provides a good example of how a durable goods manufacturer views the links described in our framework. In 1991, Volvo was performing poorly in the global automotive market. It ranked as low as twenty-sixth out of thirty-four brands in the J. D. Power Initial Quality Study in the United States, and sales and profitability were suffering. In its comeback effort, Volvo began to develop a customer orientation from a total quality management foundation.

Formerly, Volvo had emphasized changing internal quality to improve productivity and reduce costs. Its management realized, however, that just focusing on internal quality was insufficient. Internal improvements had to matter to the customers before they could create improved external quality, customer satisfaction, and loyalty.

Volvo's approach is just one example of the variety of tailored models that are consistent with the framework. Like Volvo, Sears has attempted to radically transform itself into a more customer-focused organization. But since Sears is a retailer that competes primarily on service, its model has evolved quite differently. Internal quality at Sears is primarily about its people and the service they provide. The Sears model draws directly on a service-profit chain that links internal quality (including employee satisfaction and loyalty) to service quality, and the satisfaction generated by service quality to loyalty and financial performance.

In developing its model, Sears has discovered both direct effects of satisfaction on financial performance and indirect effects through loyalty, which is consistent with our framework. A quantitative employee-customer-profit model at Sears has helped the company to establish very specific links that have enabled it to improve financial performance. The model shows, for example, that a 5-point improvement in employee attitudes (on a 0 to 100 scale) drives a 1.3-point improvement in customer satisfaction, which in turn drives a 0.5 percent improvement in revenue growth.

The Volvo and Sears models share a common logic, but each model is uniquely tailored to the organization's own situation. Both models link internal quality through to profitability. At the same time, each reflects the nature of a specific company, its customers and offerings, and the contexts involved. When you look at your own company, you will see that the same logic will work for you when you develop a similar understanding of your own customers and what you can offer them.

The best measurement system can only provide information— it can't make decisions for you. People make decisions, whether it is the convenience store executive who sets corporate priorities, the front-line service manager who translates these priorities into policies and procedures, or the service worker who translates policies and procedures into concrete actions. At all three levels, decision makers are much more likely to choose to do something that will help the store chain succeed if they understand what matters to customers and how the job at hand can enhance that value.

The process of moving from information to decisions draws heavily on *importance-performance analysis*. According to this analysis, the most cost-effective areas of product and service performance to improve are those that are important to customers *and* on which, at the same time, the company is performing poorly. Executives and managers must identify these priority areas of high importance and low performance. As an output of this selection process, they can categorize and display the drivers of satisfaction and loyalty using a strategic satisfaction matrix.

The matrix identifies four categories of performance drivers with different market action implications. Again, the aspects to improve first are those where impact or importance is high and performance is weak. This focuses resources and quality improvement efforts likely to have the greatest impact on satisfaction and thus on loyalty and profitability. Those aspects where performance and impact are both high reflect a firm's competitive advantage. It is essential to maintain if not improve performance on these drivers. When impact and performance are both weak, on the other hand, there is no need to waste resources on improvement.

More interesting is the low impact–strong performance category. This may be an area where resources have been wasted in the past because the benefits and attributes are not important to customers. Alternatively, this category may contain drivers of satisfaction that customers see as basic and necessary—so much a part of the product or service that they ignore it as long as it's there when they want it, like electric power or water on tap. Although such drivers are important in an absolute sense, they have little to no impact on satisfaction because there is little variance in their performance. The danger is that a reduction in performance quality would increase the impact on satisfaction (this danger is often referred to as a "slippery slope"). Another possibility here is to find a new target market segment for the product or service. For example, if the quality of an electrical system is so constant that it has no impact on satisfaction in one application, the system might be used in applications where minor fluctuations in this quality are more important and therefore likely to have a real impact on satisfaction.

There is also a danger that something in this category may become important in the future. For example, few customers considered "environmental friendliness" to be an important factor until recently, but more and more people are beginning to pay attention to this aspect of the goods and services they buy. In a growing variety of fields, companies that predicted the importance of this area and prepared their business accordingly clearly have an advantage over those that did not.

The circular nature of the process reflects the continuous nature of a customer orientation. Customer needs, competitive offerings, and business technologies change constantly, so customer focus is an ideal of constant growth rather than static achievement. The cycle in is thus a continuous process of planning, researching, analysing, deciding, implementing, and learning. This includes identifying the system's purpose or goals within a more balanced set of corporate performance measures (including financial goals, employee satisfaction goals, process improvement goals, knowledge and learning goals, and so forth).

Who should collect your customer data, analyze it, and use it to set priorities and allocate resources? It often seems logical to delegate the satisfaction and loyalty measurement operation to outside research firms and consultants. This is especially true early in the process of becoming a customer-oriented organization, because outside specialists offer specific skills related to collecting and analysing customer data that you do not have. Unfortunately, if you delegate the system, your company does not take ownership of it, and you and your people may fail to learn or acquire the skills necessary to measure and manage customer data on your own. The consultant's bills, heavy as they are likely to be, are only a small part of the cost of handing off a customer information system.

Bear in mind that when customer information is the key to strategy, it should reside within the company. Your best teachers about what is right and wrong with your products and services are your own customers. Direct contact with customers and customer data is a critical part of learning what it takes to satisfy customer needs. No matter how good the consultants are, they will always function as filters.

An important part of establishing a customer orientation as a core competency is creating, over time, internal specialists to measure, model, and manage quality, satisfaction, and loyalty. Early in the process, external experts are apt to be a necessity. They can provide the interviewing, surveying, data warehousing, statistical analysis, and interpretation skills that you may lack or not yet want (or be able) to invest in.

Over time, however, continued reliance on external specialists becomes costly and also fails to develop customer measurement and management as a core competency. Internalization of the process allows you to adapt to changing market needs and competitive environments in a cost-effective fashion. More important, your organization accepts ownership of the process and the data—and the decisions that emerge.

This is not to say that all parts of the process should be brought in-house in all cases. You may not want to try to run a survey that involves computer-aided telephone interviews or a Web-based system with highly specialized personnel (such as trained interviewers) and potential economies of scale. Even in the most customer-savvy organization, it may be best to outsource certain parts of the process. At the same time, a truly customer-oriented firm should own rather than rent the ability to observe and to talk to customers, formalize survey instruments, analyze and interpret customer data, and use the output to make resource allocation decisions.

Over the last three decades business organizations have evolved from a focus on quality to a focus on customer satisfaction, and onward to a focus on loyalty as a means of creating value. A customer measurement and management system views each of these areas as an indispensable link in a chain of causes and effects that runs from internal quality through to profitability.

The goal of this book is to help you and your organization create an integrated customer measurement and management system for making effective resource allocation decisions and increasing profitability. In the process of building a system, organizations develop internal specialists capable of gathering, analysing, and interpreting customer data. Truly customer-oriented companies should, over time, add these skills to their core competencies.

A systems approach to customer measurement and management also requires that you tailor the system to your unique purpose, customers, and contexts. As an illustration, Volvo's model incorporates the positive effects of improving internal quality on both productivity and customer perceptions of quality, satisfaction, and loyalty. In contrast, a major retailer such as Sears incorporates the central role that satisfied employees play in delivering quality and value to customers.

These measurement systems and models are not substitutes for decision making. Rather, they provide the information you need to make resource allocation decisions and manage the process. The system provides information on how the company and its competitors are performing in different areas and how important the areas are to customers.

When combined with cost and strategy considerations, the system allows both enablers and doers to create organizational value through a continuous focus on customers. To maximize the value generated by the system, make sure your company's own staff perform the bulk of the work of collecting and interpreting customer data, so that you get the full benefit of the insights generated by the effort.

Before you dive in and start conducting customer interviews or surveys, you must know how your measurement system will be used. This chapter focuses on the strategy and planning for such a system. Since a customer orientation builds on internal quality, we'll start with a brief overview of quality management and its role in driving company strategy and customer measures. We'll then discuss two related approaches to translating strategy into action: policy deployment and balanced performance measures. Then we'll focus on the process of getting started on developing a customer measurement and management system—or improving an existing one—which involves taking a look at the breadth and depth of the proposed system and the role of market segmentation in it.

In our customer satisfaction framework, internal quality is the first in the chain of events that drives financial performance. It's important not to underestimate the role of *total quality management* (or TQM, also known as *company-wide quality management,* CWQM, and as *total quality control,* TQC)—nor to exaggerate it. For longterm survival, businesses have been forced to improve their abilities to change and innovate. But internal quality management is not in itself sufficient to assure success.

Internal quality improvements must be linked to improvements in external quality, satisfaction, loyalty, and financial performance. And the links must be established in an environment of constantly evolving customer preferences, markets, competitors, and technologies.

The broad principles and methods of quality management apply directly to the development of a customer measurement system. The concept of quality should unify all of a company's activities. After all, only your customers can ultimately define quality for you! In the end, it doesn't matter how well the production system works, how well marketing functions are performed, or how good the company's strategy is. If no one buys, there will be no revenues.

Quality experts emphasize three basic strategies for successful quality management: use reference models or benchmarks, set priorities for quality improvement, and focus your resources.

Do not try to do things completely on your own. Instead, make use of reference models or benchmarks when they're available. Benchmarking is particularly important in developing a customer measurement and management system.

Process benchmarking—finding out how things are done— works as well in developing a customer measurement and management system as in any other area of business. When you can manage it, arrange visits to firms with strong reputations to gauge their practices and learn what they are doing, see how they are doing it, and understand what is possible. Devote some time to reverse engineering their products as well. And don't limit the benchmarking to competitors—in a general area such as customer measurement, you'll find individuals or organizations in many fields who excel in areas that you are interested in improving. Benchmarking on their processes can help you to learn how to conduct better customer interviews, develop and administer more effective surveys, and analyze customer data in more productive ways—and they're likely to be much more willing to share information with you if you're not trying to sell the same offering to the same customers.

For *output* or *performance benchmarking,* you will measure your product or service against direct or indirect competitors on various dimensions such as internal or technical quality, external or perceived quality and value, and overall customer satisfaction, loyalty, and retention. As noted in Chapter Six, external benchmarks will help you interpret your findings regarding your own customers and decide just where to devote your resources to get the most mileage from your improvement efforts.

SET PRIORITIES FOR QUALITY IMPROVEMENT

The second basic strategy of quality management is the universal law of priorities. In a quality context, it is often said that 20 percent of parts, processes, or people account for 80 percent of quality problems (often called the *Pareto principle*). Each customer and each market will react differently to the various drivers of satisfaction and loyalty, so one of your primary goals in customer measurement is to identify the drivers that are most important to improve. As described in Chapter One, you need to find out where the impact on customers is high and your current performance is poor. Your goal should be to set priorities and *optimize* rather than *maximize* your quality and satisfaction improvement efforts.

FOCUS YOUR RESOURCES

Once you have chosen the area or areas to change, the third basic strategy of quality management is to concentrate your resources to maximal effect. The goal is to create a company-wide focus on the things that matter most for performance and survival. This is one of the most important yet also most often neglected aspects of quality management. Increasingly, managers face a common problem in that their customer measurement systems point out specific needs for improvement, but their organizations don't respond. The manager knows what area or areas to attack, but has difficulty getting anyone to do anything about it. This is where the lens of the customer shows its usefulness. Once the concept spreads through an organization the independent actions of each individual and department are much more likely to fit into the overall improvement effort.

Two Ways to Translate Strategy into Action

Since no amount of information will do you any good if no one will act on it, creating an environment where resources get focused on quality management is in many ways the key element of the process. One basic approach to this problem, called *policy deployment,* has proven very effective where a company has a clear priority regarding what policy to deploy. A variation known as *balanced performance measures* allows a company to determine and deploy a balanced mix of quality improvements.

Policy deployment, or hoshin planning *(hoshin kanri)* as it is sometimes called, is a powerful quality management process that converts a company's strategy into operational change and effectively moves different units within the company in the same direction. Customer policy deployment, in particular, aims to move the entire organization to focus more on customers in order to increase their satisfaction and loyalty. Policy deployment includes four major steps:

- *Mission and Vision:* Clearly state the organization's philosophy, mission, and vision (also called the *president's diagnosis*).
- *Goals:* Understand exactly where the organization is today and where it wants to be in the short, medium, and long term with regard to specific criteria or goals.
- *Communication Strategy:* Communicate the mission, vision, and goals throughout the organization.
- *Priority Setting and Implementation:* Set priorities, align the incentives, and implement quality improvement projects accordingly (using project management).

Making customers a priority became a strategy for Volvo's survival in the intensely competitive global automotive industry. Back in 1991, the question was how to create a customer orientation in a traditionally engineering-driven company. Volvo quickly realized that policy deployment was a natural means of building on its quality management foundations to move the company from an engineering focus to a customer focus. Here is a summary of how Volvo implemented the four major phases of policy deployment:

- *Volvo's Mission and Vision:* "To be the world's most desired and successful premium car brand."
- *Volvo's Goals:* "To be number 5 in customer satisfaction (according to the J. D. Power IQS study) in 1995 and number 3 in 1997."
- *Volvo's Communication Strategy:* Stop keeping secrets about customer complaints; give employees an open information system and a broad view of the customer value-added process that encompasses the vehicle sales and service experience throughout the life of the vehicle.
- *Volvo's Priority Setting and Implementation:* Use quality teams to focus on the two hundred highest-priority areas (out of two thousand possibilities identified in an initial review), and reward team members based on the degree to which Volvo met its corporate goals as well as on the degree to which the team met its own goals.

Once mission statements work their way through various levels of management, they often end up reading like the Boy Scouts' oath. Companies want to be all things to all people. In contrast, Volvo's vision was specifically to be the most desired successful specialty car brand. While abstract and forward-looking, the vision nonetheless pointed to a particular segment of the automotive market in which Volvo wanted to excel. Quantitatively,

Volvo's goal was defined in terms of placement in a specific independent survey—to be number 5 in its industry by 1995 and number 3 by 1997. Although any measurement system has its strengths and weaknesses, by defining customer satisfaction using the J. D. Power IQS study, Volvo effectively defined where it was (twenty-sixth out of thirty-four makes) and where it wanted to be at different points in time. Volvo effectively aligned its mission and vision to concrete measures and goals.

Volvo's next step was communication. Stellan Flodin, the senior vice president in charge of quality, and Jan-Olof Nilsson, senior vice president of Business Area 900, led the effort to create a communication process and culture of openness across the company. Volvo abandoned its hush-hush approach to quality and customer data in favour of a more open system in which information was made available to anyone who could influence customer satisfaction. This was critically important at Volvo because its employees perceived their company as doing quite well. Internally, they had been improving products and processes from year to year all along. But externally, relative quality was falling and the company was losing ground to competitors. This decline was a well-kept secret until Volvo decided to change policy and speak freely about its problems.

Many of the problems reported in the IQS studies involved customers' experiences with sales and service, so it was essential that Volvo encompass the entire value-added chain (from production to delivery and dealer service) in its policy deployment process. Over a period of about two years, the company created an environment in which individuals from very different value-adding areas worked together to solve a variety of customer problems. Reported quality problems came to be viewed as opportunities to learn and improve rather than as negative reflections on any particular area, team, or individual.

As noted, Volvo's customer data revealed over two thousand areas in which quality improvements might be made. The final stage of the process, project management, set priorities and put quality teams to work improving approximately two hundred of the most glaring problem areas. On the Volvo 850, for example, customer data revealed that the manual transmission alone generated a surprising number of complaints (about twenty per hundred vehicles). For example, many customers said the manual gear box was too stiff, and people of below average height added that the stick shift was too far away and difficult to reach in some gears. A project team was therefore deployed to improve the quality of the transmission. Additional customer surveys allowed the team to translate customer perceptions into design and part changes that, when introduced, decreased the incidence of complaints by over 50 percent.

A key to making all this happen, however, was that Volvo aligned the project teams' and individuals' goals with overall policy goals. Team members were compensated based on whether their teams met project goals (such as reducing transmission problems per hundred cars from twenty to ten to five over time) and whether Volvo met its overall corporate goals such as reducing overall problems per hundred cars to reach the number 5 position by 1995 and the number 3 position by 1997.

The policy deployment process that Sears is using to create a customer focus is similar to the process at Volvo. The main difference is that, whereas Volvo built on its knowledge of quality management to implement policy deployment from the top down, Sears is using the development of its employee-customerprofit chain (the idea that satisfied employees make for satisfied customers and thereby increase sales and profits, described in Chapter One) to drive the deployment process from the bottom up. The process has been more implicit than explicit.

Retail-service companies have not gone through the same quality management revolution and training as manufacturing companies such as Volvo. But once Sears's employee-customerprofit chain was developed, it became an important tool to drive change in the company's mission, vision, goals, and communication. Everyone from senior managers to store employees had to be taught the logic of the model and its implications, including how the company's competitive environment had changed. The company held town hall meetings and used learning maps to help employees grasp the logic behind the model so that they, in turn, could apply it at the store level. In the end, the deployment process has helped build a leadership model that incorporates the various aspects of the employee-customer-profit chain. The leadership model is to make Sears a compelling place to work, shop, and invest.

Yet the deployment process has progressed more slowly at Sears than at Volvo. The process at Sears has been more data driven, working from the bottom up. Only after the employee-customer-profit chain was developed did Sears executives confront many of the challenges in deploying policy, from a lack of buy-in among top executives to communication problems among their retail employees. And arguably, Volvo has been more successful at implementing its customer orientation and turning the corner on profitability. After some initial success, financial performance at Sears remains weak.

These results aren't surprising, and they provide a useful warning to those in service industries. Product companies tend to have a history of quality management when they begin to implement customer policy deployment, and this gives them a strong head start.

Few service companies have gone through the same quality revolution, although there are important exceptions. Disney, Fidelity Investments, and USAA, for example, have long-standing commitments to quality management and its principles. Disney has used policy deployment in the development of its theme parks for many years. But most service firms simply did not get the wake-up call that hit manufacturing firms in the 1970s and 1980s, when they were confronted with competitors producing higher-quality products in less time and at lower cost.

If you manage or work in a service industry such as telecommunication, insurance, or banking, very likely your company is now experiencing or will soon experience the same type of global competition and cost pressures as your counterparts in the manufacturing world. Technology such as the Internet now provides a basis for delivering cost-effective global service. The warning from product companies is clear. If you hope to continue to prosper, establish a culture that emphasizes quality as your foundation for using customer information to drive organizational change.

Balanced performance measures or BPMs share many of the principles of policy deployment. But whereas policy deployment has always been an explicit means of translating strategy into action, BPMs were initially developed as a way of balancing the needs of multiple stakeholders in an organization. Rather than focusing mainly on customers, BPMs recognize that a customer focus must be balanced against the needs of other stakeholders, such as owners, employees, and suppliers. A popular approach to developing BPMs is the balanced scorecard.

Companies use the balanced scorecard to assess their performance and strategy in a highly integrated fashion. The scorecard's four main components are the company's financial perspective, the customer perspective, the internal business process perspective, and the learning and innovation perspective.

The *customer perspective* includes those customer measures that are most important for the company to improve, such as targets for customer satisfaction or account penetration. The *financial perspective* includes targets the company sets with respect to both financial (market value) and accounting (revenue and profit) measures. The *internal perspective* includes internal quality and business process measures, such as the number of hours the company spends talking with customers about current or future projects, or the level of employee satisfaction. The *innovation and learning perspective* include goals and measures for investments in training and new product or service development. For each perspective, goals and measures are developed and drilled down to operational levels for teams and individuals ("personal scorecards").

As balanced performance measurement systems evolved through the 1990s, their relationship to policy deployment has become clear. For example, in more recent versions of the balanced scorecard, a company's vision and strategy drive a management process that includes strategy feedback and learning, clarifying and translating the vision and strategy, communicating and linking rewards to performance measures, and planning and setting targets. These stages obviously parallel the four main steps in policy deployment described earlier. Yet important differences remain. Whereas a full policy deployment moves an organization in a completely new direction, such as focusing more explicitly on customers, BPMs balance various stakeholders' needs. In this sense, BPMs are a weak form of policy deployment. They more or less presume that the organization is headed in the right direction and align its activities accordingly. A balanced scorecard approach keeps an organization on course through an integrated management and budgeting process.

BPMs also lack any guiding framework or model of the drivers of financial performance. The approach focuses generally on synergies among the various perspectives or stakeholder needs. As emphasized in Chapter One, it is important that you build your measurement system on an evolving understanding of the drivers of financial performance that is tailored to your company and competitive environment, as Volvo and Sears did.

Although this book's focus is primarily on the customer perspective, balanced performance measures do serve as a reminder that the measurement and management process described here can be applied to other stakeholders as well. In the Sears model, for example, employee attitudes and beliefs are critically important in driving employee behaviour. The processes and tools described in this book for developing the lens of the customer can certainly be applied to develop the lens of the employee, supplier, or equity stakeholder as a basis for developing and administering surveys, analysing data, and setting priorities for improvement.

When you embark on a strategy of customer-driven quality improvement, questions will arise about how to set up a system to collect the data you need to work with. Many of these questions can be broadly categorized as relating either to *system breadth*— the range of internal and external customers and market segments that you want to measure—or to *system depth*—the level of detail and nature of the information that you gather.

Companies typically serve a range of very different customers both inside and outside the organization. Internal customers may be in the same physical location, as when marketing and finance are customers of information services, or in different locations, as when manufacturing plants are customers of the home office. External customers range from wholesalers and retailers to end users. The customer chain shows three levels of customers: plant customers, retailing customers, and end users. We have kept this example simple to make the relationships easy to see on paper; in practice any given organization or network is likely to have a much larger number of customer levels, as any individual might be considered someone else's customer. And it isn't enough to track exchanges of funds for goods or services, as even external customers don't necessarily pay to assume that role—regulatory agencies are customers for reports, for example, and people downstream (literally or metaphorically) from traditional end users are the ones likely to be customers for ecological and recycling efforts.

To determine just which customers should be your primary measurement and management focus, refer back to the framework in Chapter One. What links in the customer chain drive your financial performance? Where are the links from quality to satisfaction to loyalty and profitability the strongest? Those are the places where you're likely to get the most mileage out of any investment in improved quality. Even without a detailed measurement system, you probably have some knowledge or understanding of where to start looking.

Think about the nature of the competition and customer choice at each level. The logic of a customer orientation (the idea that quality, satisfaction, and loyalty drive profitability) is based on two critical assumptions. First, the customer is relatively free to choose products and services. This assumption holds for most industries in the developed world today—customers face a dizzying variety of brands of cars, soap, phone service, and most necessities and luxuries, and if one alternative doesn't satisfy there's always another to try. This assumption doesn't always hold true, however—when customers face significant switching costs in moving from one provider to another, or there is only one supplier available, they are essentially hostages. That is, when it's expensive or difficult to find another supplier, only a very dissatisfied customer will switch to a competitor. Airline customers are often held hostage to the hub-and-spoke system of air travel, where flying on other than the hub airline imposes significant costs in terms of time and convenience. However, no company can count on keeping its customers hostage indefinitely. In the gas and electric supply business, for example, many customers still have few options to choose from—but recent deregulation means that the situation is changing rapidly, and customer satisfaction and loyalty are likely to become drivers of profitability soon.

The second important assumption in the logic of a customer orientation is that the important customers are the ones who will generate new business if they're satisfied with their experience—buy replacements for past purchases, buy new offerings, or inspire potential customers to try the company's wares. Investments to satisfy more transient or one-time customers may not generate future revenues or cost savings. The benefits of increasing satisfaction are thus greatest at the level in the customer chain where your customers have both a choice and a potential to reward you with future revenues at lower costs.

Related to the notion of customer choice is the relative *push* versus *pull* of your products and services through the customer chain. Consider a service provider such as Fidelity, which places investment instruments through a variety of independent retailers. In one region, the end users—the individual investors— may have strong brand attitudes and perceptions that have been created over a long period of time through experience, advertising, and word of mouth. In this case, the most important customer in the chain is probably the end user who goes to a retailer (whether an agency or a Web site) in search of a particular offering. The choice in this case resides primarily with end users who pull the product through the chain. Although all customers are important at some level, relatively speaking, the satisfaction of the retailer is not as critical in this case as the satisfaction of the end user. To satisfy and retain their own customers, the retailers need to make the Fidelity offerings available to them.

Elsewhere, investors may be much more likely to follow the advice of the retailer about which brand to purchase. The retailer may be more established and trusted in the end user's mind than any individual brand. If investors are more likely to defer their choice to a trusted retailer, Fidelity is in a position of pushing the product or service through the chain. In this case, the most important thing to measure and manage may be the satisfaction of the retailer and its willingness to push the brand on to the end user. The same logic applies regardless of the product or service—if the offering is seen as interchangeable at the end-user level, you have to give the retailer a reason to favour your brand over others.

At each level in the customer chain, the market segmentation scheme is the key element in your strategic market plan to build a customer measurement system. Market segmentation is the process of identifying and targeting unique populations or *segments* of customers and developing tailored marketing strategies to meet the individual segment needs. To identify and target segments, take the following steps:

- Group customers into segments based on customer needs, benefits sought, or personal values served.
- Identify or describe the segments according to their behaviours, lifestyles, or demographics.
- Evaluate the attractiveness of each segment in terms of, for example, profit potential, risk, capacity utilization, and core competencies required to serve the segment.
- Determine strategically which segments to target and pursue and, as a result, which segments to measure, analyze, and manage separately.

These steps bring you to a framework for just which customers to measure, analyze, and monitor. Because the drivers of satisfaction and loyalty may be very different from segment to segment, be wary of averaging across segments. Averages can be deceiving. If customer data are aggregated too highly, they provide a profile of an average customer who simply does not exist. If the segments are different enough, they will require separate survey development and analysis. Even when the same survey is applicable to more than one group of customers, be sure to analyze importance and performance levels separately for each group.

SEGMENTATION IN A HOTEL CHAIN

Consider, for example, the needs of business customers and vacation customers at "Wolverine Inns" a fictitious name for a major mid-priced hotel chain we worked with recently. The chain recently segmented its franchisees according to which segment of customers they are most likely to serve, based on the idea that downtown properties cater more to the business customer segment and leisure-area properties cater more to the vacation customer segment.

The matrices are used to set priorities for quality improvement. The company's satisfaction and loyalty survey covers eight general quality areas or customer benefits (reservation process, staff, facilities, grounds, bathroom, room, breakfast, and perceived value) and each area is rated on a variety of attributes. For the moment, just look at the impact and performance aspects of the eight types of benefit. Later we will take up the issue of setting priorities among the attributes that provide each benefit, such as the friendliness, helpfulness, efficiency, and grooming and appearance of the hotel staff.

The vertical axes show how each type of property performs on each of the eight benefits using a weighted average of customers' attribute ratings (on a scale where 1 is poor and 5 is excellent). Both downtown and leisure-area properties, for example, perform very well on the quality of the reservations process. The horizontal axes show the relative importance of each benefit as revealed by its statistical impact on overall satisfaction. For example, the impact score of.75 for quality of the room for the downtown properties shows that as room quality increases by 10 percent, satisfaction increases by 7.5 percent (10 percent ×.75). (This example is based on standardized scale values.)

The results reveal vast differences in the drivers of satisfaction across the two property types. Business customers who frequent downtown Wolverine Inn locations look for the hotel to simply provide a clean and comfortable room. They use the hotel for a place to get a good night's sleep and have little interest in its other services. In contrast, a much wider variety of factors drive satisfaction for the vacation customers who frequent the chain's leisure-area properties. The quality of the room is secondary to the quality of service and advice that the staff provides. The quality of the grounds, bathroom, and breakfast are also more important for the vacation customer.

As hotel manager at any given property, you would certainly want to know impact and performance levels for your target customers. Assuming the described results for individual hotels, the downtown manager would see improving the quality of the rooms as the greatest priority, given its high impact and currently moderate performance. In contrast, the manager of the leisure-area property would see improving the quality of the staff as relatively more important. Neither manager would have much incentive to do anything about perceived value—the customers' view of the price they are paying for the experience—even though it is far and away the lowest performance area in both cases, because the survey results show that neither group of customers cares much about it. Lowering prices would be costly for the hotel and would make it more difficult to sustain improvements in areas that matter to the customers, so it's best to avoid this step unless the hotel has an incentive to change its customer base to one that regards the current price level as a barrier rather than a minor irritant.

After deciding which customer levels to include in the measurement system and what customers or market segments to include, the next step is to ask what level of generality or detail about the lens of the customer the system should contain. Customer satisfaction is a complex matter, made up of the way the customer perceives the concrete attributes of a product, the benefits the customer derives from those attributes, and the personal values that the product supports. All these elements reside with the customer and are beyond the company's direct control, so we refer to them as *external quality factors.* Measurement systems vary in the amount of detail they provide about external factors such as these.

For example, macro-level measurement systems such as the American Customer Satisfaction Index (ACSI) only include very general differences in external perceptions of overall quality and value as drivers of satisfaction and loyalty. Quality is itself measured using customer ratings of the levels of customization and reliability provided, while value is measured using customer perceptions of the price or prices paid for the quality received. The purpose of measurement systems such as the ACSI is, however, to provide quality, value, satisfaction, and loyalty benchmarks across a very wide range of firms, industry groupings (including products, services, retailers, and government and public agencies), and even countries. Such broad-based comparisons require a measurement system that emphasizes generality and comparability as opposed to depth and detail.

If your goal is to improve or radically reinvent goods and services, you'll need a more detailed and comprehensive information system. It should include information on the range of concrete attributes and abstract benefits that might drive satisfaction and require improvement. Chapter Three will return to the convenience store example and discuss perceived convenience, merchandise quality, and safety as just three of the benefits that directly affect customer satisfaction.

In subsequent chapters we will discuss how to develop these more detailed or in-depth measurement systems for the purpose of measuring and managing customer data for a particular product or service and market segment. Remember that the information in the measurement system is designed to leverage either incremental (evolutionary) or innovative (revolutionary) activities, or both. For example, when Volvo discovered that its customers found its manual transmissions difficult to shift (an attribute-level problem), it translated the problem into one of changing certain parts that immediately reduced complaints. In contrast, when product or service designers are pursuing major innovations, they shift upward from the attribute level to more abstract customer benefits and personal values as input to the design process. Developing a fuel cell or electric vehicle, for example, requires matching the benefits and consequences that the new technology provides (such as zero emissions and moderate performance) with the benefits and values that are important to target customers (such as a willingness to trade off vehicle performance for environmental impact). Product or service design is then a process of developing a whole new configuration of product and service attributes to better serve customer needs.

We are often asked when to engage in revolutionary innovation rather than more evolutionary continuous improvement. The key, of course, is to avoid focusing on one to the exclusion of the other, but rather to balance both activities. Masaaki Imai, who was instrumental in developing the *kaizen* or continuous improvement process, emphasizes the importance of maintaining a balance among three activities: maintaining the quality of existing products, services, or processes; achieving kaizen or continuous improvement; and achieving innovation. The temptation, Imai argues, is to focus only on innovation as a means of making rapid changes and leapfrogging the competition. This ignores the long-term benefits that continuous improvement brings to a company.

When all three activities are balanced, the result is a formidable competitive advantage. Disney is a great example of an organization that consistently manages to balance all three activities. The regular development of new characters for use in movies, television shows, and theme parks is a constant source of innovation. At the same time, Disney works to maintain or keep improving every stage of its customers' experience. The combination has created a legendary service organization that is built on a quality foundation *and* reinvents itself on a regular basis.

Measuring quality, customer satisfaction, and loyalty should be an ongoing, repetitive process. It is difficult, however, to make general recommendations about just how frequently to measure. The frequency varies from company to company and depends on the audience, the stability or volatility of the product or service, and the nature of the market. For instance, if you have relatively few customers it may not be desirable to survey them too often. Needless to say, your customers should never feel that the process is burdensome. And once you do a survey and set some priorities, be sure to implement the changes before you launch another survey. Otherwise, your customers will ask the obvious question: "Why should I bother filling out this survey when you didn't pay any attention to the last one?"

A product's life cycle also affects the frequency of measurement. You need frequent contact with customers early on, when the market is evolving and changes to the product or service can have a great impact on a company's success. Consider the battle between Ericsson and Nokia in the cellular phone market. The early adopters of cellular phones were businesspeople. They simply wanted a reliable phone, which gave Ericsson the edge. But Ericsson did not keep up with the evolution of customer needs in the market and emergence of new market segments that demanded more features and design improvements. This allowed Nokia to achieve a greater advantage as the market evolved.

Later in a product's life cycle, customers are much harder to attract, more valuable to keep, and more costly to lose, so again you want close and frequent customer contacts. And, of course, it is always important to listen carefully to customers when the threat of competition has increased. The general point is that contact with customers should become more frequent during certain critical stages of the product life cycle and market dynamics.

Keeping these contingencies in mind, we recommend a customer satisfaction survey at least yearly. More frequent surveys are likely to have little effect on your improvement efforts when the product and the market are stable. If competition is really active and is moving quickly in a market, it may be necessary to carry out more frequent studies—perhaps even on a quarterly basis. But make sure you have enough resources to process and implement the findings, or the efforts are wasted. It is often a good compromise to measure every six months in times of change.

Finally, remember that there's a difference between customer measures and surveys as the basis of a measurement and management system and more informal surveys or methods designed to take a quick pulse or to identify problems as they occur. The latter methods typically focus on the most recent episode or transaction with a customer (such as the latest stay at the hotel or visit to the bookstore), and are often loosely structured (an informal interview by the manager or an open-ended "opinion" card). Their value towards allocating resources and deciding strategy is limited. At the same time, they may be a valuable source of information for service managers or front-line service personnel to catch and resolve certain classes of problems as they occur.

Providing external quality and customer satisfaction depends directly on the quality of your company's internal processes, operating policies, strategies, and plans. Whether your company provides products or services (or both), quality management provides a solid foundation for developing and deploying strategy and measuring quality through the lens of the customer. As you move through subsequent chapters, you will see the three basic strategies of quality management. We will describe the use of reference models or benchmarks to interpret and analyze customer data. We will show you how to optimize rather than maximize customer satisfaction and loyalty by setting priorities for quality improvement. Finally, we will describe ways to maximize use of available resources to implement the change. Policy deployment and its variants, including balanced performance measures, are important tools for creating a more universal and consistent focus. These approaches provide companies with a means of translating their customer strategies into action.

Just where to begin building the system requires decisions regarding which customers to include, or system breadth, and how much detail to provide, or system depth. You want to include the kinds of customers that drive business performance. To do this, you will need to ask "which of our internal or external customers are both a source of future profits and have a choice about where they take their business?" To drive profitability, produce and deliver high-quality products and services to satisfy and retain these customers. When including customers in the measurement system, remember that customers do not all value the same things and behave in the same way. Build your customer measurement systems on an understanding of how your customer base at any given level (such as retail or end-user) is segmented.

Segmentation is a process of identifying individuals or populations of customers with unique needs and wants. By paying attention to segment differences you will avoid the pitfall of setting priorities based on "average" customers who don't exist. In your planning process, also consider just how much detail you will need to measure and how you will use your measurement system. At a general level, macro-level customer measurement systems provide for broad-based comparisons and benchmarking but give only general guidance about what companies should improve (such as product or service quality or value). In this book, the focus is on measurement systems that are more specific to the company or segment; they provide detailed information regarding concrete product or service attributes as well as information about more abstract consequences and benefits. By continually improving the concrete attributes of existing offerings and finding completely new ways to provide customer benefits, you can leverage your customer data to create a truly exemplary level of performance and competitive advantage.

To link internal quality to profitability, you have to find out how customers see the products and services they purchase and consume. Your first step (and the subject of this chapter) will be to develop a model of how customers view your firm's products, services, and activities—the "lens of the customer" that will guide the rest of your efforts.

As discussed earlier, people inside an organization too often develop customer surveys from their own perspective, or how they believe customers view their products and services.

The result is a survey or measurement instrument that embodies the lens of the organization rather than the lens of the customer. You'll often see airline surveys organized in this fashion, for example, full of questions broken out by organizational activity (check-in, preflight service, food and beverage, flight crews, and cabin environment).

A survey that aligns question areas with organizational responsibility in this fashion does have the advantage of producing recommendations that are fairly straightforward to implement. If the survey results and prioritysetting process indicate that flight crews are most in need of improvement, then the responsibility for making improvements within the organization is clear.

Unfortunately, this type of survey may warp or entirely miss issues that cross organizational boundaries, as when flight crews get blamed for being short-tempered about carry-on baggage that should never have been allowed into the cabin in the first place. Customers tend to form opinions regarding such benefits as service, convenience, and safety that cut across the functional areas of an organization.

It is essential, therefore, that the measurement system be based squarely on the lens of the customer. In addition, having a survey instrument that better captures the customers' perception of the company makes the data easier to analyze.

We are able to explain more variation in key customer evaluations and behaviours, such as satisfaction and loyalty, when the questionnaire is based on the customers' view. For an airline, such a questionnaire might address a whole range of activities from seat reservations through boarding to baggage claim under the heading of convenience, and everything from the gate lobby staff to the seat cushions under the heading of comfort.

The concrete attributes of a product or service and the abstract benefits it generates occupy different levels in the customers' lens. This distinction is very useful but may take some getting used to.

The rectangular objects at the left-hand side represent the concrete aspects or dimensions on which customers can readily report performance via survey measures (such as whether a sales staff keeps its appointments and returns telephone calls and e-mail messages). The circular objects to the right of the attributes represent the relatively abstract or *latent* variables that capture the benefits or consequences that the attributes provide or, at an even more abstract level, the personal values that they serve. For simplicity, we will refer to all the abstract drivers of satisfaction and loyalty as *benefits.*

As in a traditional marketing perspective, the customer satisfaction model embodies the view that products and services compete primarily on the benefits they provide or the needs they fulfill. The concrete attributes of the product or service are only the means to these more abstract ends. Letters, e-mail messages, and faxes all, for example, provide the benefit of communication. You can thus view benefits as the primary drivers of satisfaction in the lens. Notice, however, that benefits may be measured using different numbers of concrete attributes.

Satisfaction in the model is defined as a customer's overall evaluation of the purchase and consumption experience with a product, service, or provider. This definition is quite different from transaction-specific definitions of satisfaction that capture a customer's immediate reaction to a particular episode or experience. Why discard the immediate response in favour of a more cumulative or overall definition of satisfaction? Although it seems more remote, the latter turns out to be more directly tied to customers' repurchase intentions and behaviour. Customers' repurchase decisions are affected by their entire purchase and consumption history with a company or brand, not just the last trip to the restaurant or last shipment from a supplier. Although we list loyalty, broadly defined, as the desired outcome of satisfaction, there are other constructs we could have shown there as well. Customer satisfaction may also lead to an enhanced reputation and greater brand equity for the company, which will in turn attract additional customers who are disposed to develop loyalty of their own.

The also see overall satisfaction and loyalty in circles, treating them as abstract constructs that can be measured in concrete terms. Overall satisfaction is reflected in different concrete satisfaction measures, which might include a satisfaction scale, how the product or service performs overall versus customer expectations, performance versus an ideal product or service in the category, and performance versus "best in class" competitors. Similarly, loyalty may be measured using a variety of behavioural intentions (ratings of the likelihood that customers will return, will purchase other products and services from the company, or will speak positively of their experience to others) or actual behaviours (such as whether customers do return, how often they return and how much they purchase when they do, and whether they bring or refer additional customers).

Note the dotted arrow that runs from an attribute-benefit cluster directly to customer loyalty. This captures the possibility that customers' intentions or decisions to repurchase are affected directly by certain benefits. In a recent study of satisfaction with hair care providers, for example, we found that the quality of the haircut, the relationship with the stylist, and the atmosphere of the salon all affect loyalty via overall satisfaction. However, the timeliness and ease of scheduling an appointment have direct effects on loyalty in addition to their effects on satisfaction. Price can also affect loyalty directly— customers are likely to weigh price or value much more when evaluating loyalty than when evaluating satisfaction. "I love his work, but I can't afford to go back every month"

You can't develop the lens of the customer by sitting around and reflecting on how customers view the world. Instead, you need in-depth, qualitative research to show you the issues from the customers' own perspective. Keep in mind that the goal of conducting qualitative research (such as interviews and focus groups) is not to immediately set priorities for quality improvement— it is to identify a comprehensive range of issues (benefits and attributes) that potentially drive satisfaction, loyalty, and profitability. The customer sample that you use at this stage of the research should represent a good cross-section or range of customers from the population or target market of interest, but it need not be truly random as you're not looking for statistical validity at this point. The lens or model that results from this qualitative research provides the foundation for more systematic survey research, which in turn becomes the primary basis for setting priorities when you get to that stage of the process.

Marketing books offer a wide choice of qualitative methods that you can use to identify product and service attributes and the customer benefits they provide—one-on-one interviews, group interviews or focus groups, protocol methods (having customers "think out loud" while using or evaluating a product or service), and a variety of observation techniques. Here, we focus on one qualitative technique that is particularly well suited to the development of a customer model or lens: the *critical incident technique* (CIT).

The CIT can be used to identify satisfaction drivers for a range of internal and external customers. It typically involves an interview in which individuals or groups of customers are asked to provide a list of the things that they like and dislike about the product, service, or company in question. According to Bob Hayes, an expert on the CIT approach, "A critical incident is a specific example of the service or product that describes either *positive* or *negative* performance. A positive example is a characteristic of the service or product that the customer would like to see every time he or she receives that service or product. A negative example is a characteristic of the service or product that would make the customer question the quality of the company."

The critical incidents themselves should be as specific as possible in describing a single feature of the customer's purchase and consumption experience. Hayes argues that a good critical incident should cover a single behaviour or characteristic, and should either describe the service provider in behavioural terms or describe the service or product using specific adjectives. Consider two examples from the case study in Appendix A, which describes CIT interviews with tire retailers. One retailer noted positively that "the range (variety) of products is good"—pointing to a particular characteristic of the tires (the available range) using a specific adjective (good). Another retailer noted negatively that "regional representatives arrive too seldom"—pointing to a specific behaviour of the local salesperson (waiting too long between visits).

If the critical incidents are too general, the interviewer needs to ask additional questions to clarify what the customer really has in mind. For each specific incident, it is also useful to ask the customer for comments on the significance and consequences of the incident. Such questions will elicit valuable information for the next stage of the process, categorising the incidents into attributes and benefit groupings.

When encouraged to elaborate, for example, the retailer who praised the product range pointed out that carrying a range of tire products allowed him to offer "a tire for almost every customer that walks into my store." The one who said the regional representative arrived too seldom said that "he should come every month ...just to see how things are going."

Overall, the CIT process involves a number of steps that are helpful to describe using an activity-based flowchart. Step 1 is to compile and assess whatever relevant secondary research or knowledge pertaining to the lens of the customer already exists within the company.

(One should avoid, of course, any biases from the lens of the organization.) Perhaps similar studies have been conducted in slightly different research contexts that shed light on how customers view the product or service. Step 2 is to make initial visits to different customers early in the process. We have found this important for two reasons. First, the visits will provide firsthand observations of the

QUALITY-SATISFACTION

You'll usually need several sources of data to establish all the links from quality through to profits. Consider the experience at Sears and Volvo. Sears uses one survey to measure internal quality in the form of employee perceptions and attitudes and a second survey to measure external quality and satisfaction from the customers' perspective. Information from both sources is then combined with financial performance information for individual stores to trace the links in the employee-customer-profit chain. Volvo tracks internal quality with engineering-based measures of vehicle performance, and uses customer surveys to track external quality.

Now we focus on ways to develop and administer the survey that measures customer perceptions of quality, satisfaction, and loyalty. The lens of the customer—built from the qualitative research in Chapter Three—will serve as a blueprint for your survey, identifying the attributes to include and the order they should appear. To make the survey results useful, however, you will also need to specify and include measures of satisfaction and loyalty so as to be able to combine the individual customer responses into a meaningful pattern of causes and effects.

Step 1: The Preliminaries

As in any other activity, if you don't know what you want to get out of customer measurement, it's going to be hard to tell if you've found it. So before you develop the survey itself, you need to figure out what information is required—which is a function of what you're planning to do with it—as well as how to segment your customer base, what survey method or methods to use, and how to sample the population.

What Information Is Required?

Start by restating in simple terms what you want your customer survey to tell you, and what you plan to do about it. This might be as generic as "We want to know what our customers want so we can give them more of it—and what they don't want, so we can avoid including it, " or it might be tailored to your particular business. Then look back at the lens of the customer and list the attributes and benefits it identifies as having the potential to drive customer satisfaction and loyalty.

Then list some direct questions about customer satisfaction and loyalty. From a statistical standpoint, these are the primary dependent variables that the model is to explain based on customer perceptions of attribute and benefit performance.

Make sure that the things you're asking about are at least partially under your control, so the results will be meaningful and useful. There is no point in finding out that your customers are uniformly unhappy that every day they get a day older, unless you're in the business of providing some way to preserve youth and prolong life. So consider just how the results will affect areas and individuals in your organization and what actions you may need to take based on the results.

How to Segment Survey Respondents?

The next step is to figure out which market segments to include in the survey—and just how to classify respondents into those segments. The choice of segments should be based on their importance in your strategic market plans. Beyond the choice of key segments (such as "daily" and "weekly" convenience store customers), another important question related to segmentation and sampling is whether to include current, past, or potential customers in the research.

Companies are often content to focus only on current customers. Unfortunately, if current customers are systematically different from those you've lost or those you would like to pursue in the future, your results from a currentcustomer survey could be misleading or incomplete.

Market segment classifications may be based on information collected prior to the survey. Existing research may already have determined which customers are classified into which segments. If survey respondents can be identified and classified into segments beforehand, then it is perhaps unnecessary to have segment-related information in the survey itself. Otherwise it will be critical to include information in the survey that allows you to sort or select customers by segment. The sorting or selection criteria may be direct or indirect.

The Indirect Approach

Using the indirect approach, you might include descriptive items in the survey such as demographic variables (age, sex, income level, education level, ethnic background), geographic variables (city, country, or geographic area), and experience-related variables (frequency of purchase or consumption of the product or service, confidence in evaluating the product or service, and so on). These measures would then be analyzed *after* the surveys are administered to develop distinct clusters or groups of customers that differ on the variables of interest (such as male versus female or frequent versus infrequent convenience store customers).

This approach is indirect in the sense that the descriptive measures are only proxies for identifying more needs-based segments. A disadvantage of this approach is that it can lead to the inclusion of so many descriptive variables that the survey becomes long and cumbersome.

An advantage of the approach is that it provides a database that can be used to develop and identify new segments. This allows you to *cut,* or sort the data, in various anticipated and unanticipated ways. Descriptive variables are typically collected near the end of the survey.

If a customer feels sensitive about answering particular questions (such as age, income, or education level), encountering such questions up front may bias the responses to the whole questionnaire or lead the customer to give up on it entirely.

The Direct Approach

Using the direct approach, you provide an existing segmentation within which customers place themselves in a needs-based segment. Often companies have some existing knowledge of the major segments or populations in their customer base. If simple descriptions of each of the different segments can be included in the survey, customers can indicate directly which segment they most identify with. For the convenience store survey, for example, independent research conducted prior to the survey helped us define five major segment profiles. We then used the profiles to develop descriptive statements for each segment:

- *Segment 1:* I tend to visit a convenience store several times a day for snacks as well as meals.
- *Segment 2:* I am a parent who occasionally goes to a convenience store mainly to buy fill-in items, emergency items, or things for the kids.
- *Segment 3:* I visit a convenience store daily to buy one or two items such as a soda, coffee, cigarettes, or candy.
- *Segment 4:* I go to a convenience store once or twice a week to buy a snack, soda, or coffee.
- *Segment 5:* I shop at a convenience store less than once a week, mainly to buy snacks and party items or items for a trip.

In the resulting convenience store survey (presented in Appendix B at the end of the book), we asked survey respondents to indicate which of these statements best described their behaviour. The primary advantage of this approach is that it is based directly on an existing segmentation scheme. This greatly simplifies the analysis of the survey data. The responses are simply sorted according to their segment identification and analyzed. The disadvantage of using existing segment profiles is that it assumes that the profiles provide an accurate description of the underlying segments. If the nature of the segments changes between the segmentation study and the quality-satisfaction-loyalty survey, the results of the latter will be skewed in unpredictable ways.

We recommend using a hybrid of the direct and indirect segmentation approaches when possible. Using existing segment profiles simplifies subsequent analysis and bases the analysis squarely on a segmentation scheme. But it is helpful to include some additional descriptive questions. The convenience store questionnaire, for example, augments the segment-level questions with a small number of demographic questions used in U.S. census questionnaires. The hybrid approach allows for some exploratory analysis using the demographic variables to sort or cluster respondents into new segments. The demographics also provide descriptive details of the segment profiles, such as whether "daily" convenience store customers tend to be male, female, older, younger, and so on.

Prior to developing the survey, you also need to decide just how to communicate with customers and administer the survey. The choice of survey methods has important implications for the nature of the questions and scales involved. There are various approaches, the more common being one-on-one interview surveys, telephone surveys, Web-based surveys, and written surveys. Each method has its strengths and weaknesses. The choice of methods should depend on the context.

One-on-one interviews are well suited to business-to-business applications, where the population of customers is relatively well defined (such as those customers who purchase a certain type of chemical or part). Conducting personal interviews is a good way to increase response rates; it shows customers that you are deeply interested in their opinions. This is important if your organization has a reasonably small number of key customers that you want to take special care of. A disadvantage of one-on-one interviews is that they can become difficult to manage when the sample of respondents is large.

Problems also arise when the individual conducting a survey interview has a vested interest in the results of the survey, as when the salespeople's bonus system is tied to the data that they collect from customers. Anyone who has purchased or leased a new automobile in the last few years might remember the pleas from salespeople to "give me 10s on the survey—my bonus depends on it!" It is crucial to maintain independence and objectivity in these cases through the use of a third party within the company (such as a manager or a salesperson who does not serve that customer) or an independent data collection agency to conduct the actual interviews.

Telephone surveys, particularly those using a computeraided telephone interview or CATI system, are particularly well suited to end-user products and services where representative samples of consumers are needed from a large population. The convenience store survey script in Appendix B is taken from a CATI application. The advantages of telephone interviews include their relatively low cost per completed interview and the control the interviewer has over who is responding to the survey (compared, for example, to written or mail surveys). A human interviewer can clarify any misunderstandings or problems that a respondent may have in answering a survey question. And when they encounter respondents who are simply not able or willing to respond to the survey, trained interviewers can quickly say thank you and terminate the interview. The disadvantage of the telephone interview approach is that interviewers may generate unpredictable effects of their own. They must be carefully trained, as the way questions are stated is likely to have an impact on how customers respond.

Through the use of randomization techniques (such as random-digit dialing), telephone interviewing typically yields more representative samples of customers in a population than you get with other methods. Using this approach, time zones and area codes can be systematically sampled. The American Customer Satisfaction Index survey, a large national survey, uses this approach to obtain valid cross-sections of U.S. consumers. The survey samples are checked against census data using demographic profiles to ensure that they are properly balanced with respect to age, sex, income and education levels, and ethnic background.

Internet-based surveys are growing in importance as the population of Web users becomes more representative of specific customer groups. Web surveys offer significant advantages in that data can be collected, transferred, and updated continuously online. And unlike CATI survey participants, Web respondents have a written version of the survey available on the computer screen to help keep the questions and scales clearly in mind—and they all see exactly the same questions, which eliminates the danger of interviewer bias. Web surveys have already become the preferred method of data collection in those industries where Web samples are representative of the customer base (as for certain financial services and online retail operations).

Yet many customer populations continue to contain large percentages of individuals from lower income and education categories that do not have direct access to the Web (such as convenience store and mass merchandise retailer customers). This situation is likely to change in the near future. Infrastructure changes, such as the diffusion of broadband cable, will broaden the population of Web users in the years to come. Even now, creative solutions can be used to give more customers Web access for the purpose of conducting a survey. For example, a kiosk system can be placed in a location that all customers could access (such as a convenience store or an employee lounge). A crosssection of customers could be encouraged to use the kiosk using personal communication or incentives (such as store coupons). Easy-to-read touch-screen displays can be used to collect, transfer, and even analyze the data on-line. Another alternative is to use printed versions of the survey that can be handed out or mailed to customers and later scanned and processed on-line.

Written surveys, particularly mail surveys, remain a popular approach to data collection. An advantage of written surveys is their relative low cost *per targeted respondent,* or survey sent. Written surveys can be mailed or distributed efficiently to a relatively large number of customers. The problem is that response rates tend to be low for this approach. Because of the low yield, direct mail often proves more expensive than telephone or Webbased surveys and the respondents are not as representative of the customer population. The quality of the survey data also suffers in that, compared to phone or interview surveys, written surveys offer less control over the interview itself. Written surveys may be passed along for others (subordinates or other family members) to fill out and there is no easy way to clear up misunderstandings or ensure that the respondent is responding carefully to the questions.

One solution to the weaknesses inherent in any one method of data collection is to combine elements of more than one approach. For example, one-on-one or small group interviews can be used to explain the purpose of the survey and motivate participation. To ensure anonymity, written surveys could then be left with the respondents to fill out and return after the interview. Another successful approach in retail contexts is to use store intercepts in combination with written, telephone, or Web surveys. The store intercepts are used to explain the survey and motivate participants to participate in it, while the follow-up survey (in writing, by phone, or by Web page) allows respondents to participate at their convenience.

Sampling is the process of selecting respondents or customers from a population for inclusion in the survey. Naturally, then, sampling starts with the customer population or populations of interest. Your market segmentation scheme and the specific segments that you have decided to include in the research largely define your customer population.

The wide variety of techniques for sampling from customer populations fall into three General categories:

- Census samples
- Judgment samples
- Statistical samples

Census samples involve gathering information from every possible member of a population, such as all of an organization's customers—or all customers in a given segment. Census samples are perfectly representative because the sample and the population are one and the same. Census samples are feasible primarily when the population size is relatively small (such as potential purchasers of jumbo jet engines or highly specialized industrial tools). If you define your population as all customers who have recently recorded transactions, your own records can supply a census sample of current customers.

When the population of customers is too large for a census sample, judgment or statistical samples are called for. Judgment samples involve—as you would expect—using your judgment to decide who should and should not be included. One common method of judgment sampling is to take a list customers and pick people well dispersed with respect to age, sex, income, education, and so on. The drawback is that the inclusion of respondents in the sample is at the discretion of the researcher. This makes it difficult to generalize any results to the population at large. At the same time, this approach is useful when the goal is simply to identify potentially important issues, as when conducting qualitative research. Recall, for example, that the primary goal of using the CIT (critical incident technique) method is to find out what attributes and benefits to include in a more systematic survey.

Statistical sampling involves using statistical probability to determine a sample. Hayes tells us that the primary differences between judgment and statistical sampling are that statistical sampling involves the use of random selection to include cases or respondents in the sample, the ability to statistically determine an appropriate sample size, and the ability to determine how representative the sample is of the population. Thus statistical sampling allows for greater generalization of the study results to the population as a whole. Examples of statistical sampling methods include random-digit dialing of customers (as through CATI systems) and systematic sampling from a customer list (start at a random point and then pick customers at set intervals, say, every tenth or hundredth name, until you have the number you need for your sample). Respondents in the ACSI survey, for example, are selected using random-digit dialing. Naturally, the choice of a sampling method or methods is a function of both the size and accessibility of the customer population or populations of interest and the purpose of the research.

Once you've cleared away the preliminary survey questions, the next issue that you face in developing the survey is just how to measure benefit and attribute performance and importance. With respect to performance, the survey results should provide reliable and sensitive measures of customer benefits, customer satisfaction, and loyalty. When measuring importance, you must choose between direct customer measures of importance (using, for example, scales or other rating tasks) and derived importance or impact measures based on statistical analysis.

There are two important factors to consider when you measure perceived customer benefits, customer satisfaction, and loyalty.

First is the abstract nature of the constructs involved. Recall from Chapter Three that customers do not obtain satisfaction directly from the concrete attributes and features that describe product and service offerings. Rather, satisfaction and loyalty are a function of the benefits and consequences that the attributes provide. These benefits (such as convenience, safety, and service quality), being abstract or latent constructs, cannot be observed or measured directly using single survey items and scales. The same is true for such overall evaluations as customer satisfaction and loyalty. Abstract or latent variables are reflected in a variety of concrete measures. Benefits are reflected in the attribute ratings that make up the benefit, satisfaction is reflected in a variety of overall performance ratings, and loyalty in a variety of behavioural intentions.

The best way to empirically measure these latent variables is to use multiple concrete *proxies,* or survey measures. For example, qualitative research shows that a convenience store customer's perception of convenience is reflected in ratings of store location, hours of operation, speed and efficiency of employees, and the availability of parking. A latent variable can be measured using a weighted average or *index* of these survey measures. The convenience index of a convenience store thus becomes a weighted average of a customer's ratings of store location, hours of operation, speed and efficiency of employees, and the availability of parking. Overall satisfaction becomes a weighted average of a customer's ratings on such measures as satisfaction, overall performance versus expectations, and overall performance versus a "best in class" competitor.

The second factor to consider when measuring perceived customer benefits, customer satisfaction, and loyalty is the distribution of the data as it relates to your need for *sensitive measures*—measures that can differentiate among fairly small differences in the underlying conditions. This is an ongoing problem in customer surveys because perceptions of quality and satisfaction almost never fall on a normal distribution. That is, there are typically no bell-shaped curves in the data. In a competitive economy, only those competitors with relatively high quality and satisfaction ratings tend to survive. As we know this results in quality and satisfaction data that is strongly *skewed* (where most of the responses are bunched near the high end of the quality and satisfaction scale and the tail of the distribution trails off towards the low end of the scale).

The measurement challenge is to be able to distinguish among customers that are crowded together at the high end of the scale. To illustrate the problem, consider what happens if you use a very insensitive measure of satisfaction. When asked yes-or-no questions (say, Are you satisfied?), the overwhelming majority of customers answer yes. In a recent study of airline passengers we found 95 percent of customers responding yes when asked to evaluate their satisfaction on a yes-no scale. Unfortunately, yes-or-no questions give you no way to distinguish among customers that range from moderately to very satisfied.

The sensitivity of the scale improves when you move to a 5-point scale (where 1 = poor performance or very dissatisfied and 5 = excellent performance or very satisfied). Research on quality and satisfaction scales suggests that using a 10-point scale is better still. Going beyond 10-point scales, however, is not beneficial as respondents have trouble using all the scale points.

Most sensitive of all is the use of multiple 10-point scale questions to form an index. Consider that any given survey measure is composed of two sources of variation, that which is supposed to be measured (what statisticians call the "true score") and that which is not meant to be measured (the "error"). The *true score* is what the various items in an index have in common, while the *error* is more a function of the biases or problems inherent in individual survey questions. By averaging the measures into a single index, you can increase the amount of true score and reduce the overall error variance (relative to an individual survey measure or question) as error from the individual questions is canceled out.

As a result, in statistical analysis and modeling, when you use indices in place of single item measures, you explain more of the variation in satisfaction and loyalty, and the relationships involving quality, satisfaction, and loyalty are stronger. In state-of-the-art quality and satisfaction modeling, the use of indexing to measure abstract or latent variables has become the norm.

Consider a simple example of the value that indices bring to an analysis. When you assess the financial health of your company, you know that any one marketing, accounting, or finance measure (customer retention, return on investment, return on capital employed, stock price) is an imperfect reflection of overall state of the company. Taken together, however, the measures provide a more accurate picture of financial health than is possible using any single measure.

The next step is to decide whether to use direct or derived measures of attribute and benefit importance. Many satisfaction measurement systems rely heavily on the "gap" model, in which the measure of what needs improvement in quality or satisfaction is the difference between customers' direct ratings of attribute importance and direct ratings of performance (performance minus importance). There are three kinds of direct measures commonly used in marketing research:

- *Direct scale ratings:* Respondents rate the importance of a product or service's attributes on a scale ranging, for example, from "not at all important" to "very important."
- *Point allocation methods:* Respondents distribute importance "points" (say 100 points) among a given set of attributes where the proportion of points allocated to an attribute indicates its importance.
- *Paired comparison ratings:* Respondents rate the relative importance of attribute pairs.

Paired comparison ratings can place tremendous burdens on respondents because of the number of attribute pairs involved. They have also been heavily criticized for producing arbitrary measures of importance.

Direct scale ratings are considered more accurate (less biased) than point allocations and easier for respondents to provide than either point allocations or paired comparison ratings. These factors make direct scale ratings the more popular choice, so the remainder of this discussion will focus on this method of assessing customer responses.

The primary advantage of direct importance scale ratings and the gap model is their ease of implementation. They require minimal analysis (plotting averages and taking difference scores) and can be easily understood at various levels in an organization, from front-line service personnel to CEOs. Yet there are several problems associated with using direct measures. The method assumes that customers understand what you mean by "important" and also that they know just what attributes are important to them—and are willing to tell you about it. In the end, we find that asking customers directly to rate the impact that an attribute has on their satisfaction and loyalty is an extremely difficult task. Direct importance measures often result in socially acceptable or status quo answers and poor discrimination. Using direct scale ratings, for example, respondents have a difficult time differentiating among those attributes that are most important to them. We have rarely found significant differences in importance among the top-rated fifteen to twenty attributes in a survey. Research also shows that the importance measures or weights that people report and those that they use when making a decision often differ dramatically. The insight that direct ratings provide drops off as the number of attributes increases.

We illustrate both the strengths and weaknesses of the gap model using a study in which we examined the drivers of satisfaction for a pharmacy. Approximately a hundred customers evaluated twenty-nine attributes of a retail pharmacy.The mean values of rated attribute importance are ordered from least to most important and plotted question by question (where 1 = not at all important and 10 = very important). The corresponding attribute performance measures are also plotted (where 1 = poor performance and 10 = excellent performance). The key attributes to improve are those where the "gap" (performance minus importance) is lowest.

On the positive side, gap models are relatively easy to implement, analyze, and explain. The analysis simply involves plotting the two dimensions, importance and performance, and examining their differences. This often makes gap models a good option for companies that are just beginning to develop a customer orientation. The models identify the "low-hanging fruit"—the obvious gaps that need to be closed—and get the company into the habit of monitoring customers. The prioritysetting logic is also the same as for the strategic satisfaction matrix. Attributes on which both importance and performance are rated high are core competencies, while attributes with high importance and low performance need improvement.

However, a major problem with the approach is that customers rate most everything as important. The conclusion is that the company needs to improve most of the items with low performance ratings, and it's hard to tell which ones would make the most difference to results. Basically, importance scales are effective at highlighting the *least* important attributes but ineffective at highlighting the *most* important attributes. The direct importance ratings are simply not diagnostic. It is primarily the *performance* measures that drive the priority-setting process.

Another problem with direct importance measures and the gap model is that the survey has a tendency to grow. Because the approach requires at least two ratings for each attribute, the survey becomes nearly twice as long as a survey where importance measures are derived by other (statistical) means, as described in the next section. One question is required to rate an attribute's performance and another to rate its importance. Direct importance ratings may be the only option when the customer population (or the sample size) is too small or ease of implementation is an overriding concern. Where feasible, however, it is much more economical to take the statistical approach and add good dependent variables, such as satisfaction and loyalty, for use in a regression analysis.

Importance measures do not need to be measured directly. They can be derived statistically from attribute performance ratings and ratings of overall satisfaction. Because statistical estimations are more objective and less biased, they are often superior to direct customer ratings. Statistical analysis provides estimates of importance as the impact that one variable has on another. Customers indicate how they perceive a product or service to perform on a number of attributes as well as their overall satisfaction and loyalty. Variation in performance and satisfaction across customers allows the researcher to estimate (using regression or regression-based statistical techniques) the impact that different aspects of quality and value have on satisfaction and loyalty. Statistically determined importance ratings can avoid many of the problems that you encounter with direct importance ratings.

But the quality of the statistical estimates can vary significantly. *The important question is whether or not the estimation builds on the lens of the customer!* The lens should be viewed as a blueprint for both survey development *and* analysis.

A major problem facing regression-based estimates of impact or importance centres on the correlation among the drivers of satisfaction. If attribute ratings are too highly correlated, that is, if changes in one rating tend to follow changes in another without regard to outside factors—what statisticians refer to as lacking sufficient *independence*—the statistical estimates of impact may be poor.

The lens of the customer, which is based on thorough analysis of qualitative research, shows just which attributes go together in the customer's mind. By combining multiple attribute ratings together into benefit indices, the lens provides a means of reducing correlation among the satisfaction drivers; it increases their independence. The result is a set of benefit and attribute importance weights that are superior to those that can be collected directly from customers.

Once you go through the background analysis outlined thus far, you'll be in a position to develop a survey instrument you can use with confidence. The process described here follows the flowchart which we have found useful in developing and administering our own quality-satisfactionloyalty surveys. The first part of this chapter covered Step 1 (the preliminary decisions regarding what information to collect and how to collect it), so the discussion here starts with Step 2 and goes through the rest of the process.

Appendix B at the back of the book provides a sample output in the form of a finished survey script from the National Association of Convenience Stores (NACS). We refer to this survey throughout the process to illustrate our recommendations.

The primary purpose of the opening statement is to persuade your targeted respondents to take part in the survey. There are three main messages that can be communicated in an opening statement to help maximize the response rate:

- Emphasize the importance of the topic or problem area to respondents.
- Emphasize that the primary purpose of the research is to better understand the problem.
- Emphasize that the organization or entity conducting the research will use the results to improve the situation.

In the convenience store survey, the emphasis in the opening statements is on the latter two points. The statements point out that the survey is meant to understand what quality areas are important to convenience store customers and that the results will be used to guide quality improvement efforts.

The opening statements may also include screener questions needed to identify customers. The convenience store survey screens respondents to include those individuals who have visited a convenience store within the last three months. The screener in the survey also provides an explanation that convenience stores do not include grocery store chains, drug or discount stores, or mass merchandisers. If asked, the interviewer explicitly defines a convenience store as "typically a small franchised market that is open long hours." These explanations and definitions were added as a result of pretesting and revising the survey.

Once respondents have been screened and agree to participate, their first task is to evaluate attribute performance levels. In some cases the ratings may only apply to the product, service, or retailer of interest (say, stores in the Seven-Eleven chain). In other cases the ratings may apply to multiple competitors (say, Seven-Eleven, Quik Stop, and other widely known chains). Before providing the information, the survey must instruct respondents on how to perform the task. This includes who or what is being rated and how to use the scales.

The types of scales and their explanation depend partly on the method used to collect the data. If, for example, it is important to explain multiple anchors on the scale (such as what a 1, 2, 3, 4, or 5 actually means in the context of the survey), it is easier to do this in a written or Web-based survey where respondents can refer to the written anchors. It is more difficult to do so in a telephone survey. Because the respondent has no written list to refer to, the emphasis is typically on keeping only the two endpoints in mind. In the convenience store survey, for example, it is explained that a rating of 1 means poor performance and a rating of 10 means excellent performance.

Keep in mind that the choice of scales and the need to label scale points depends on the researcher's approach to measurement. Given the abstract nature of the constructs and the need for sensitive measures, we strongly advocate using indices to measure customer benefits, customer satisfaction, and loyalty. The use of indices gets you away from very concrete, individual scales where each point on the scale is ascribed some meaning. Indices resemble temperature scales—they just show that the reported value is higher or lower than some benchmark. The meaning you attach to the index levels is based on how a product or service performs against competitors and over time. By deemphasising concrete scale points in favour of more sensitive indices, you have less need to ascribe meaning to anything more than the end points. We recommend using 10-point scales, where 1 is poor and 10 is excellent, to evaluate performance across data collection methods.

The next sections of the survey present all of the attributes the lens of the customer research recommended for evaluation. The lens of the customer provides a blueprint as to how the attributes are organized— how they go together in a customer's mind. The survey should leverage this lens and present the attributes in clusters defined by the benefit categories (quality of the service, product offerings, store layout, and so on). Particular to the convenience store survey is the inclusion of two questions at the beginning of this section to assess customer perceptions of store reputation. As described in Chapter Three, these ratings will be used in combination with overall satisfaction to explain customer loyalty.

Satisfaction is the customer's overall evaluation of his or her experiences with a product or service provider. In your subsequent analysis, it will be a major dependent variable that you will explain using your measures of attribute and benefit performance. Satisfaction is a latent variable that will be manifested in a variety of more concrete performance ratings. As we have said, it is critical to combine multiple measures of satisfaction in a satisfaction index. In addition to a simple rating of satisfaction, other measures include evaluations of overall product or service performance against different benchmarks. You might ask customers to evaluate performance versus their expectations, versus an ideal product or service provider in the category, or versus a "best in class" competitor.

Notice that we do not advocate using any one of these as a proxy for satisfaction. Rather, satisfaction as a latent or abstract construct is what all of the various evaluations have in common. The measures simply represent different benchmarks that customers use to evaluate performance and from which an index can be constructed. The convenience store survey has respondents evaluate performance using three different questions. The first asks them to express overall satisfaction, the second asks for an evaluation of performance versus expectations, and the third seeks an evaluation of performance versus an ideal product or service in the category. These questions were modeled directly on those used in the ACSI survey, which have been shown to provide a very reliable and sensitive measure of satisfaction. An added benefit of using the ACSI questions is that it allowed us to benchmark the survey results for convenience stores against other industries and firms included in the ACSI survey.

Whereas satisfaction measures apply more or less universally across industries and contexts, loyalty measures do not. As discussed in Chapter Three, the desired outcomes of satisfaction are highly specific to the nature of the business, product, and service involved. Volvo, for example, has specified a range of desired customer outcomes, from the repeat purchase of a Volvo vehicle to the purchase of Volvo financing, Volvo insurance, the purchase and use of a Volvo gas card, and the spread of positive word-ofmouth advertising. If your customers are retailers who turn around and sell your product to end users, loyalty may take the form of the *push*—the sales effort they make on your behalf—as in the "Råtorp Tire Company" case in Appendix A. If your product is a once-in-a-lifetime purchase (a piece of jewelry or a collector's item), loyalty may involve the customer's willingness to buy other products or services from you (cross-selling) and to tell other potential customers about your offerings. In an industrial context, the level of satisfaction may have little effect on whether a customer buys at least some of your products and services. At the same time, it may have a great effect on just how *much* they buy (account penetration). Another desired outcome may include the trust that customers place in you and their resulting commitment to maintaining a relationship.

Our point is simply that, whereas satisfaction measures are more or less universal, loyalty measures must be customized. In the convenience store survey, the desired outcomes for the store chains and franchisees are rather straightforward. They include enhancing the customers' likelihood of visiting the store again in the future and their likelihood of recommending the store to others. The measures used in the Råtorp Tire Company survey were quite different. As in the convenience store survey, they included the likelihood that the customer (in this case a retailer) would continue to purchase, but they also included whether the proportion of products ordered from the manufacturer would likely increase or decrease in the future (account penetration) and the degree to which the retailer would recommend the manufacturer's products to its customers (push).

Descriptive questions (including market segment profiles and demographic questions) are typically added near the end of the survey. As noted earlier, the main reason for this placement is that the questions, being more personal in nature, are apt to lead a respondent to terminate the survey if asked early on. Once the interviewer has developed some rapport with the respondent and the interview has the momentum provided by answering the performance, satisfaction, and loyalty questions, descriptive information is often easier to get.

The primary purpose of the descriptive questions is to group customers by characteristics such as age and income level for later analysis, so as to track their representativeness and discover possible new segments. Recall that the convenience store survey contains both a direct question regarding segmentation and a group of indirect demographic questions that can be used to segment or describe customers. The direct question presents the five segment-defining statements listed towards the beginning of this chapter and asks respondents to select the one statement that best describes their use of the convenience store. As noted earlier, the primary benefit of having respondents selfselect into pre-existing segments is the ease of subsequent analysis. The drawback is that it presumes that the segments do not change or evolve significantly over time.

A golden rule of survey research is to conduct one or more tests before you put any survey into the field. The primary purpose of preliminary testing is to identify and resolve whatever problems respondents might have in answering the questions. Pretesting tells you whether the survey is able to collect the desired information, and where you need to reword questions to make them simpler and easier to understand. If the pretest is weak and major revisions are required, the revised survey should be tested again before being put into the field.

Pretesting is not just the domain of those who administer the survey; it can raise questions of strategic relevance to top management as well. Another rule we like to follow is to involve both those directly involved in the survey process and those who will use the information to make resource allocation decisions. In pretesting the convenience store survey, for example, we learned several lessons. One was that many people were unclear as to just what a convenience store was in the first place. Does it include gas stations that sell some other merchandise? Grocery store chains that sell gasoline? This led to the inclusion of more specific screening questions and definitions that the interviewer could use as needed.

Pretesting also raised questions about what benchmarks the customer should use to evaluate the competitiveness of a convenience store's prices. Should the benchmarks be limited to other convenience stores, or should they include other stores that sell similar merchandise (such as grocery stores for bread, milk, and soft drinks). Based on top management input, it was decided to let customers compare prices to other stores at which they may buy similar merchandise.

The reason was that executives at the various chains were very interested in the gap between perceived and actual price differences between convenience stores and other types of stores. Whereas convenience stores are often perceived as having relatively high prices, actual price differences are often small or nonexistent.

Just how the survey is arranged and conducted is largely a function of the method of contact. Telephone surveys often involve random-digit dialing or random selection from a customer list.

The interviewer makes a pitch for participation and, if the time is not convenient, can arrange for a better time to call back. Before collecting survey data in a one-on-one interview, the respondent is usually called and an explicit appointment is made. Recall that store intercepts are also a valuable tool for selling the survey—persuading people to take part in later administration either by phone, Web, or mail. Web surveys may use an e-mail message to introduce and gain interest in the survey and then instruct the respondent on how to access the survey. Customers may also self-select to participate in surveys that are available on a company's Web site.

Just who administers the survey is a function of both the sheer number of respondents and the need for objectivity. We suggest that people within the sponsoring company administer the survey themselves as long as the number of respondents is not too large and administrators can remain objective. As argued in Chapter One, a truly customer-oriented company should not routinely leave the job of collecting customer data to outsiders. But for a large-sample survey, it will be more cost-effective to use a professional data collection firm. If the interviewer's compensation is a function of customer responses (the number of "10s" on the survey), the objectivity of the responses and resulting data will be compromised. If a more objective interviewer cannot be found within the company, it would again be best to use a third party to collect the data.

The development of a quality-satisfaction-loyalty survey builds directly on the lens of the customer. Survey development should not be a process in which people from different parts of a company sit around and decide what they would like to see on the survey. Rather, the lens of the customer provides a blueprint for deciding which attributes to include and the benefit categories to use for organising them. Even before developing a survey it is important to understand what populations or market segments to survey, what data collection method or methods to use, and how to sample from the target populations.

In leveraging the lens of the customer, the construction of a quality-satisfaction-loyalty survey should follow certain guidelines. Benefits, satisfaction, and loyalty are abstract constructs that cannot be measured directly using any one concrete survey item. They are best measured using an index of multiple measures or proxies. Indices also provide for more sensitive measures than single survey items, so they can explain more of the variation in satisfaction and loyalty and are better at identifying important satisfaction drivers.

The importance that customers place on attributes and benefits has traditionally been determined by two different approaches: direct measures of importance and those derived from statistical analysis. Among the different direct measures, direct scales (ratings from "not important" to "very important") are often preferred. They are straightforward to collect and as good as or better than other direct approaches (such as point allocation or paired comparisons). Yet, when done properly, statistically derived measures of importance are better than direct measures at objectively capturing the impact attributes and benefits have on satisfaction and loyalty. It is important for statistical analyses to leverage the lens of the customer when grouping variables for analysis. Otherwise, even the most rigorous statistical estimates may be a poor reflection of reality.

With the lens of the customer in mind and the data collection methods chosen, you can complete the survey instrument in a systematic way. First, assess attribute performance by benefit category. After that, obtain overall evaluations of satisfaction. Then select loyalty measures and customize them to fit the product, service, or context. To some, loyalty is simply a matter of whether a customer comes back to buy the same product or use the same service. To others, loyalty is a matter of how much more customers will buy (account penetration) or what else they will buy (cross-selling). After adding descriptive questions to help identify market segments, pretest the survey to identify any unforeseen problems. Arranging and conducting the survey yields the data that serves as input to the next phase of the process. In Chapter Five we focus on using this data to derive the information needed to set priorities and improve product and service quality.

W hen it comes to analysing your customer survey data, you have a lot of options. We recommend a variation on *principal-components regression (PCR)* that is relatively simple to use and provides as much detailed information as you need to make quality improvement decisions. It combines two statistical methods: principal-components analysis and regression analysis. *Principal-components analysis* is a data reduction tool that shows what any group of survey measures have in common, so you can develop the benefit, satisfaction, and loyalty indices. *Regression analysis* relates these indices to each other and lets you determine the benefit, satisfaction, and loyalty impact scores.

As in earlier chapters, we present a flowchart to illustrate the necessary steps used to apply PCR to the lens of the customer. To support our recommendation, in Appendix C at the end of the book we compare results achieved using this method against the results of other approaches.

We begin by describing just what information you can and should be obtaining from your analysis. After describing our data analysis method, we end the chapter with a discussion of how to link survey data to financial performance measures, illustrating the links with examples from Volvo and a major hotel chain. These financial links, which highlight the payoff from investments suggested by customer measurement, will help you inspire people to make real quality improvements based on the information the survey process develops.

When you analyze satisfaction and loyalty data, you're really looking for answers to two relatively simple questions. Where does your company need to improve quality or value to increase satisfaction and loyalty? And once satisfaction and loyalty are improved, what are the payoffs? The basic assumptions are that improved quality leads to increased satisfaction, which in turn makes customers more loyal, and that you get more profit from loyal customers than from those who don't care where they get the product or service you're selling.

Now, how do you quantify the links? The prerequisite is that your measurement system should provide sensitive *and* reliable measures. Your goal is to provide managers with truly diagnostic information—with levers they can push to improve quality and satisfaction. You don't want results that suggest that everything (or nothing) is important, or results that show differences (as among competitors) or changes (over time) that are not valid and meaningful. In other words, you want a system that produces results you can trust. Finally, you want to be able to predict what happens when satisfaction increases. How likely are customers to come back and how much more revenue or profit will they generate?

To make your measurement system a reality, you will need to analyze your survey data to produce multiple levels of information in the system. The circles labeled "satisfaction" and "loyalty" are the key to understanding your customers' overall consumption experience. Best measured using indices made up of multiple concrete measures, these abstract constructs are important in benchmarking performance versus competitors and tracking performance over time.

These benefit-level indices are the heart of the lens of the customer. They provide an overall view of how you are performing in quality areas as defined by your customers. But because these indices are abstract, they cannot be acted upon directly. Action requires moving down to the level of the underlying concrete attributes.

Attribute values are obtained directly from the quality-satisfaction-loyalty survey ratings. Each is measured using a 10-point scale like the ones in the convenience store questionnaire in Appendix B. For the benefits and attributes, 1 is poor performance and 10 is excellent performance. But setting priorities requires you to measure impact as well, that is, the extent to which a change in an attribute will lead to a change in satisfaction, loyalty, and other desired customer outcomes. As there are attribute and benefit levels of performance, so there are also attribute and benefit levels of impact. The benefit-level impacts (obtained from the regression analysis described later in this chapter), indicate how much impact each benefit has on customer satisfaction. It is helpful to focus initially on these benefit-level impacts to gain an understanding of the consumption experience. Looking at the attribute or question level impacts (obtained from the principal-components analysis also described in this chapter) will help you relate your improvement efforts to the everyday activities of the company that have the highest payoff. Attribute impacts are more the focus of continuous improvement efforts, while benefit impacts are the focus of innovation efforts—attempts to find completely new ways to deliver the benefits that customers value.

A benefit-level impact of 0.5 shows that a 1-unit change in that benefit index is associated with a 0.5-unit increase in the satisfaction index. Once you have impact information at every level of the model, you can quantify the change that improving an attribute or benefit would make in loyalty (and subsequent profitability, once this data is added to the model). The impact of changing an input to the model (an attribute) on the output of the model (loyalty or profitability) is simply the product of all impacts in the chain of causes and effects. (Where there is more than one path or chain of cause-and-effect relationships, it would be the sum of the different impact chains.)

If you are familiar with traditional PCR, you will see that our approach to principal-components regression has some unique features. Traditional PCR factor-analyzes all the attribute ratings simultaneously to produce a set of independent components or factors. It ignores benefit clusters of the type we recommend you develop using qualitative research to create the lens of the customer. The problem is that the approach is too data driven; the factor analysis dictates the lens. In contrast, our approach uses the benefit groupings or clusters in the lens as a theory or model to structure the PCR analysis. This approach provides the technical sophistication and diagnostic information that your analysis requires.

The main alternative to using our version of PCR is *partial least squares* (PLS). Both our PCR approach and PLS use the lens of the customer as a guide to structure the analysis. PCR is a two-step approach in which the benefit, satisfaction, and loyalty indices are first estimated using a series of principal-components analyses. The researcher then uses these indices or latent variables in a series of regression models to estimate a causal chain of events (as from quality through to financial performance). PLS performs both of these steps for the researcher. It estimates an entire causal chain or model using an iterative estimation procedure that integrates aspects of principal-components analysis and multiple regression. Researchers in the areas of quality, marketing, and consumer research regard PLS as the state of the art in customer satisfaction modeling.

The disadvantage of PLS is that it requires special software and training, and the software is neither user-friendly nor easy to find. If you have mastered PLS, by all means use it. At a conceptual level, our flowchart and procedure for evaluating the quality of your analysis still applies. Otherwise, we recommend that you use PCR, which is straightforward to do using easily available and user-friendly software packages. In Appendix C we demonstrate just how similar the results are with PCR and PLS. Comparing the two approaches we find a 0.99 correlation in estimated benefit-level impacts and a 0.98 correlation in estimated attribute-level impacts. In other words, the results are virtually identical. The following sections describe how to analyze a customer satisfaction model using our PCR method.

The sole purpose of analysis is to make sense out of the data you collect. This section includes a step-by-step guide to analysing data sets that you can use if you're in charge of performing or managing the data analysis. Even if you're remote from the actual research and your responsibility is to create an environment where customer data will be developed and used, the guide will still be useful as it will demystify the process and, as a consequence, make you more constructively critical when evaluating the output of an analysis.

The first major accomplishment will be to create the latent variables for benefits, satisfaction, and loyalty. Then the process will go on to derive the actual values for the impact of one level of the model on the next, and to establish benchmark values for the benefit, satisfaction, and loyalty indices. The combination of impacts and indices will provide the cause-effect chain.

Once you've built the lens of the customer for your products or services and seen the valuable information it can help you produce, it's tempting to sit back and ask, "Well, now what do the numbers say we should do?"

But it's not that simple. The critical next phase of the process is to use the information to set priorities for improvement. And don't underestimate the importance of obtaining top management input to your action plans at this point. This may require some persistence. Too often managers view measurement systems, including the quality-satisfaction-loyalty model we present here, as a means of avoiding tough decisions—but "the numbers" don't pay the bills, and they don't make decisions, either.

Managers who are in charge of implementing their company's strategies and hold the authority to budget and who allocate resources to improve quality and satisfaction cannot absent themselves from the process. The numbers simply help managers base their decisions on facts.

Here in this chapter we close the loop. We first discuss management's role in using the output of the measurement system to set priorities for improvement. We then discuss how to implement the priorities. We bridge the gap between the customer benefits and product or service attributes that need improvement and the internal changes they require.

As we said in Chapter One, setting priorities requires both impact and performance information for the various drivers of satisfaction and loyalty. But to set priorities, you must make some critical decisions regarding just what constitutes high versus low impact and high versus low performance. These decisions require you to consider a number of factors beyond the information in your impact-performance chart, including your strategy and competencies as well as relevant benchmarks, costs, and market dynamics.

Recall that the basic logic is to categorize the various benefit and attribute drivers of satisfaction into one of the four cells of the matrix, each of which is associated with its own market action implications. Generally, the essential areas to improve are those where impact or importance is high and performance is low. Customers are essentially telling us that we are falling short in these important areas. Improvements to these areas will effectively focus resources where they have the greatest impact on satisfaction and subsequent loyalty and profitability. This is also the cell in which you are most competitively vulnerable. If competitors do an excellent job in these areas, they will lure your customers away.

Those areas that are important to customers and in which your performance is strong represent your core competencies and competitive advantages. It is essential to maintain if not improve performance on these drivers. The implications for the opposite cell, where impact is low and performance is weak, are also clear. Generally, there's no reason to waste resources on improving these areas. According to the customers, performance here just doesn't matter.

The implications for the remaining cell, in which impact is low yet performance is high, are less straightforward. This may be an area where resources have been wasted in the past because the benefits and attributes are not important to customers. In one recent application, for example, we found that customers at an IKEA furniture store in the United States rated traditional Swedish amenities—a child-care facility and a Swedish bake-shop—very positively. Nonetheless, these amenities had little to no impact on satisfaction and loyalty. From a cost-benefit standpoint, we concluded that having the amenities was not costeffective for the U.S.-based store.

Alternatively, benefits and attributes in the low impact-high performance category may contain drivers of satisfaction that customers consider to be basic and necessary (as in Kano's model described in Chapter Five). Customers may find these benefits and attributes everywhere they look and take them for granted. Although important in an absolute sense, these features offer no differentiation because there is little to no variance in their performance across customers and competitors. Airline safety is a classic example here—as long as the planes aren't falling out of the sky, passengers tend to regard one airline as much the same as another. That doesn't mean that any airline can afford to ease off on safety! The same sort of consideration can apply in less dramatic circumstances as well. In the IKEA project, we found that "ease of assembly" was also rated highly and had little impact. Our conclusion here, however, was to make certain that we assure continued high performance on this benefit. Withdrawing resources and reducing performance would only serve to put us on a "slippery slope" and decrease satisfaction. The area would quickly return to the high impact–low performance category. Another possibility in the high performance–low impact quadrant is to find a new target market segment for the product or service. It may well be possible to find new customers who would especially value these benefit areas (such as customers who would value the child-care and bakery facilities in the IKEA store).

But data analysis does not determine where to draw the cell boundaries. Managers must draw the lines and decide just where the improvement should occur. Again, the impact-performance charts are a primary input to this decision process, but there are several other factors that you need to consider.

Your strategic market plan leads you to focus on particular segments of customers to leverage core competencies. But what if your customer data analysis suggests that you improve in areas that are inconsistent with your basic strengths? Management must decide whether or not the areas that need improvement are those in which core competencies and a competitive advantage can be achieved. If not, you may be pursuing customers you can't please with your strengths, at the risk of alienating customers who currently value your offerings. Perhaps you should reconsider your entire strategic market plan instead.

At the same time, the information may be very valuable in deciding on network partners who can help provide customers with the benefits they need. Think back to the convenience store survey, which revealed that safety is the primary driver of satisfaction for customers.

In practical terms, safety is not something that a convenience store can completely control, so the implication may be to network and collaborate with those who can have more effect. In some cities, for example, convenience stores provide an area where local law enforcement officers can take a break, make phone calls, and do paperwork. This win-win solution saves the officers time and creates a greater atmosphere of safety than the stores could provide on their own.

It is also critically important to benchmark both impact and performance when using this information to set priorities. In the Råtorp Tire Company case (Appendix A at the back of the book), impact-performance charts are supplied for three main competitors in the market. As the reader quickly finds out, making decisions for Råtorp requires a careful consideration of impact and performance levels for the competitors as well. In an absolute sense, impact may be high and performance low in a given area, suggesting the need to make improvements. But what if your closest competitor shows even lower performance and higher impact? It may be a mistake to improve that area if there are others that also call for attention. Relatively, it may be a competitive strength, at least in the short run.

At the same time, do not ignore the absolute levels of impact and performance. Over the long haul, the absolute levels of performance and impact highlight your vulnerabilities, as well as those of your competitors, and suggest where new competitors may enter or improve to take customers away.

In Chapter Five we briefly discussed how to incorporate cost considerations into the analysis. When you tie your model and analysis to increased profit per customer, you then have some idea that the costs typically incurred to improve quality are covered. But in most cases, managers must consider the relative costs of making improvements when deciding which areas to improve. Remember that the goal is to optimize rather than maximize satisfaction and loyalty. If two areas show equally low performance and high impact, managers should ask, "Which is more cost-effective to improve?" One source of cost information is management itself. Another is through the use of tools such as QFD (quality function deployment, described later in this chapter) that translate product improvements into internal change and explicitly consider cost information.

Finally, consider where your market is headed over time. Just what factors will become more or less important? For personal computers, will processing speed become less of a differential advantage going forward? For convenience stores, will prepared foods become a greater source of differentiation and impact? Both social and technological forecasting are important bases for predicting these market dynamics, but are beyond the scope of our discussion.

Appendix A at the end of the book concludes with a prioritysetting exercise that makes use of the Råtorp Tire Company information discussed in Chapter Three. The exercise provides the output of a survey and data analysis for Råtorp and its two main competitors. We strongly encourage you to work through the data in the case and set priorities for Råtorp. Based on the data, consider what you expect the competition to do as well. The case will force you to consider several factors, including what Råtorp's strategy should be, how the benchmarks influence interpretation of the results, how the competition is likely to evolve over time (such as the role filled by import brands), and what the improvements might cost. The case emphasizes that the task of moving from information to decisions is far from trivial. It requires significant reflection and input from managers in a position to set and implement a strategic market plan.

Once you have targeted which benefits and attributes to improve, you have to figure out just how to improve them. In effect, you need to build a bridge from your model of customer perceptions and behaviours to your internal metrics, parts, processes, and people. When you do this, you'll soon find that—as with any bridge—the traffic on this one flows both ways.

The framework integrates aspects of two leading approaches to improving quality and satisfaction: *quality function deployment* (QFD) and customer satisfaction modeling (as detailed in Chapter Five). Together, the two approaches illustrate qualitatively different steps in the overall process of translating satisfaction into its means of accomplishment. Our satisfaction models translate overall satisfaction down into the customer benefits that drive satisfaction and into the product and service attributes that provide the benefits. These are the uppermost stages of the framework. The lower stages, taken from QFD, translate these attributes further down into their means of accomplishment or production.

It is important to consider what we mean by *translation* in the framework. Consistent with the arrows is a process of moving from the most abstract information of interest to the most concrete. Customer satisfaction is customers' overall evaluation of their purchase and consumption experience. Moving downstream in the framework from satisfaction to production is, therefore, a process of translating abstract, subjective evaluations into concrete, objective means of accomplishment.

In contrast, the process of moving up in the framework from concrete processes and attributes to abstract benefits and overall satisfaction is more of an inductive or *change monitoring* process. After determining what changes to make, it is important to track the changes back upstream in the process. Did, for example, the changes we made internally have a subsequent effect on customer perceptions and satisfaction? To what degree did our improvements to production processes improve process operations, parts deployment, engineering or design characteristics, and ultimately attribute and benefit performance? As we see, the combination of translation and change monitoring forms a two-way traffic that is essential to close the loop on the quality improvement process.

A central point of the framework is that QFD picks up where satisfaction modeling leaves off. The product and service attributes that are the output of the priority-setting process represent the input to QFD. The four houses or phases of QFD thus represent phases four through seven of an overall translation process. The translation is, however, different for pure products than for pure services. For products, targeted attributes must be translated into engineering or design characteristics, parts characteristics, process operations, and finally production requirements. Because services are co-produced by customers and employees at a time and place of the customer's choosing, service production is a different beast. In service applications of QFD, targeted attributes for improvement must be translated into service qualities (for example, hotel arrival), service functions (airport shuttle service), service process designs (number of shuttles, routes, and personnel), and operating policies and procedures (daily schedules and contingency plans).

An important implication of the framework is that for a given product or service, there are at least seven conceptually distinct stages in the overall translation and change monitoring process. It highlights the difficulties and challenges that we face even after a satisfaction model is analyzed and priorities are set. Our goal here is not to exhaustively discuss the implementation phases, but rather to introduce you to QFD as one tool that has helped thousands of companies around the world to link their customer data to product and service improvements. A thorough treatment of how tools such as QFD are used to implement product-driven product and process changes is beyond the scope of this book. It is, in fact, the subject of our next book in the UMBS Management Series.

The work is usually documented in a series of matrices. Its primary benefits are reduced design costs and development time. Other benefits include improving communication and cohesion within a product development or improvement team and solidifying design decisions early in the development cycle.

Generally there are two variants of the QFD methodology. The first is the four-phase system captured and presented in more detail later. In this approach, QFD starts with an input list of customer-desired attributes. These attributes are often ordered hierarchically to handle the large number required to describe a product (such as an automobile door system). At a higher level of abstraction are the benefit categories similar to those used in our satisfaction model (such as that a door system "operates well"). At a lower level of abstraction are the more concrete attributes (such as that a door system is "easy to close from the outside").

The QFD translation process begins in Phase 1, the "House of Quality, " where attributes are translated into engineering characteristics. In subsequent phases—often called *houses*— engineering targets are translated into parts characteristics; targeted parts characteristics are translated into key process operations; and key process operations are translated into production requirements or work instructions. As mentioned, this system is altered when applied to services.

The second variant of QFD recognizes that the four-phase system that only fulfills a portion of the planning that is needed for a new product. Separate matrix systems are required to incorporate product quality deployment, technology deployment, cost deployment, and reliability deployment throughout the planning, design, trial, manufacturing, and service phases of product development and launch.

7

Customer Knowledge Management

Among other reasons firms have a low return on their information technology investments is that they only poorly understand what the technology makes possible. The objectives and role of information in customer-focused management must be understood. Customer-intelligent firms use their customer knowledge to drive all of the firm's activities and decisions.

When firms have so much opportunity to interact with their customers, why is it that they treat their customers like strangers? The reason is not lack of information on their customers, but a lack in a firm's managing of that information. Firms may have the ability to capture that information, but may not process and utilize the knowledge to manage relationships with their customers. Information technology has only placed this realization in sharp focus. On the other hand, the power of information technology has also raised the ugly specter of abuse of privacy when firms have access to a vast amount of customer information. Network Solutions, the first company that registered addresses on the. com,. org, and. net domains for the Internet, now a unit of VeriSign, raised eyebrows when it planned to sell names, street addresses, and other information gathered from businesses and individuals who signed up for an Internet address.

There are several examples of Internet companies that have been reined in for their use of customer information. DoubleClick Inc., decided against combining Web-tracking data with offline databases. Toysmart was not allowed to sell its customer database when it shut down.

Hagel and Rayport suggest that customers will become savvy about their personal information and be reluctant to divulge it unless they receive some value for it. They predict that customers will win the battle over their information and firms they call "infomediaries" will "become custodians, agents and brokers of customer information, marketing it to businesses on consumers' behalf while protecting their privacy at the same time

" Nevertheless, customer information is crucial for a customer focus because of the need to make and execute customer-focused decisions in all aspects of the business. Firms will continue to require customer information to do business. Information technology will continue to challenge a firm's judgment in obtaining and using customer information.

Traditionally, research on the customer has been at the aggregate level, most utilized during the new product development process, to test new product ideas, in test marketing, and to test new campaign concepts in the realm of advertising. Marketing research has been standard practice preceding the launch of new products or advertising campaigns. Most firms conduct regular market research activities to direct segmentation decisions such as targeting and to determine how to reach segments.

This chapter does not limit itself to data from market research studies, nor is it about how to conduct market research studies. Instead, this chapter is about the consolidation and utilization of information on the customer to align all the activities of the firm to meeting customer needs. The key issues discussed in this chapter are central to designing and implementing effective customer knowledge management: the sources and avenues from which customer information is available to the firm; in what form is it available; how this data can and should be analyzed and interpreted; and how the information should be utilized.

BENEFITS OF CUSTOMER KNOWLEDGE MANAGEMENT

Scholars have implored managers to "spend a day in the life of your customer" and to "get inside the lives of your customers, " so as to obtain a deeper understanding of customers. The quality of the knowledge on the customer is much greater because of direct observation. Obtaining that knowledge is only the first step. The basic skill of listening involves competence in sensing, evaluating *and* responding. A study of 500 new car buyers found customer perceptions of these three dimensions of listening to be strongly linked to trust in the salesperson. There are also benefits within the firm when the practice of listening to customers is emphasized by senior managers. Senior managers at First Chicago discovered that in emphasising listening to the customer they found a cultural change within the organization. Customer knowledge gained from firsthand customer contact is very persuasive. Smart CEOs at firms like IBM, Cisco, and EMC intuitively realize this, and their senior managers contact their major customers on a regular basis. These firms also act on that information to improve relationships with those important customers.

The benefits of customer knowledge management have concentrated at the individual level. For example, Dreyfus, like other mutual fund firms, keeps track of client activity, claiming that they can predict when a client is going to shift money out of their mutual funds. Clients receive a call from a Dreyfus representative, who wants to know how the client feels about the investment and if his or her goals are being met. If Dreyfus is able to track clients at all stages of the consumption process, then the firm has a better chance of retaining the customer. A number of CRM- and ERP-type software programmes allow companies to track processes in the life of a specific sales order from order entry all the way to delivery to customer. Of course, FedEx introducing package tracking is a well-known example from years ago. There are a number of benefits of information technology for firms of any size.

Siebel software allows Honeywell to spot problems and opportunities by tracking and analysing all customer interactions; and at Marriott, Siebel empowers sales reps to respond more quickly to customer needs by integrating customer information from different departments. Lexmark International used Microstrategy software to help build what they call a data warehousing solution that accomplished a reduction in product delivery time by 70 percent, a threefold improvement in being able to deliver a customer's order on the desired date, and a 60 percent reduction in the information costs. Package delivery firm UPS's selfservice tracking system, built by IBM, saved the company $450,000 a day in customer service expenses; and, the Clarify call centre software helped payroll-processing firm ADP improve customer retention rate by 5 percent and increase revenues by $100 million in 1999 simply by providing its customer service reps with customer information on its 8000 clients. There are numerous such examples of technology-based customer information management systems having a profound impact on a firm's productivity and in customer retention. Both outcomes are the basis for achieving and sustaining profits.

The marketing research practice has undergone a major transformation in recent years. A primary function of marketing research activities is to collect and analyze customer information. Technology has enabled all phases of the marketing research process ranging from sampling and data collection to analysis and reporting. With newer technologies and faster cycle times, firms conduct research at all stages of the product life cycle and not just at the product development stage or the test marketing stage. This is at the aggregate level, whereas there is another change in research on the customer at the individual level, where technology is enabling customers to interact with the firm in a multitude of different ways not previously possible. These interactions can now occur during all stages of consumption. At every interaction with the customer, a firm has the opportunity to acquire valuable customer information, as well as to process and utilize the information for creating and delivering superior customer value.

Once the data is available, the challenge is to provide the user of the information and decision maker with targeted information. Enter rulesbased approaches, which are simply programmes that make sense of data using preconceived models. Sadly, the majority of CRM and ERP packages fail the firm not for lack of data, but simply because the firm does not have the appropriate understanding and appreciation of the fundamentals of customer-focused management. The rules for decision-making should be founded on customer-focused management principles. The better the understanding of the customer and the utilization of that knowledge, the more customer focused the rules are. The best technology is only as good as what you tell it to do. CRM and ERP packages are really knowledge management software, tools to manage knowledge of the customer and enable the processes within the firm that are working to meet specific customer needs. To be more effective with these tools, firms need to gather the information, analyze and process it to obtain a good understanding of the customer, and utilize it at every opportunity in the value-creation and delivery process. Therefore, for a thorough understanding on how to manage customer information, it is important to understand the principles of knowledge management, in general.

What is knowledge management? To answer this question, we have first to deal with a more fundamental question: what is the difference between data, information, and knowledge? Are these terms just synonyms that are interchangeable? No, they are not! The simplest way to understand the differences among these terms is to picture a continuum. As we add value to data, it becomes information; and as we add value to information, information becomes knowledge. When we interpret data in a context, we convert that data into information that has some meaning. When we categorize and elaborate on that information with explanations, then we have added more value and the information can now be considered knowledge. Thus, *knowledge management* is the management of data and information so that a firm can optimally capture, process, and utilize its knowledge for effective decision-making and operation. *Customer knowledge management* is the management of the acquisition, processing, and utilization of customer information for effective customer-focused decision making. Knowledge management practice has been studied in the context of how organizations learn. Before we discuss the methods of managing customer knowledge, it would be useful to understand knowledge management and, specifically, information processing from the perspective of organizational learning. Organizational learning can be broadly depicted as a three-stage process:

- Information acquisition or generation
- Information transmission or dissemination
- Information analysis or interpretation

Studies have demonstrated that a customer-focused firm has a formal and systematic method for gathering, interpreting and using customer information. To be customer-focused, therefore, firms need to be committed to the importance and value of customer information and to the use of customer information in guiding the creation and delivery of customer value. Thus, recognising information's value to the firm and realising when and where it is accessible is a prerequisite for knowledge management.

Richard Schulze, CEO of Bestbuy, the runaway success in electronics retailing, says: The best way to find out whether a store is running smoothly is by asking the cashier. "The cashier really understands where the problems lie. They're the last people to see the customer. "To consider all of the sources of customer information we also need to first identify the natural state of the information. Customer information is available as tacit and as explicit knowledge. The explicit knowledge is present in the databases of the firm or as documented information. Customer information files in databases are usually quantitative data. More and more firms are also using qualitative data when the technology is used to accommodate that type of data. Otherwise, most of this rich information remains as hidden knowledge. This information that is not recorded is the tacit knowledge that is usually resident with the employees and managers of the firm. For example, records of customer service interactions capture the actual transaction, complaint, or feedback from the customer. At the same time, employees, based on their prior experience, will unconsciously record and bring to bear their judgments of the situation, which are not necessarily documented. The knowledge that employees have that is not recorded anywhere is deemed the tacit knowledge of the firm.

Table. States and Forms of Customer Information.

	Individual level	**Aggregate level**
Explicit - Documented knowledge	Customer Information Files	Research Reports
Implicit - Tacit knowledge	Knowledge held by employees and intermediaries about individual customers that are not recorded	Knowledge held by employees and intermediaries about groups of customers that are not recorded

Table. Customer Information Sources Based on Consumption Stages.

Sources of Information Salespeople	
Preconsumption	Channel intermediaries Referral data Frontline service personnel
Consumption	Service delivery personnel Service failure and recovery data Customer satisfaction surveys
Postconsumption	Customer complaints Customer service logs Frequent user profiles

While at the individual level information is available from customer information files in the firm's databases, other types of information at the aggregate level may be gathered during the course of product development activities and other specific projects and reside in research reports. There is information on the customer at several locations within the firm, from sales to customer service, to name the most obvious areas. As we know besides this explicit knowledge, there is a wealth of information at both the aggregate and the individual levels. Wherever the firm has interfaced with the customer, the "touch-points, " there is information on the customer. It immediately becomes apparent that several product and service delivery contact points within the firm have access to customer information, but not all are part of the customer information management system.

CRM software packages enable the firm to capture all of the information gathered at each touch-point into a central database and make it available at any touch point. To determine all of the opportunities for gathering information on the customer, firms can develop a blueprint of the order delivery or customer service processes depicting all of the touch-points from the consumption cycle when the customer interacts with the firm. Knowledge gained on the customer from each and every customer interaction when recorded and made available can be valuable in improving the customer focus of any of the firm's decisions or actions. The major sources for customer knowledge are discussed below.

Customer Information Files are typically transaction-related and purchase-related individual-level customer data found in sales records, customer interaction records, and customer service incident records. What is perhaps not in these files, which needs to be considered as a necessary component of individual customer profiles where available, is information related to the activities of preconsumption, consumption, and postconsumption.

Research Reports have segment-level aggregate data that are found in product development reports, advertising research reports, sales and marketing reports, and customer service reports. What needs to be seen is whether research on market segments is an ongoing pursuit of the firm—to indicate that the firm is proactively assessing customer value being delivered by the firm.

Knowledge held by employees and managers: Tacit knowledge of the customers—is by definition not completely identified and its utility not realized. If there is no formal process to regularly capture and utilize this information, a wealth of knowledge resident in the firm is being ignored.

Upstream and downstream sources: When suppliers and intermediaries are regularly included in discussions of value-creation and delivery decisions, there is an opportunity to discover information on market trends, technology, ideas for product improvement, and so on that are useful at the aggregate level. At the individual level, where there are (downstream) intermediaries, if it is possible, it would be highly valuable to obtain individual customer level information.

Now let us look at opportunities that may be missed by firms that are not proactive in looking for customer information. For example, how many firms capture and utilize data on referrals? If it is appropriately captured and analyzed, firms can use this information to proactively stimulate referrals. Firms can identify customers who could be bringing in new customers. Firms can determine what incentives would be effective in stimulating referrals. From the referring and referred customers, firms can learn what messages are being conveyed about the firm and which messages are most effective in stimulating product trial from new customers. Firms can learn what types of customers are most liable to switch from their current patronage based on word of mouth. Firms can track and follow the patronage behaviour of these new customers and nurture their loyalty and referral behaviour. Firms can also find out from these new customers valuable information on the competition as well. Similarly, what about prospective customer queries? How well is this information captured and utilized? What would such information contain? They are a good source of what customers look for in a product, a reflection of their choice criteria. How many firms systematically record information on complaints and praises? This type of information would be very helpful in understanding how the firm is faring on creating and delivering customer value. It could highlight failpoints in the value-creating processes and provide input into frontline evaluation and motivation activities.

Many firms have loyalty programmes to reward the frequent user. What sort of frequent-user data do these firms maintain? How many firms really use the frequent-purchase data? Some firms who know their customers well recognize the importance of sorting out the most profitable customers from their customer base and treating them differently. Some customers are indeed more equal than others! Most firms use frequent-purchaser data for targeting specials and promotions. However, this data can also provide invaluable information on customer value and customer profile information to align the firm's value-creation and delivery processes.

Traditionally, firms have gathered routine customer information only at purchase and when a customer returns a product for a refund or mechanisms. Feedback forms and customer surveys are administered on a regular basis in some firms. However, most often the information gathered from these efforts is worthless because of faulty designs and worse, sometimes even result in misdirected decisions because of flawed survey methodology. More often than not, the surveys are neither reliable nor valid. While reliability and validity as statistical measures of the psychometric stability of a scale are important for a scientific, unbiased study, management can improve the utility of customer surveys with a rather simple analysis. Examine the design, administration, and use of any survey along the dimensions of structure, content, and process. Structural features such as length and the time it would take the respondent to fill out the survey, the layout of the various questions in the survey, and the response format for the questions affect the effectiveness of the survey. Content decisions, such as the categories of information sought from the respondent and information identifying the type of respondent filling out the survey, affect the utility of the survey, which will only be as good as the effectiveness of its administration and its usability.

Table. Guidelines for Customer Information Surveys.

Elements	Analysis
Structure	*Length* - What are the research objectives; recognize the trade-off between amount of information needed and impact on response rate
	Layout - Examine the construction of the survey in terms of appearance and feel
	Format - Examine question construction and response format; open-ended questions invite top-of-mind issues from customer, whereas close-ended questions focus on issues that are of specific concern; in close-ended questions, avoid a "yes or no" and adopt at least a 5-point scale if you want to do any serious statistical analysis
Content	*Categories* - Compare the types of information solicited with the research objectives; recognize which aspects in the customer's consumption activity cycle are covered or not covered
	Profile - Examine whether there is adequate and appropriate information obtained from the respondent to allow for some segment-based analysis of the responses
	Identity - Examine whether it is appropriate to ask for the identity of the respondent to allow for response to customer inquiries or customer complaints
Process	*Input* - Ensure that the appropriate users of the information have contributed to the research design; examine also whether the customer's perspective has been incorporated into the design of the survey
	Administration - Examine how the survey is being distributed as well as returned, and the impact on who will be responding (for a representative sample) and who is receiving the completed surveys (for a nonbiased information)
	Output - For what purposes will the information gathered be used; determine the best reporting format and procedure for maximum benefit to the user

Thus, the process of survey delivery, customer response delivery mechanisms, and the customization of the reports to the decision maker and user of the information in their value-creating and delivery roles is critical to the success of the customer feedback exercise.

There are other sources of customer information that the firm has access to and may not fully utilize. The systematic way of determining what these sources might be is to list all the possible touch-points where customers interact with the firm and placing them in sequence in the three phases of consumption. In the preconsumption phase, customers may interact with salespeople or customer service or other frontline personnel. Recognising what these touch-points are and what kinds of information is shared between the firm and the customer is an important step. Firms must decide what data needs to be captured at the touch-points and how it is to be used in guiding decisions and activities.

How many firms systematically utilize frontline operations personnel for gathering customer information? Frontline operations personnel are in an ideal position to gather customer information. They can be trained on when, what, and how to observe or elicit information from customers. They need to be motivated and recognized for their ability to obtain, process, and disseminate such information. Similarly, there are also the intermediaries or resellers of the firm's products and services that represent the firm in different ways. These intermediaries might perform functions of delivery and distribution, promotion, or customer service on behalf of the firm. Walmart recognized and wielded the power it held with such customer information in negotiating terms with powerful packaged goods manufacturers, including Procter and Gamble.

In the consumption phase, customers may call for assistance in using the product or on some aspect of how the solution works. This information needs to be captured and incorporated into customer education activities such as product directions-for-use instructions, or used in product development and improvement efforts. There is also a wealth of information within the firm available from customer complaints and suggestions. Service failures and recovery situations provide valuable information on customers and their experiences with the firm and its solutions. If these are recorded and maintained on a systematic basis, they can be "mined" for patterns that yield insights not otherwise available. For example, recurrent complaints about customer service response time might suggest that the customer service process needs redesigning.

Often when the data is not available on which to base a decision, the firm has to collect that information. For example, say the firm has received several complaints about customer service access and wants to determine what changes need to be made to the customer service operation. In this case, the firm may want to conduct some research in order to determine the customer needs and preferences with regard to customer service. For each decision that directly relates to a customer, the firm has first to determine what kind of information is needed to make the most effective customer-focused decision. Some of this information is available in existing databases, while some may have to be gathered. To gather information, the firm needs to set up a method of determining what information needs to be gathered, how it can be obtained, and in what form it will be available.

When the information is not available from the day-to-day activities of the firm, then research needs to be conducted on the customer on a project-by-project basis. There are a number of choices and decisions to be made regarding the methods available in researching the customer. For example, to determine what changes are needed to improve customer satisfaction, there are formal and informal customer satisfaction measures. There are qualitative and quantitative methods to obtain the information. For unique project-based decisions, there are several datacollection methods. Among the quantitative methods typically used are paper and pencil surveys administered over the telephone or by mail. On the other hand, qualitative methods typically utilize structured and unstructured interviews, focus groups, or observation methods. A number of innovative qualitative approaches are being introduced. For example, Kimberly Clark for its diaper market, Intuit with its personal finance software, and Patagonia for its outdoor gear have used the method of "story-telling" by getting customers to tell real-life stories expressing how they use the product and feel about it.

Customer case research is another method that conducts chronological case studies of actual purchases to discover previously unknown purchase drivers by systematically capturing all events leading up to the purchase decision. These approaches can uncover customer experiences and thought processes that may not be accessible through a pencil-and-paper survey approach. Any research project should take a systematic approach for maximum benefit and to reduce errors (such as measurement and sampling errors) and biases and follow the following approach.

- *Framing the research*—Management needs for the decision or objective
- *Examining existing and available information*—For hypotheses, specific research questions and to guide research design
- Specifying the research questions
- *Determining the research design*—Questionnaire construction, sampling frame, data collection method, and plan of analysis
- Administering the research and collecting and analysing the data
- Reporting the results and findings

First, the research objective frames the management decision to be made. Information already available is used to guide the research design. The research is then designed by making decisions on what information is needed and how and where to collect the information. The research design includes determining the questions to solicit the information, the method for administering these questions, the sample of subjects, and a plan of analysis. Qualitative research designs are appropriate when there is a need to generate ideas on what to focus on, or to get in-depth information on specific issues. Qualitative research, such as focus-group methods, can complement quantitative research, such as surveys.

Quantitative research designs are useful when a broader cross-section of the customers needs to be polled about a broad range of issues. Sampling techniques are used when it is not possible or necessary to contact all the sources of information. Statistical techniques allow for generalising inferences and conclusions on the entire population of interest based on data from a representative sample of that population. The research instrument or questions and response format are constructed and pretested on a small subset of the population for validity and reliability before obtaining responses from the final sample. The responses are tabulated and statistical procedures applied to the data for analysis. The findings generated are then made available to guide the decision maker. The appropriate format of tables and the report are predetermined in the plan of analysis, so that the data is collected and analyzed according to the needs of the user of that information.

Especially in service firms and in the service component of manufacturing firms, where there is a significant opportunity to interact with the customer and to customize value, firms have used customer information in a number of ways. Observe any service encounter and you will see tacit or explicit customer knowledge being used. When the data from these interactions are systematically documented and analyzed, patterns in customer data can detect the dynamics in consumption behaviour. When aggregated, customer data provides an opportunity to analyze customer segments for anything from price sensitivity to demand patterns to why, when, and how customers behave in the various activities within each of the consumption stages. Firms can divide their customer base into segments based on profitability. When customer purchase information is mapped onto capacity utilization data, for example, a deeper analysis of the firm's value-creation and delivery processes can help determine which of the firm's marketing and operations practices contribute to its profitability. Which frequent customer promotion programmes are most/least effective? Where are the low and peak demand periods? A yield analysis of the utilization levels at the various price levels would help determine the most effective pricing decisions.

Each customer has a value to the firm, and that information is also valuable to the firm to determine the right customer. The lifetime value of the customer to the firm is a function of what they bring to the firm as revenues over the lifetime of the customer. By the same token, it is also important to know what it costs the firm to serve that customer. Loyal customers with a favourable disposition towards the service provider are also likely to engage in favourable word-of-mouth behaviour. They are valuable in trying new products being offered by the firm. They are also less costly to serve because they are familiar with the firm and are socialized into the procedures of the firm that they encounter in their consumption. As customers' loyalty with the firm grows over time, the firm also has a better knowledge of the customer and is more efficient and effective in serving that customer.

Firms that have the data on their customers are able to engage their best resources for their best customers. For example, firms have used information on a customer's profitability to the firm to determine the level of service appropriate for each customer. A *Business Week* (October 23, 2000) special report titled "Why Service Stinks" cites several examples of firms pampering their premium customers. Charles Schwab's premium customer waits no longer than 15 seconds for a phone call to be answered, while others could wait as long as 10 minutes. Centura Bank's most profitable customers—rated 5 on a scale of 1 to 5—get an annual call from the CEO; customer retention in this group improved by 50 percent in five years. Even utility companies, believed to be less sophisticated in their marketing than the consumer packaged goods firms, have a higher proportion of service representatives per customer for their higher-revenue customer groups. In each example, unless the firm knew what each customer was worth to the firm, it would not be able to proportionally allocate its resources to the "right" customers.

A grid guided by the three consumption stages can be a useful framework for determining what decisions need to be based on what customer information. All the functions and processes that affect the creation and delivery of customer value in each of the stages need to be aligned with customer information.

Technology has revolutionized customer information management. Information technologies allow firms to gather, store, and interpret demographic and behavioural data so that each subsequent interaction with the customer is customized, based on historical data gathered from each customer interaction. Digitized purchase transactions in commerce have enabled numerous opportunities to track customer interactions. Chip technology has progressed so rapidly that soon there could be a computer chip in just about any product that would enable mindboggling links to improve customer value and the customer-firm relationship. For example, take the Internet and e-commerce. Most Web sites will ask simple unobtrusive questions of customers when they browse the site. This information identifies the customer and tracks the customer's activities or "clickstreams" on the Web site. Subsequently, software can use this information to personalize the Web site and the experience for the customer.

A number of firms have emerged that provide customer information management software. Such software can customize Web pages for each customer depending on the customer's profile, which is created based on the customer's previous interactions with the firm and the Web site. Vignette's software allows Web sites to dynamically generate pages that are custom-made for each customer. Silknet's virtual sales assistant guides customers through a series of questions about their need situations and then makes product recommendations. Marriott has an enterprise-wide software that integrates information on customers from different departments so that its sales reps can anticipate and respond more quickly to customer needs. Similarly, HandR Block uses software from Clarify to combine and coordinate customer records from its tax offices, discount brokerages, its customer service centre, and its Web site so that customer interaction personnel in each department have access to all of the information on the customer.

There are a variety of methods for analysing data. Data mining techniques attempt to discern patterns in the data where one set of characteristics affects another set in a certain way. SAS Enterprise Dataminer software helps detect patterns in databases and construct models to predict customer response to the firm's actions. Software from iMarket looks at customers' most recent or most frequent purchase decisions and the monetary value of these purchases for the firm and helps decision makers select a subset of customers for targeting specific promotions or new product introductions. Epiphany and Digimine are examples of firms that use a set of their own proprietary algorithms to analyze customer data for their clients. Early clients of Epiphany included Charles Schwab and Hewlett Packard, and for Digimine include Nordstrom. Edify has software that will link customer feedback such as survey responses to individual customer profiles for anlaysis. There is also software such as Nudist available for the analysis of qualitative data. When firms are able to sort through their customer databases and group customers by the relevant characteristics with such datamining software, the power of segmentation and targeting is fully realized with such datamining software.

In general, data is useless for decision making unless it is organized for interpretation. When organized appropriately, data can be contextualized so as to be transformed into information. Displaying and disseminating information is critical to the firm's success. Without proper reporting procedures, decision makers do not benefit from the information that the firm has. For example, ESRI has a programme called Arcview that allows the user to spatially display numerical data. The user can view the data in his or her preferred format to match individual cognitive styles. As Peter Drucker notes, no two executives organize the same information in the same way. Therefore, software that allows the users to display information in their own preferred formats is valuable in customer information management.

The task of the customer information management system is to generate intelligence on the customer so that firm can be more customer-focused in its serving the customer. Intelligence generation capability has been shown to be positively correlated to superior customer value. In a study that involved hour-long in-depth interviews and surveys of sixty-six of the largest one thousand electronic firms by scholars interested in the characteristics of the market-oriented firm, firms are urged to treat learning about the customer as an investment.

Table. Framing the Customer-Focused Analysis: Using Customer Information.

Business Process	Customer Information	Strategic Decisions Needs
Core Value Creation	What are the specifics of the customer value in terms of core product?	Keep core of customer solution ahead of competitive offerings.
Delivery of Solution	What are the specifics of customer value in terms of augmentation to the core product?	Keep augmented customer solution ahead of competitive offerings.
Customer Service	What are the customer identity, background, and consumption profiles?	Personalize customer interactions with recognition, acknowledgement, and gratitude for patronage by caring for the customer and serving customer needs based on potential and long term value to the firm.
Communi-cations		What types of information are relevant and important for updating customers? Keep customer informed about firm's activities regarding customer solution.

Ultimately, customer information is useless unless it is available to the user. Scholars researching the value of information have called this the "value in use" metric. The more the information is used, the more value it has! Customer information management, therefore, involves determining how the information needs to be made available, to whom, when, and in what form. The focus here is on who needs the information

In the spirit of customer focus, the information system serves an internal customer—the decision maker. What will the user need the information for? What specific information is needed for the firm's decisions and activities? Is the user of the information able to enhance customer value with the information? At what level of aggregation is the information used: policy level and customer level, segment level, and individual level? Such decisions need to be made so as to prioritize the customer information according to its impact on customer value. In making judgments about committing resources to managing and leveraging customer information, the firm should consider the worth of the information in terms of how it would help the firm provide superior customer value at a reasonable profit.

Customer information must drive any business process and activity, as suggested in Table Customer-focused management requires a customer-focused analysis of the information necessary for designing processes and making decisions regarding value creation in the firm. These run the gamut of decisions regarding creating and delivering customer solutions, product improvements, attracting and retaining customers, customer service, recovering from product failures, hiring and motivating employees, and ensuring a customer-oriented climate and culture.

CUSTOMER DEFECTION MANAGEMENT IN HOTELS

A customer-focused firm with a good customer defection management system can use customer information to monitor customer interaction incidents and pre-empt customer defection. Customer service is critical. Firms need to give it strategic importance and take a proactive stance with customer service to obtain its numerous benefits for marketing research, product improvements, and customer recovery.

Why would McDonald's create "customer recovery teams?" Internal company documents posted on the firm's intranet revealed that a whopping 11 percent of the firm's customers are dissatisfied and complain to the management. Consistent with the TARP research, this is only the tip of the proverbial iceberg, since only a small proportion of dissatisfied customers ever bother to complain. What is worse for McDonald's is that their internal documents admitted that nearly 70 percent of the complaining customers were even further dissatisfied with the way their complaints were handled. The crowning irony is in the nature of the complaints. They were about the key feature of the core product in a fast food restaurant—slow service. Other issues affecting customer value included wrong orders, dirty stores and, worst of all, rude and unprofessional employees. Earlier that same year, the University of Michigan's customer satisfaction survey (ACSI) had ranked McDonald's among the poorest-performing retailers.

In contrast, it is not surprising that this classic Nordstrom story is often quoted to exemplify exceptional service. A lady goes to a Nordstrom store and complains that the tires she bought at the store are no good and demands a refund. The store clerk refunds the customer, without asking a question, what she claims she paid for the tires. What is remarkable about the story is that Nordstrom does not carry car tires.

It is usually customer service that gets the rap when a product fails or when a firm fails its customer. With the advent of online brokerage services, customer service complaints from investors are on the rise. In the first half of 2000, the SEC received 2,803 complaints against online firms. These complaints were mainly about operational and service-related failures, as opposed to sales-practice complaints that were the norm prior to the availability of online brokerages. Public service is notorious for poor customer service. When none of the seven customer service employees at the Massachusetts Bay Transportation Authority (MBTA) acknowledged rude treatment of a customer, the MBTA suspended all seven and officials prepared to install a recording system to monitor service calls. The story broke in the local press when a customer experienced a rude MBTA operator who twice hung up on him when he had called to learn why his train was late. This is an example that is probably not uncommon in public transportation. Employee indifference to customer discomfort in the wake of a product failure is a chronic problem with firms that are not customer focused.

The airline industry is frequently chastised for poor customer service. Northwest Airlines got into some real choppy weather when it badly mishandled customer service during a major snowstorm in the winter of 1999. Thirty planes that landed in Detroit during a storm that deposited 14 inches of snow were in trouble when planes already at the landing gates were not able to leave. Some planes with passengers sat on the tarmac for as much as eight hours. One pilot even phoned the chief executive of Northwest from the cockpit asking for help.

Lousy customer experience almost always brings with it severe consequences to the firm. Firms suffer from the drain of customer defection, and when customers feel they were particularly wronged, firms can also expose themselves to lawsuits. Firms must find a way to be proactive to protect the more profitable customer relationships. This chapter covers an important component of managing customer relationships—retaining customers. Since products, especially the service components of products, are bound to fail customers in different ways, firms are vulnerable to customers switching to other firms. It is therefore important to understand switching behaviour of customers. Customer service in recovering from product failures and making amends to the customer is critical to managing customer defection in the customer-focused firm.

A customer defection management system must be designed into the value creation and delivery process.

Where we fail customer service

When products fail, customers are aggrieved and will react. What their actions might be is a function of a number of things that are hard to anticipate. At the extremes of satisfaction and dissatisfaction, customers can react with delight or outrage, conceived to originate from the handling of three basic customer needs: security, justice, and selfesteem. Security is the need to feel unthreatened by physical or economic harm; justice is the need to be fairly treated; and self-esteem is the need to maintain and enhance one's self-image.

In a study of about 300 customers regarding how their customer complaints were handled, researchers found that satisfaction with complaint handling is significantly associated with both trust and commitment that customers have towards the firm. They found that their theoretical framework, based on the concept of "justice, " com-prising distributive, procedural, and interactional elements, were useful in explaining customer assessments of complaint handling by the concerned firms. The researchers found that customers related distributive justice to compensation for financial loss and an apology. Procedural justice they found to be related to aspects of customer convenience and firms' follow-up and accessibility. Interactional justice related to several aspects of (un)fair communication and behaviour such as honesty, empathy, and politeness. These relationships reflect the meaning of the terms in the context of customer service. An important finding of this study is that 65 percent of the complaints were received by customer-contact or frontline employees. Firms that have extensive training for customer-contact employees on how to handle complaints will find these investments in frontline education most worthwhile. Where firms fail customer service is when it is not placed in the larger context of customer acquisition and retention, but instead it is seen in its narrowest context as being necessitated by product failures.

Assess customer service by customer recovery

Acquiring the right customers is only the first step in managing customer relationships. A large percentage of new customers—up to 50 percent in some sectors—was found to defect before their third anniversary with an e-commerce site. Once acquired, firms must do everything possible to keep that customer or prevent itself from doing things that force or even allow the customer to switch. When a customer switches to another firm, not only do you lose the remainder of that customer's lifetime value, but you also incur the costs of attracting a new one to replace the lost customer. The costs of serving a customer are high in the initial stages, as the firm sets up procedures for the new customer and becomes familiar with the needs and situations of that customer. As time goes by, the costs of serving that customer go down. To replace a lost customer, the firm has to incur all these costs again before costs to serve the customer go down. So adding the cost of attracting new ones and bringing them to the same level of profitability as the old ones doubles the cost of losing a customer. When you consider the *total cost* to the firm in terms of the opportunity cost of lost customers, it behooves firms to pursue the retaining of customers as a relentless endeavor. The first step in retaining customers is to understand why they would want to switch in the first place.

Most firms have established procedures to recover from product failures. Typically, these customer recovery procedures are a part of customer service, a business function that is generally relegated to the status of a necessary evil. It is typically associated with unpleasant situations like product complaints, product returns and refunds. With the way firms are organized, it might fall upon the customer service department to ensure that these processes are in place and that they work properly. Product-focused firms may be focused on their core product and may view complementary services of the product as customer service. But service is not customer service. As we saw in Chapter 6, facilitating services such as customer service is just one of the various services that a firm might offer its customers as part of the total solution.

The customer service function is a significant factor in the efforts to retain customers. Firms may see it as a function to handle customers' special requests or complaints. However, customer service from a customer's point of view is more broadly defined than from the firm's point of view. Some scholars have defined customer service as all customer interactions that enhance the core product other than proactive selling. Even in its narrowest definition, customer service as complaint management is very beneficial for the firm. Not only does it provide the mechanism to make amends to the customer for a botched job, it also provides information to the firm for service design improvements. When the firm goes out of its way to compensate the customer for its failures, it creates an opportunity to obtain a lifelong customer.

Traditionally designed for complaint handling and refund/exchange for product returns, customer service as a function serves other important uses. If one takes the perspective that customer service is at the tactical level of customer retention, there is a very important by-product from these customer retention efforts. It can be a powerful research source to obtain information on the customer and on customer value delivered by the firm. This information can be used as input for product and service design improvements. We know that that the customer service process and what many firms struggle to do with it. The customer complaint management process discussed is generalized for any firm. When a customer complaint is received by the front line in any firm, it is important to take the approach that a dissatisfied customer is an opportunity—an opportunity to alleviate the customer distress and compensate for it in such a way that the customer is impressed with the service recovery and is satisfied with the process. A first step in the whole process of customer service is to acknowledge and apologize to the customer. If the customer is in the presence of other customers, it is important to isolate the complaining customer so as not to disrupt the service delivery process for other customers. Let the unhappy customer vent and explain the nature of the product failure. Fully document the customer's complaint and explore the likely actions that the firm and the customer may have committed to cause the unfortunate situation.

Customer-focused firms will want to gain as much information as possible about the situation and to indicate to the customer that the firm is taking the problem seriously. A commitment to customer satisfaction from a customer-focused firm is also evident in the firm asking the customer for suggestions on how the customer may be compensated and how the product and service may be improved for other customers in the future. The firm then initiates remedial action and promises to rectify the situation for the customer and make product and process improvements such that it will not happen again. Finally, it is important that the firm follow through with its promises and follow up with the customer to ensure that the recovery process met with the customer's satisfaction. It is also a powerful message to the customer if the firm is able to inform the customer about what it has done to prevent such product failures from happening again. Such would be the case when the product failure has indicated a systemic problem with the firm's operation. An important outcome of this whole customer service process is that valuable information has been obtained, recorded, and utilized for permanent product and service improvements to improve customer value created and delivered by the firm.

The TARP study concluded that only 4 percent of dissatisfied customers complain; dissatisfied customers share their story with about 9 or 10 other people. If a complaint is satisfactorily handled, about 70 percent of them will continue to do business with the firm, and if resolved quickly, this figure goes up to 95 percent and they will tell about 5 people about their fair treatment. Thus, it is safe to say that what the firm does in its complaint handling has serious consequences for customer equity. Many firms seem to offer customers avenues to provide feedback. The customer-focused firm will even proactively encourage customers to complain. The Bank of New Zealand, for example, has complaint procedure brochures available at every teller window that show the customer what to do step-by-step if they need to complain. There are instructions on who to call or write to if the problem is not resolved at the first service encounter. If not resolved by senior management, it lists the address and phone number of the CEO for good measure!

Customers will act when they are emotionally charged, either because of the importance of the solution to their need situation or because of the degree of their dissatisfaction. If the product failure was avoidable, customers are more likely to act. Customer action may be in the form of a customer complaint or defection without complaint. The recovery is likely to be effective if the firm has provided the frontline personnel dealing with the complaint or customer action with the appropriate skills and motivation. Effective recovery requires customer knowledge and freedom to exercise the discretion they require to satisfy the complaining customer and remedy the consequences of the product failure. Customers are likely to forgive the product failure if the firm demonstrated a customer-caring attitude in its handling of the complaint and if the recovery options offered the customer were appropriate. Nevertheless, preventing dissatisfied customers from defecting to a competitor is a challenge.

Why do customers switch? A study of 526 responses covering 45 different service industries, using the critical incident technique to explore the question, found eight main reasons for customer switching behaviour. These were categorized under price, inconvenience, core product failures, service encounter failures, failed employee responses to service failures, competitive issues, ethical problems, and involuntary factors. The study found that even satisfied customers switch providers for reasons such as price, competitive issues, convenience, or access. The bottom line is that managers need to develop customer retention strategies or customer defection management programmes to pre-empt customer switching, and to minimize or eliminate systemic reasons for customer switching behaviour. They need to understand why their customers switch. Firms need to be able to identify those customers who are at risk of switching. It is imperative that they set up alerts and remedial mechanisms to reach those customers to prevent them from switching to a competitor. Ensuring a high retention rate must be a treated as a constant endeavor for the customer-focused management. Striving to sustain long-term profitability means ensuring a stable and growing customer base. Growing the customer base by targeting the right customer is only the start of customer relationship. Enhancing the value of each customer to the firm presumes that the customer is retained by the firm. Retaining the customer base requires a close monitoring of how each customer is feeling and behaving in terms of product purchase and consumption. The defection management system should comprise of a means

- To assess customer value changes so that it can alert the firm about the possibility of customer defections,
- To assess the extent of long-term revenues at risk, and
- To determine and execute the appropriate recovery methods for each type of customer.

Customers switch when the customer value they receive at the individual or segment level is inferior to an alternative. Thus, it is necessary to conduct a continual assessment of customer value as the critical first step. Failpoint data on customer experiences is a metric that could serve as a barometer for customer value changes. Customers who have experienced the service when failpoints have failed are at risk of switching. The firm has failed to deliver the expected customer value for these customers. Customer defection management is proactive—its purpose is to identify customers who are at risk of switching and to initiate an assessment of the status of customer value to the firm, followed by an analysis to determine how to increase customer value to those customers. One of the functionalities required in a good customer knowledge system is to alert its users when there might be a problem with a customer, and to provide the information necessary to rectify that problem. Customer defection management begins with designing into the customer information system alerts that are triggered by customer switching indicators. These alerts can be based on thumb rules suggested by the information on successful and unsuccessful customer recovery captured and stored. Thus, any time there is a change in the customer's situation, a thumb rule-based trigger sets off a defection alert that indicates the customer is at risk of switching.

As we saw earlier, customers switch for a number of reasons. Customer-focused firms with good customer information systems would have identified reasons for switching behaviour in their customer base. Causes of switching behaviour can be grouped into firm-induced reasons or environmentally induced reasons. Firm-induced reasons are really customer value changes that could be from price changes, product failures, service encounter failures, or problem resolution failures. Environmentally induced reasons can be those that are customer life events. For the individual consumer it could be events such as change in professional or marital status, income changes, relocation, or change in lifestyle—or in other words, change in need situation in general. For the business customer it could be change in value creation and therefore consumption of productive factors or change in value creation processes, including change in the buying centre, a change in the buying process or criteria, or individuals making the buying decision. Environmentally induced reasons could also include competitor actions that have changed the relative worth of customer value in the firm-such as a price change or a product feature change by a competitor making the firm's own customer value less attractive than the competitor's promise of customer value. Legal, social, or technological factors in the environment could also result in customer switching. Wherever possible, the firm must attempt to integrate alerts into the customer knowledge for system for when any firm-induced or environmentally induced changes occur portending a negative change in customer value.

Once a defection alert is activated, whether related to a specific customer encounter or not, the firm initiates an analysis of whether the customer is in fact at risk of switching. If the customer is at risk, the firm must now determine if this customer is worth the effort, so to speak. If the loss in customer equity outweighs the retention costs, then the firm must attempt to employ the means necessary to alleviate the switching triggers. Incidentally, this thumb rule could apply at the segment level or to a specific customer. When the switching triggers are related to a specific encounter with a customer, it usually involves a critical incident, a product failure of some kind. Either the core product has failed or there was a service encounter failure or a failure to resolve a problem for the customer. For any of these reasons, a service recovery procedure needs to be in place to retain the customer. Customer-focused firms should consider it a functional requirement from investments made in any CRM technology that it is able to power a rich recovery database. The recovery database should yield costs and benefits of the various recovery options for this particular customer either based on segmentspecific information or information related to this specific customer.

A recovery database is utilized to determine possible recovery programmes, where specific retention options are assessed along with customer input. Once the retention plan is selected and implemented, it needs to be assessed for effectiveness and employed until the point where customer equity does not exceed retention costs. The recovery database must consist of all the information regarding customer switching behaviour and recovery successes as well as failures. Customer switching behaviour information should contain the reasons for customer switching obtained from customer satisfaction surveys, from exit interviews, and from customer research in general. All methods of recovery that have been tried need to be recorded for their effectiveness. A matrix developed to record what recovery procedures worked and didn't work for each switching trigger should determine a recommended retention programme. To accomplish this, retention reports from each customer recovery experience will need to be recorded, analyzed, and stored in the recovery database. The analysis would deal with the costs of the retention programme and the effectiveness assessment of the programme. Each customer switching trigger needs to be calibrated so that when a segment or customer is at risk the defection alert will move the firm to act with its recovery procedure. A well-planned customer recovery procedure is crucial to a sound customer defection management system. Customer service is considerably enhanced by such a knowledge-based decision support system.

Corporate strategy is about core competencies being leveraged to meet corporate goals. When analyzed into its parts, corporate strategy is about how the core competencies are leveraged in the operations and marketing strategies. Customer service is lost in the shuffle and usually ends up in neither strategy, primarily as a consequence of misplaced definition. Customer service has its unfortunate connotations because of its history and original intent as a business function, and the label does it a tremendous disservice.

Customer service is where most of the interactions with the customers occur for a manufacturing firm, whereas for a service firm not all customer interactions need be customer service. There are interactions whose task is the value creation and delivery of the core product. If firms find that customer service is where most of the customer interactions occur, then customer service should be the most crucial business function for the firm in managing customer relationships. Wherever there is a customer interaction, there is an opportunity to gather information about the customer and how the product meets the customer's needs. The knowledge of the customer's experience with the product in a customer database, if properly utilized, could serve to improve the product. With improved quality and customer value, customer loyalty is nurtured. With the knowledge about specific customers, firms can become intimately familiar with specific preferences of each customer, allowing for customization where possible. Customers can also provide knowledge about how the firm is doing compared to the competition in the customer's eyes. They provide an access to market information not otherwise possible. Firms develop market competence in understanding their competitive advantage and seek the loyalty of the customer by employing this knowledge. As summarized earlier, any manager should be able to look at the good sense in incorporating customer service in the overarching task of managing customer interactions and customer relationships.

Generally, in firms that are not customer focused, customer service has not transcended its image of a necessary evil involving a firm's obligations to take care of the annoyance of product failures. Customer-focused firms elevate customer service to a strategic level by placing it in the context of customer retention and giving it the prominence in the firm that it deserves, alongside customer acquisition, an integral part of customer relationship management.

Elevating the status of customer service function within the firm to a strategic level requires senior managers to practice and perform customer service as well. MBNA requires its senior management to handle four hours of customer service phone calls each month. Folklore in Freeport Maine has it that the founder of L.L. Bean had piped in customer service phone calls to his home! The customer-focused firm makes customer service the responsibility of everyone in the firm. Ritz-Carlton says to its employees, if you are the one to receive a customer complaint, you own it—follow that complaint's resolution process to its conclusion. It is a good practice to regularly involve the backstage personnel in handling customer service. Firms need to construct integrated knowledge management systems that obtain and utilize information from customer service experiences to improve the design and delivery of its value-creating processes. All customer touchpoints in the firm need to be involved in the planning and control functions of the product and service design and delivery.

The customer-focused firm needs to have several things in place to be able to implement a strong retention programme. It needs to have a rich recovery database, the processes to implement the retention programme and the people appropriately trained in recovery procedures. As we will see later, the best-designed processes will not work unless the people involved in the execution of these processes are empowered not only with the knowledge, support, and skills but the motivation and inclination in a customer-focused climate.

Operationally, retention programmes and the actual customer service activities must prioritize attention for its most valuable (customers) relationships so that all assets of the firm are dedicated at all times to maximum long-term profitability. The problem is that not all firms are proactive in their management of customer relationships. As a result, customer defections go unnoticed and customer service is the only desk at the firm that handles a customer defect risk. Customer service as an operation of the firm needs to be viewed as within the scope of customer relationship management. It should participate in the firm's retention activities with a much broader scope and higher status. A key consideration is what status the firm has given its customer service function.

Customer-focused quality, when combined with customer-focused productivity, ensures that the firm views operations with a customer focus for an outside-in view of the firm. Productivity is defined differently—not in quantity of customers handled but in quality of their lifetime value. Customer service productivity should not be measured by how many complaints were handled in a certain amount of time, but in terms of how effective it was in retaining customer equity. Costs and efficiencies are measured in terms of customer lifetime value.

A short-term orientation is discarded in favour of acquiring and retaining the more profitable customers for the long term. Short-term losses in a customer relationship are accepted if the long-term relationship with that customer will yield large and sustained profits over the duration of the relationship with that customer.

No customer-focused management decision can be executed without the appropriate customer-focused culture within the firm. The people in a firm, its managers and employees, should be provided with a customer-focused environment. The commitment begins with the CEO. The task of creating and delivering superior customer value must be complemented with the selection of the appropriate employees and the effective management of relationships with those employees. Employee equity, the value of the employee to the firm, should be linked to customer value by valuing an employee based on the individual's contribution to customer value and sustainable profits.

Strategies and tactics that are discussed from the customer-focused perspective are not deliverable unless there is the right kind of environment within the firm. Ultimately, for all of this to work, the people and indeed the corporate culture need to be customer focused and service oriented.

John Chambers runs CISCO Systems, one of the most successful among the largest firms in the world. Rated among the top firms as a "most admired company" and "best company to work for, " by *Fortune* and *Financial Times*, Cisco has grown to over 35,000 employees from about 3,000 when Chambers assumed leadership in 1995. During the same time, sales increased from $2 billion to $22 billion in fiscal 2001. When asked about how he manages growth, Chambers ranked "make your customers the centre of your culture" at the top of his list. To demonstrate the CEO's focus on the customer, Chambers regularly reviews customer satisfaction data and has a daily critical list of customers for whom the firm's products are in jeopardy of failure. He has access to a customer knowledge system that allows him, as he says, to explode critical information on each customer. Chambers focuses on recruiting, developing, and retaining the leadership team that can implement his customer-focused strategy. He ties manager and employee compensation to customer satisfaction.

Over and over again, it is very clear that the successful firm focuses on its people and ensures that new hires fit its corporate culture.

Southwest Airlines' director of field employment says: "We hire for attitude and train for skill." Candidates are put through a rigorous interview process, taking as much as six weeks sometimes. After that, the training period rejects 20 percent of the new hires because they don't fit into the corporate culture. Like CISCO, Southwest has a culture of teamwork and cooperation.

This final chapter is about the glue that keeps the entire firm collectively focused on the customer and on delivering a service-oriented customer value that is superior to the competition. Each chapter in this book thus far has outlined and discussed the critical business decisions and processes in the customer-focused firm. The success of the firm in executing and delivering on the goal is predicated upon the ability of its people, managers and workers, to make it happen. Without the employees, workers, and managers, individually and collectively sharing and believing in a cohesive culture or climate conducive to performing as a customer-focused firm, none of what has been covered in this book would have any meaning.

The CEO sets the tone for the climate within a firm. Senior managers take their cue from the CEO. You can tell how strong the culture is by observing how senior managers refer to their CEO. If you have had the opportunity to hear or watch Jeff Bezos, CEO of Amazon, you will have noted his playful nature and "we can make it" attitude. This attitude is also evident in how the people in his firm approach their tasks. Another CEO credited for his firm's customer-focused culture is Fred Smith, of FedEx, who says: "Customer satisfaction begins with employee satisfaction." Lou Gerstner talked about changing IBM's culture as critical to competing in the information age. By most accounts, he appears to have succeeded.

GE's Jack Welch, one of the great CEOs of our time, talked about shared values as critical to realising his vision. If the culture is not customer focused, the firm cannot be customer focused. The German ERP software company SAP almost disappeared into oblivion until its CEO, Hasso Plattner, who founded the company around an engineering-focused corporate culture, began to heed customers who had been asking for changes in the way its product was configured and were demanding a Web-enabled interface for the product.

When CEOs who have been successful in getting a firm to the top or keeping the firm at the top of their industry are asked about how they did it, there is always some mention of the attention they gave to the culture of the firm.

The importance of culture in the performance of a firm comes to the fore following mergers and acquisitions. In a survey of 1,200 adults, Andersen Consulting (now called Accenture) reported that customers of recently merged firms compared to other customers in the three telecom sector players—cable companies, Internet service providers, and phone companies—felt that service was worsening. The telecom industry had been and is still going through some pretty significant series of takeovers, mergers, and consolidations, causing the customers, even the goldplated and special ones, to suffer from lack of customer focus. CEOs who have been successful in leading a firm through a merger are likely very good at also shaping cultures. Such CEOs are much sought after and financially well rewarded by firms going through dissolution, turnaround, consolidation, acquisition, a merger, or some other form of asset reorganization. The clash of cultures is perhaps the most important challenge for this CEO.It takes a capable CEO who understands the importance of corporate culture and renders it prominent attention to successfully lead and shape the culture of the firm.

To ensure a customer-focused culture, the CEO must commit his attention to it. Fleet bank CEO Chad Gifford pledged $75 million in 2002 "to improve the overall customer experience, " recognising the severity of the customer service problems it had after its merger with BankBoston. Through a number of mergers, Bank of America's CEO, Kenneth Lewis, said he has been insistent on "one culture" and feels that he has succeeded in bringing the previously disparate entities with their respective cultures into one single culture. A major cornerstone of his efforts was the six-sigma programme and the "Spirit to Serve" customer service training at the bank. As of this writing the jury is still out on how successful Carly Fiorina, CEO of Hewlett Packard, is with her reorganization and change, involving everything from strategy, structure, and culture to compensation, following their controversial merger with Compaq in 2002. It had only been a few short years since Compaq itself had acquired Digital Equipment Corp. Even Wall Street has not been kind to its darling, HP. The challenge is tremendous and the rewards are huge. The task of shaping culture is perhaps the most important and fundamental challenge for any CEO. For a successful corporate culture that emphasizes a focus on the customer, the commitment has to begin at the top and be reflected in how the CEO runs the shop.

How an organization behaves depends on what Peter Drucker calls its "theory of the business." He says that the assumptions that a firm makes about its markets, about its technology, and about the strengths and weaknesses of the firm are what define its behaviour. He draws evidence from IBM creating the computer industry in the 1950s, Apple bringing personal computers to the household in the 1980s, and GM inventing lifestyle segmentation in the 1990s. These companies had the right theory of their business because the assumptions they made about the world around them were the right ones. The characteristics that define a customer-focused firm align closely with the assumptions that Drucker is talking about. Drucker's three assumptions centre around markets, technology, and firm. In customer-focused management terms, these relate directly to customers and to the firm's value-creating assets. Firms must understand their customers and be open-minded about the technology of the value creation and delivery in their business to leverage its core competencies towards superior customer value.

The strategic decision making process begins with assessments of markets and firm to determine the customer value that can be created profitably from its productive assets. These assessments serve to define the customer in terms of consumption activities and to define the solution or value bundle it will provide the customer through the core and supplementary product. Value-creating and delivery processes are designed according to these definitions of customer and product. What follows from the definition and analysis of the customer is the estimate of the lifetime value of all customers or more appropriately the long-term profits of the firm. In parallel, the product definition will guide the asset and resource allocation towards the more profitable products. Firms seek to maximize the value to the firm by serving the most profitable customers with the most profitable value bundle that can be produced with its assets.

The strategic decision-making process incorporates a customer focus to guide value creation and delivery decisions. As developed and emphasized throughout this book, the principles of customer-focused management are the following:

- Obtaining and utilising information about customers, especially with respect to their consumption cycle
- Designing value creation and delivery strategy and processes that are based on that customer knowledge
- Implementing the strategy and processes that provide superior value to customers so as to meet the firm's goals

To make any of this work, the entire firm has to get behind believing in these principles of customer-focused management. To become customer focused, the firm must really change the way it thinks and behaves, such that the customer is always the centre of the value creation and delivery. The firm must have in place the appropriate people with the appropriate attitude. When the goals, structures, processes, and rewards are also in place, the culture and climate should follow for the firm to become customer focused. Two underlying fundamental concepts defining organizational behaviour become evident here in the processes and people requirement: organizational structure and corporate culture. *Organizational structure* refers to how firms define the roles and relationships between the various functions or processes and the individuals responsible for and given the authority to fulfill them. *Corporate culture* refers to the values and beliefs held in the firm that dictate how the firm operates.

Value creating and delivering processes may be designed so that firms can be customer focused. But if the culture does not provide the climate, the firm cannot be customer focused. Just about everything in the firm from the office and building design to social hours can affect the culture of the firm. Nokia, the wireless devices giant from Finland, went so far as to instruct its building designers to design and construct an environment where individuals are immersed in the corporate culture and can interact with the company and fellow employees on a variety of levels. Notice the company's slogan: "Connecting People." Citibank has "pulse lunches" at its banks where managers have a weekly lunch with employees and listen to their concerns and then act on them. These are two examples of how climate can be created for the firm to be customer focused.

ORGANIZATIONAL DESIGN

For the value creating and delivering process to be customer focused as intended, the organization design should follow the way that people who execute the processes need to relate to each other. Traditional organizational structure may not be designed for a customer-focused operation. McKinsey introduced the notion of the "horizontal corporation" in 1996, citing examples of firms that had reorganized around natural workflows rather than conventional functional areas. What is interesting about the principles behind their horizontal organization model is that most of them would translate very well to the customer-focused firm. Among other things, such firms, they say, must focus externally on the customer and realign organizational roles and resources around the processes that deliver customer value. They offered the following as evidence of the benefits of reorganising into a horizontal corporation.

- A division within Motorola reduced cycle time by 80 percent and late supplier deliveries by 30 percent.
- A GE production facility improved productivity by 50 percent, reduced manufacturing cycle from three weeks to three days, and customer complaints from 2 to 0.2 percent.
- Ford's customer service division increased productivity by 20 percent and improved customer satisfaction performance by 20 percent to 60 percent.
- Saab Aircraft reduced lead times by 50 percent, value-added costs by 20 percent, and customer complaints by 70 percent.

The point to be made with these examples is that the benefits from an organizational structure that is designed to focus on the customer can be very powerful. A structure that integrates both suppliers and customers and is conducive to a focus on creating and delivering customer value is a prerequisite for customer-focused strategies to work. An interesting support to the logic of making radical changes to the traditional functional, geographic, or product-based forms of organizational structure can be drawn from the following example. The manufacturing chief at Rowe Furniture in Salem, Virginia, disassembled the assembly line and allowed the factory workers to figure out their own processes to get the furniture built. The result? The shop floor seemed to be crazed, but productivity and quality went up dramatically! Organizational structure and design including such things as hierarchy, power structure, and decision making and hiring, training, and rewarding are critical to ensure that the firm is customer-focused.

Organizational design can take various forms depending on the value creation and delivery process. With the recent revolutionary advances in information technology, newer forms are becoming evident. In what is also referred to as the knowledge economy, virtual organizations are commonplace today. A new model has emerged where organizations draw knowledge-based assets from entities outside the firm to create and deliver value to the customer. Clearly, information technology plays the crucial pivotal role in making this possible. Scholars have suggested that in such a virtual organization, three vectors—customer interaction, asset sourcing, and knowledge leverage—are the key components in the strategy and structure of the successful business model. The organization structure must be designed so as to perform its value creation and delivery processes in a customer-focused culture.

Customer-focused culture

To understand what customer-focused culture is, it is important to first understand what "culture" means in the context of organizations. One commonly accepted definition of corporate culture among scholars studying organizational behaviour is: the pattern of shared beliefs and values that guide the way the firm behaves. Mrs. Fields would say, "It's the way we do things around here." Culture is deeply rooted in values and translates to "climate" in a day-to-day "feel" of the place. Climate is a manifestation of culture. Schneider and Bowen, two wellknown scholars from the fields of psychology and organizational behaviour who have done a great deal of research on customer-focused culture and service climate, view climate as the "tangible layer on top of the organization's underlying culture."

Culture, along with mission and strategy, is also seen as an important piece for the vision of a firm to work. Corporate culture has been proven to be predictive of the performance of an organization. For example, in a sample of 102 companies, it was found that corporate culture was strongly linked to innovativeness. In this study, investment in technology was found to be influenced by corporate culture when firms provided the climate that fostered innovations. When Snapple, the beverage industry's surprise breakthrough firm, fell on hard times, Michael Weinstein of Triarc Companies, who took over the firm, focused on corporate values to turn the firm around.

Cultures are relatively stable, and it takes a long time to shift core values of a firm. The resistance to change has led to the demise of such former giants such as Polaroid. Polaroid's I-Zone instant pocket camera zoomed to number one status in less than three months after its introduction. This product almost didn't happen. During its development at the firm, the marketers who brought this idea to the table faced powerful resistance from old-line scientists and engineers at the firm who could not imagine what the founder of the firm, Edwin Land, would say about moving away from creating elegant products based on high technology. At one of the design meetings, the chief engineer was said to have asked, "Have we lost our minds?" He wondered why the same firm that Land had founded would produce something that was small, clunky, with a cheap lens, to produce fuzzy, thumbnail-size photographs!

The culture of a firm is its soul, and it resides in its employees and managers. Home Depot founder Bernard Marcus is known for his reliance on employee empowerment to make his vision a success. But, how many firms show a real caring for their employees? The statistical analysis software company SAS is often cited as one of the few information technology companies to have weathered the technology sector-led recession in the last couple of years because of its strong culture and caring for its employees. The firm has won several "best places to work" awards over its 25-year history. The CEO of SAS, Jim Goodnight, says, "I think our history has shown that taking care of employees has made the difference in how employees take care of our customers. With that as our vision, the rest takes care of itself." Unfortunately, it is the exception when a firm is able to say this and execute those sentiments in any meaningful way. The result is that employees are left to fend for themselves and leave unhappy. The Creative Group, a firm that specializes in recruiting creative talent, reported that in their survey, two-thirds of their sample of advertising and marketing executives from the nation's largest companies said the creative professional changed jobs every other year. It is not only important to attract the right employee, it is even more important to retain customer-focused employees.

It shouldn't come as a surprise that firms that are customer-focused are also ones that take care of their employees. When firms minimize their efforts in developing employee dedication to creating and delivering customer value they face high employee turnover. Harvard researchers Schlesinger and Heskett called this unfortunate but common attitude among senior managers, the self-perpetuating "cycle of failure." Among the reasons they offered to explain why firms fall into this cycle is an inability to measure the costs of employee dissatisfaction. They cite firms such as Wells-Fargo, ServiceMaster, Dayton

Hudson, Au Bon Pain, and Fidelity Bank of Philadelphia, who have broken the cycle of failure by paying attention to their frontline employees. Recruiting, training, and rewarding practices of frontline employees at these firms are remarkably simple but different from those of the "average" firm. They pay more and reward their employees and managers who are productive and customer focused. The results in the form of employee and customer satisfaction are very compelling.

The direct correlation between employee satisfaction and customer satisfaction is often underestimated. Researchers Schneider and Bowen have shown through a series of studies of bank tellers that satisfied employees deliver satisfying customer encounters that result in employee and customer satisfaction feeding off each other. The key prerequisite is to create an atmosphere that fosters a focus on creating and delivering superior customer value. Such an atmosphere or climate comes from a firm that has a customer-focused culture and instills in its employees the values of customer-focused behaviour. Almost all top researchers in the field of services marketing, operations, and management have called for increasing attention to the culture that promotes satisfying service encounters. A firm cannot hope to satisfy its customers if the employees are not happy themselves. If the employees are not happy they leave. Guess who leaves first? The ones whose skills are most in demand are the ones who are most mobile—usually the best employees.

Attracting and retaining the customer-focused employee

Turnover at Dallas-based The Container Store is 20 percent compared to the industry average in retail operations, which generally ranges from 80 percent to 120 percent.

Full-time employees at the company get 235 hours of training in their first year and are constantly asked what they need to do their job well. The company won *Fortune* magazine's "America's best workplace" honour in 2000. Similarly, at the 60-employee sports apparel company, Athleta Corp., employees set their own schedules and handle personal matters during the workday, backed by a CEO who believes that they will make up the time.

To break the cycle of failure, firms have to value their employees. They ought to rethink the way they hire and groom their employees and managers. To do this, firms should be asking, what kind of employee do we need to attract and retain so that we can create and deliver a customer-focused solution?

Managers from the functional areas of human resources, operations, and marketing management should jointly help determine the ideal employee for any position that is directly involved in creating and delivering value to the customer.

Human resource decisions centre on hiring and training and are critical to acquiring the appropriate human capital in the firm. Study firms such as Disney,

Nordstrom, Southwest Airlines, Ritz-Carlton, and American Express, which are known for their customer-focused culture, and you will see that all of them are very careful in how they select and hire their employees.

They have in mind specific profiles that characterize the desired skills and personality traits that are necessary for the customer-focused employee in their business.

Some of them use quite sophisticated ways of assessing the service orientation of the recruit. With the training and education these companies have in place, new employees are socialized into the corporate culture, whatever that culture might be.

In a study within a large firm of five strategic business units (SBUs), 3,500 managers responding to a survey confirmed that the degree of market orientation in the processes of recruiting, training, and reward/compensation were found to strongly correlate with job satisfaction and trust in management.

A very revealing and useful exercise would be to investigate the hiring practices of the firm and check for how well the requirements for a customer-focused employee are reflected in the hiring and training practices.

Does the firm have customer-focused criteria in their employee selection process? Do the job requirements and ideal candidate description reflect a customer focus?

If the firm is well coordinated and integrated, customer knowledge is likely to be well utilized by the human resources department as well as the operations functions.

Knowledge of the consumption activities of the customer should guide the practice of attracting and retaining human capital. If this is in place then the training and education is also likely to be designed to develop the employee for operational excellence contributing to creating and delivering the desired customer value.

The operational excellence assumes the appropriate knowledge and attitude of the value creating and delivering role of the employee. Many firms now complement operations skills training with training on customer interaction skills or other customer-focused skills for the frontline employee.

Previously, for example, banks would provide operations training for tellers but not customer skills training. Once hired and trained, the operations and marketing functions take over the direct allocation, motivation, and supervision of the employee.

Employees must be able to enjoy their work and find it rewarding not just financially but emotionally as well. How well these functions value the employee will have a major effect on the efforts of the firm to create and deliver the desired customer value. The customer-focused firm ought to be very interested in the welfare of its employees. Otherwise, employees tend to disconnect from the firm and are not committed to their jobs. For example, Dupont began a programme to "re-engage" with employees by helping employees design their career paths in an attempt to win back employee loyalty.

Northeast Delta Dental is one of the major dental care insurance providers in New England. CEO Tom Raffio expresses his main challenge as "how to retain the customer-focused culture that has given us success as we continue to grow."

He succeeds by being very close to his employees. He goes to the extent of meeting the families of his employees so that he has an intimate knowledge of his employees' lives. His office is in the middle of the busiest floor of the corporate office.

He likes being accessible and close to his employees. Tom brings customer feedback directly to his employees and asks them what they thought the firm ought to be doing.

He is genuinely interested in the growth and development of the employee. The employee is empowered with the operational skills and with customer knowledge.

The customer-focused firm is proactive in rewarding employees for being customer focused. As we saw earlier, Commerce Bancorp of New Jersey gives its employees $50 to come up with any practice of the bank's that is not customer-focused.

The company almost instantly rewards an employee for specific customer-focused actions in a customer experience or incident.

Whoever has wowed the customer gets a "Wow" award hand-delivered the next day from head office. The customer-focused firm ensures that the workplace is a place where people can grow, where they are comfortable at what they are doing.

Several firms have begun to include a measure of customer satisfaction in the compensation and bonus criteria for employees. Here is an interesting example of a culture spillover from a merger that benefits the bigger company. PTC, formerly Parametric Technology, which acquired Computervision, found that their own salespeople were not concerned with managing the customer relationship after the sale while those who came from Computervision emphasized customer service.

Today, all salespeople in the company are evaluated on customer satisfaction scores as well, and PTC is focusing on solutions rather than the software product.

More than a decade ago, GE began a customer education programme at its Management Development Institute, where customers and employees are educated on the firms' goals and processes. The idea was to get the customers and employees together and explain the goals and strategies of the firm.

In this new economy, knowledge-based employees are very mobile with their expertise. Firms would be well advised to assess each employee's worth, including replacement cost, similar to the analysis in managing customer relationships, to determine the firm's need to retain the individual.

Retention efforts should be prioritized according to that worth of the employee. When firms reluctantly started laying off workers during the recent recession, employers were also offering enticements with bonuses so that they would return to the firm when it was ready to rehire workers. Charles Schwab was offering bonuses and $20,000 worth of college tuition money, hoping that these workers would come back to Schwab when the company started to hire again.

Treacy and Wiersema argued that a firm has to have at least one of the three value disciplines they organize their thesis around—operational excellence, customer intimacy, and product leadership. Either firms have to be very good at the customer value that they create and deliver, their values should be built around intimate customer knowledge, or they should be at the forefront of product innovation.

The argument that these are separate value disciplines is often commonly accepted. However, in a discussion of the customer-focused firm, the distinction appears to be irrelevant.

The customer-focused firm assumes that it has to be good at all these three value disciplines simply because they are interrelated. A customer-focused firm derives its competitive advantage from its service orientation.

Table. Framing the Customer-Focused Analysis.

Impact of Customer-Focused Culture	Analytical Questions
Customer Intimacy—How well the firm strives to understand the customer is a measure of how customer-focused the firm is.	How good is our customer knowledge? Do we proactively obtain customer information? Do we analyze our customer information? How well do we deploy that information in creating and delivering customer value? How effective are we in maximising customer equity?
Operational Excellence—Creating and delivering the desired customer value such that the firm maximizes returns from its assets is the measure of how customer-focused the firm is.	How effective are we in meeting customer needs? Are we creating and delivering the desired customer value? How efficient are we in terms of maximising returns from our productive assets?

With its intimate knowledge of the customer (customer intimacy), the firm excels in creating and providing superior customer value (operational excellence), and by anticipating and responding to evolving customer needs it continues to improve its customer value (product leadership).

In the new economy, a firm with a customer-focused culture leverages its people and its information technology to be close to the customer so that it can create and deliver superior customer value.

Its people and information technology, as the primary productive factors, have to be employed in such a way as to ensure the firm's ability to understand the customer and to use that knowledge in its value creation and delivery.

Thus, the importance of customer intimacy and operations excellence is taken as a guiding element in corporate strategy and performance. This approach requires a culture that is customer focused as a prerequisite to derive a sustainable competitive advantage.

Ensuring that the firm is staying customer focused should be a constant endeavor. It requires assessing the level of customer intimacy that the firm can claim. It requires the continuous assessment of the operational excellence that the firm is able to achieve. Key questions to ask would concern customer knowledge management. The following Table offers the key questions to help assess the customer focus of the firm. How effective is the firm at obtaining, processing, disseminating, and using customer information in guiding the decisions and activities of the firm? Only the customer-focused firm can effectively create and deliver superior value while maximising returns from its productive assets.

8

Cleaning and Cleaning Materials

Thus we know that any establishment has to be clean, well maintained and presentable at any given moment of time. But how to ensure well maintained premises?

Cleaning is the most important and primary aspect of housekeeping. It is a process of removing dirt, dust and grime by using methods such as dusting, shaking, sweeping, mopping, washing or polishing. There are certain areas you may clean daily, whereas you may clean other areas occasionally or once/twice in a year. Since there are different types of surfaces like wall, counter tops, marble floors, ceramic tiles, wooden chairs, etc, special cleaning agents are used to clean these specific surfaces. In this chapter, as suggested, discuss these various aspects of cleaning as well as the materials and equipments used for cleaning.

MEANING AND IMPORTANCE OF CLEANING

WHAT DO YOU MEAN BY CLEANING?

Cleaning involves sweeping floors, dusting furniture and other surfaces, mopping or washing floors, polishing surfaces, articles and accessories, scrubbing tiles, sinks, toilets, disinfecting drains, rearranging cleaned areas and putting things in their specific place. We can say that cleaning is a process of removing dust, dirt or any other undesirable materials like stains, spots, contents of an ashtray, etc. What happens if cleaning is not done on a regular basis?

- Yes, your house will become the breeding ground of insects such as cockroaches, spiders, ants, flies and mosquitoes. It will look dirty and will be most uncomfortable.
- Living in such circumstances can also lead to diseases such as asthma, bronchitis, etc. Thus, cleaning is necessary for a general presentable appearance and also to ensure good hygienic conditions. What do you understand by dust and dirt?

- 'Dust' collectively refers to the loose particles, which are very easily moved by air and settle on any surface. It is easily removed with the help of a dry cloth.
- 'Dirt' refers to dust which sticks to any surface with the help of moisture or grease. It is more difficult to remove dirt as compared to dust. Dirt has to be removed either with a detergent or any other cleaning agent. Let us now read ahead of some general methods of cleaning.

INTRODUCTION TO CLEANING AREAS AND TYPES OF GUEST ROOMS

As far as I know, it normally starts from the Standard, Superior, Deluxe and Grand Deluxe as the very top of the categories. The names basically vary, depending on types and locations of the hotels. You may find some 5 or 6-star hotels put "Ocean, Lagoon and etc" in front of the category names, making guests realise how this room is different from others. Also, the price is higher.

SINGLE ROOM

Comfortable yet functional Single Rooms feature a 2.8-meter-high ceiling, a large writing desk and a generous-sized bed:

- *Floor Space*: 20m^2 (218sqft)
- *Bed Size*: W1,400mm × L2,030mm(55.1inches x 79.9inches)

STANDARD DOUBLE

Standard Double Rooms have an innovative yet functional layout with a diagonally positioned semi-double bed. The large-sized desk/dresser faces the window.

All Standard Double Rooms have a limited view, and look out onto Nittele Tower, the new company building of Nippon Television Network.

- *Floor Space*: 22m^2(233sqft)
- *Bed Size*: W1,400mm × L2,030mm(55.1inches x 79.9inches)

DOUBLE

Double Rooms are an excellent choice for both business and leisure travellers. All Double Rooms have a bathroom with a separately enclosed bath/shower.

- Floor Space: 26m2(278sqft)
- Bed Size: W1,600mm × L2,030mm(62.9inches x 79.9inches)

STANDARD TWIN

The extended (2.8 meter/110.2 inch) ceiling and oversized windows promise a comfortable stay. The bathroom features a separately enclosed bath/shower, creating a space that is highly functional.

- *Floor Space*: 26m^2(278sqft)
- *Bed Size*: W1,100mm×L2,030mm(43.3inches x 79.9inches)

BUSINESS DOUBLE

Totally equipped, comfortable and spacious room, available with a double bed or two single beds and a fully fitted bathroom with shower unit or bathtub. Following the same style as the other rooms, it has been decorated in beech wood and white colours. Bright and cosy, it is also both modern and functional.

Room services:

- Flat Screen
- Security desposit box
- National and International TV
- Air conditioning with personal control system
- Sound-proofed room
- Hair-dryer

BATHROOM CLEANING

A trip down the cleaning aisle in your local supermarket can be confusing. There are scrubbing bubbles, foaming cleansers, bathroom, tub and tile cleaners, toilet cleaners, glass cleaners, mildew cleaners--and that's just a start. You could easily spend half the day just reading labels to find out which product is the best for every single job in your bathroom. There are a few things to keep in mind, however, when choosing cleaners for your bathroom in order to make the selection process a bit easier.

Chlorine and ammonia don't mix. Or at least, they shouldn't. When chlorine and ammonia get together, a chemical reaction releases harmful and potentially toxic fumes. This is important to know because ammonia and chlorine bleach are the two most common bases for many power-scrubbing bathroom cleaners. When you mix and match bathroom cleaners, you increase the likelihood of accidentally combining ammonia and chlorine. If possible, stick to either ammonia based cleaners or bleach based cleaners only and never combine the two. One way to avoid the potential for mixing the two chemicals is to choose a multi-surface bathroom cleaner that you can use on multiple surfaces. If you can find one product that removes hard water scale, eliminates soap scum, and can be used on porcelain, Formica, glass and mirrors, tiles, and many other surfaces, you'll eliminate a potential hazard and save money at the same time.

You can reduce the work of cleaning the tiled walls of your shower by applying a coat of car wax to them after they have been cleaned. Make sure you only wax the walls and not the floor of the tub, as the wax can make things awfully slippery. Glass and fibreglass are both porous, which makes them prone to staining from hard water. The car wax seals the pores, however, making them less prone to staining.

General Duties:

- Rinse out the sink after each use.
- Hang up towels and washcloths.
- Wash out the bathtub after each use.
- Flush the toilet after each use.
- Remove excess hair from the sink or tub.
- Remove dirty clothes.

Supplies needed:

- All-purpose cleaner
- Cloths or sponges
- Toilet brush
- Glass cleaner (for mirror)
- Mop and bucket
- Rubber gloves

All-purpose cleaner:

- Mix 2 tablespoons ammonia, 2 tablespoons liquid dish detergent, and 1 quart of water.

To clean the sink, faucets, tub or shower:

- Wash with a soapy cloth or sponge.
- Use baking soda and a nonscratch pad for stubborn marks.
- Rinse with clear water.

To clean the toilet:

- Wash the tank, outside of bowl, seat, and lid with a soapy cloth.
- Scrub the inside of the toilet bowl with a long-handled brush.
- Any all-purpose cleaner will work if the toilet bowl is cleaned weekly.

USE A BATHROOM STEAM CLEANER FOR A HEALTHY, SPARKLING ROOM

The average person can ignore a little dust, but when it comes to a grimy, dirty bathroom that is a completely different story and where a bathroom steam cleaner comes in handy. Nobody likes to use a bathroom that looks unkempt and dirty. At the very minimum, you should clean your bathroom at least once a week and even more often if you have a large family or the bathroom gets a lot of use. There are a few tips to follow daily that make your bathroom easier to clean weekly.

After a shower wipe the shower stall, walls or tub with a damp, soapy sponge and rinse. Rinse your sink after each use and always clean up any spills immediately. A steam cleaner comes in many different sizes, shapes and models and uses steam vapour to deep clean, deodourize and sanitize in one easy step. There are vapour steam cleaners and dry vapour steam cleaners that produce low moisture and high temperature vapour. A vapour steam cleaner does not use chemicals for cleaning so it is a healthy way to make your bathroom shine.

For allergy sufferers, a bathroom steam cleaner penetrates the object that you clean and kills any molds, mildew, fungi, viruses or dust mites instantly, which improves the air in your bathroom immediately. The wonderful thing about this type of cleaner is it is useful in every room of your home, not just the bathroom.

It is also an environmentally safe and fast way to clean your home. A steam cleaner uses very little water, as the vapour produced is low moisture, so it leaves almost no damp residue on the cleaned surface. This is especially handy if your bathroom has carpeting because, after steam cleaning, your carpets will dry completely in approximately ten to fifteen minutes. Once it is dry, vacuum the carpet to remove any particles of dirt loosened. Using the steam cleaner on hard surfaces dislodges the dirt and grime, which you just wipe up with a cloth. The bathroom steam cleaner works great around the bathroom window, on grout and kills the mold spores.

In the bathroom, it also cleans many other things such as:

- Faucets
- Floors
- Shower stall doors
- Bath surrounds
- Inside and outside of the toilet
- Tiles
- Shower curtains
- Walls and ceiling

By cleaning your entire bathroom with a steam cleaner it not only smells clean and fresh but removes germs, viruses, bacteria, mold and odours, making it very sanitary. Using a bathroom steam cleaner will make your bathroom sparkle, shine and look clean and fresh in no time.

ORGANIZE YOUR BATHROOM CLEANING SUPPLIES

The bathroom cleaning supplies needed to clean a bathroom are as numerous as the different surfaces and varieties of dirt and scum, which form in the area. There is some or all of the following surfaces in many bathrooms such as porcelain, glass, mirror, chrome, tile, fibreglass and ceramic. Some of the soils that need cleaning are soap scum, dirt, rust, hard water deposits, mildew, stains and mold. Because this can become overwhelming the best way to tackle cleaning a bathroom is by being organized and having the necessary bathroom cleaning supplies.

When your supplies are organized and together in one place, it makes cleaning the bathroom so much quicker and easier. Go through all your cupboards and drawers and gather the bathroom cleaning supplies you use specifically for your bathroom cleaning together. Throw away any products you have had for many years and never use, as they probably lost a lot of their effectiveness. Toss any that are almost finished or you do not use anymore, along with old, worn out, sponges and rags. Find a large bucket or shelf and fill it with all of your cleaning supplies.

Keep it well stocked with items you need to make your bathroom clean, fresh and sparkling. Some of the items that you may use or need on a regular basis, for cleaning your bathroom, are window cleaner, sponges and rags, toilet, sink and bathtub cleaner, paper towels, duster, floor cleaner, tile cleaner and a good all-purpose cleanser. Finding or making a cleaning product, that does more than one job, cuts down on the amount of different cleaning items needed and this saves you time in the end.

You do not need to load your shopping cart with cleaning supplies for your bathroom, as there are many great, simple, inexpensive recipes for making your own effective cleansers at home. Many are more environmentally friendly and do not contain irritating fumes and harsh chemicals. Stock the cleaning supply bucket or cupboard with homemade cleaning solutions and sprays, to get rid of household dirt and grime.

Here are a couple of great cleaning products to add to your supplies:

- In a spray bottle, mix a cup of white vinegar and one cup of water. Use this spray to clean the outside of the toilet, floors, countertops and shower stalls. For tough bathroom dirt, mix a cup of white vinegar and a cup of hot water. Spray this heated mixture on, leave it for ten minutes, so it softens stubborn hard water deposits, and soap scum, scrub and then rinse. Undiluted white vinegar also works great for cleaning toilets, showerheads and dissolving hard water deposits.
- Make a great, inexpensive glass and mirror cleaner by mixing one cup of rubbing alcohol, a cup of water and one tablespoon of white vinegar in a spray bottle. Simply spray on and wipe off with a lint-free cloth or paper towels. You can also replace the white vinegar with a tablespoon of non-suds ammonia instead, for a tough, all-purpose cleaner.
- To keep bathroom drains clear, pour a cup of baking soda down the drain, followed by a cup of white vinegar and leave this for an hour. Flush with warm water. This also works for kitchen sinks, bathtub and shower drains.

Cleaning is not most people's idea of fun but by keeping your bathroom cleaning supplies organized you will finish the job faster and have more time to relax and enjoy your day.

BATHROOM TILE CLEANER THAT GIVES YOU SPARKLING RESULTS

Cleaning a bathroom, including the bathroom tiles, is a household task that most people dislike. Because of this, they do not clean the bathroom often enough and the dirt and grime build up, which makes the job of cleaning it even more difficult when the time finally arrives. Most of us can tolerate a little dust occasionally, but when it comes to the bathroom, everyone dislikes going into that room and feeling like it is not clean and fresh.

It can be embarrassing to have company drop in and instead of enjoying yourself, you worry about someone wanting to use the washroom and noticing your stained, marked tile floor. Its time to get organized, learn some cleaning tips and also what bathroom tile cleaner to use so you have a bathroom that shines and looks fabulous. Start by gathering all your bathroom cleaning supplies.

Put them in a large bucket or on a shelf for easy access whenever you clean. Make sure you store them in a place that is child and pet safe. Remove the rugs and garbage pails, so you do not have to work around anything. Sweep your tile floor before you start to clean the bathroom so if water drips on it you do not end up with a muddy floor. Clean everything in your bathroom except the tile floor and the shower and shower floor or bathtub walls and bathtub. Always work in a well-ventilated area and wear rubber gloves when cleaning. Here are a few great bathroom tile cleaner products that are inexpensive to make, easy to use and work great for bathtub, shower and sinks.

- Combine one cup of clean ammonia, a quarter cup of baking soda, a half-cup of white vinegar and a gallon of warm water. Apply the cleaning solution, let it sit for a few minutes to dissolve the dirt and grit and then wipe off and rinse.
- In a gallon of warm water mix, a half cut of vinegar, one cup of ammonia and a cup of baking soda. Use a mop to clean the tile floor with this mixture. In the bathtub, sponge on or spray, leave it sit for a few minutes and rinse off.

If you have a grout problem, use an old toothbrush or grout brush and scrub with a solution of five parts water to one part liquid chlorine bleach. Let it sit for a few minutes and rinse with warm water. Repeat if necessary. Using a great bathroom tile cleaner and cleaning a little more often, will have your bathroom clean and sparkling all the time.

CERAMIC TILE CLEANING LETS THE TILES BEAUTY AND LUSTER SHINE THROUGH

With a little ceramic tile cleaning your ceramic floors and tiles will look as lovely today as they did the day you had them installed. Ceramic tiles come in two basic types, which are unglazed and glazed. Along with cleaning the ceramic tiles you must give some attention and care to the grout between the tiles. Grout gives your floor or walls a finished look, as it fills the spaces in between each tile. Grout comes in several colours and types but they all require cleaning and maintenance to remain in good shape.

They often use unglazed ceramic tiles on floors and countertops. Unglazed tiles require more attention than a glazed ceramic tile does. They traditionally use glazed tiles on floors, walls and countertops and these tiles have a tough, almost glasslike surface. Ceramic tiles are available in many finishes such as matte, glossy or textured. Ceramic Tile Cleaning For Unglazed Tiles Always sweep or vacuum your unglazed tile floor regularly to remove any dirt or gritty particles. Wash the floor with a mild soap-free detergent and warm water. You can also damp-mop unglazed tiles with a gentle all-purpose cleaner and dry with a soft cloth to avoid any streaking. Use the same solution on a sponge, for cleaning unglazed wall tiles.

Never use strong soaps, abrasives or acids on unglazed ceramic tiles. You should seal unglazed or matte ceramic tiles with a commercial sealer, as they are very porous and stain. On any ceramic floor, wipe up spills immediately to avoid staining. Ceramic Tile Cleaning for Glazed Tiles Sweep or vacuum your floor before cleaning. Damp mop the floor, using warm water and a soap-free mild detergent. Rinse with clean, warm water. For walls and shower walls, a mixture of equal parts white vinegar and warm water often removes soap scum and dirt.

Use chlorine bleach and water to clean dingy, dirty grout. Apply this solution, scrub with a grout brush or toothbrush and rinse. Use this only on light, non-coloured grout. You can also use a mixture of fifty-per cent hydrogen peroxide and fifty-per cent warm water in a spray bottle to clean grout. On stubborn stains, spray on shaving cream, leave for a few minutes and rinse off. Never use anything abrasive, such as scouring powders, on your ceramic tile as they could scratch the finish. By regularly ceramic tile cleaning and wiping up spills immediately you will keep your floors, countertops and walls looking wonderful.

MAKE YOUR BATHROOM MILDEW FADE AWAY

Walking into the bathroom and smelling a sour or musty odour is very upsetting and unpleasant and more than likely bathroom mildew and mold are the culprits. Mold and mildew are fungus that grow anywhere in a home but they especially love bathrooms. The reason for this is that it meets their environmental needs, which are poor or low air circulation and ventilation, low-lighting, high humidity, dampness, and warm temperatures. Mildew and mold grow on almost any surface such as tiles, grout, paint, wood, glass, material and porcelain. At one time or another, most small bathrooms end up with mold and mildew. Bathroom mildew finds a damp, dark crack or corner on the wall or in the shower, slowly starts growing and before you know it, you have a big problem on your hands. It continues growing, attaching itself to the grout between the tiles, the silicone sealer and even on the ceiling. Without getting the mold and mildew under control, your beautiful bathroom could end up looking and smelling terrible.

Controlling Mold and Mildew

Controlling the humidity in a bathroom, caused by running water and steam, is extremely important. Turn on your bathroom fan to pull steam and moisture from the air and if you have a window, open it a bit. This helps to keep the air circulating. If you do not have a bathroom vent or fan, it is a great investment but be sure it vents directly outside. Mildew loves dark areas so turn on your lights before a shower or bath and leave them on for an extra fifteen or twenty minutes after. Wipe the bathtub or shower area with either a squeegee or dry cloth after bathing and always hang up damp towels and clothing. Use either bleach or vinegar regularly, to stop future growth of mold and mildew. When the time comes to repaint, use a mildew proof paint, designed specifically for bathrooms, kitchens and other high-moisture areas

Removing Bathroom Mildew

Always wear rubber gloves and work in a well-ventilated area when cleaning. A mixture of five parts water to one part chlorine bleach is great for killing bacteria as it cleans. Use this on all the bathroom surfaces. In the shower or bathtub areas, use a stiff brush to get into the grout, tiles and hard to reach corners. If you have a corner that is difficult to reach even with a brush, soak a cotton ball in bleach. Place the cotton ball against the mildew, for twenty minutes, remove and then rinse. Wash your shower curtain in the washing machine but add a cup of bleach to kill any mildew or mold. Once your shower curtains are clean, soak them in salt water to prevent future mold and mildew growth. Keep a spray bottle of vinegar in your bathroom and after each shower or bath, spray the walls and tiles around the bath area. Clean your bathroom often with bleach, vinegar or commercial bathroom mildew cleaner to keep your room sparkling fresh, mildew and mold free.

CLEANING TOILETS, FLUSH THE DIRT AWAY

Cleaning toilets is not a job anyone looks forward to but it is very important not only for the appearance of your bathroom but also your health. As hard as it is to believe, there really is a correct and incorrect way to get your toilet sparkling. People spend far too much time worrying about the inside of the toilet bowl and too little time on the outside of the toilet. The outside of your toilet is where you need to spend the time cleaning and disinfecting because you sit on the seat, lift the lid and push the handle. The parts of the toilet you touch are more important than the toilet bowl. One thing you should never do is flush the toilet with the lid up, as it sends bacteria everywhere.

When tackling the job of cleaning toilets gather all your supplies together in one place. This makes it far easier and quicker to get started. Some of the supplies you need are rubber gloves, a stiff plastic bristle brush and holder, paper towels, cleansing powder, bleach spray and all purpose cleaner. You can make your own bleach spray by mixing 3/4 cup of bleach and a gallon of water. Fill a spray bottle with this solution. Make a good all-purpose cleanser by mixing a cup of rubbing alcohol and a tablespoon of ammonia in a spray bottle and then fill up the rest with water.

Wearing your rubber gloves, always start cleaning toilets by pouring or sprinkling cleanser into the toilet bowl, but not in the water. After leaving it sit for a few minutes, use your toilet brush and scrub, starting under the rim and clean to the bottom of the bowl.

Flush your toilet with the lid down, when you finish scrubbing. Spray the outside of your toilet with an all-purpose disinfectant spray. Using paper towels, start wiping the toilet down, beginning at the top of the tank. Pay special attention to the handle area and the toilet base. Now, spray the toilet seat outside and inside, the hinges and then the rim of the toilet. Using the paper towels, wipe this area clean, from the lid to the toilet rim. Always start at the top and work your way down. Nobody likes to use a bathroom that looks like it needs a good cleaning. Clean your bathroom weekly or more often if used a lot. Pay special attention when cleaning toilets and your bathrooms will sparkle and shine.

CLEANING BATHTUBS AND HOMEMADE BATHTUB CLEANERS

Cleaning bathtubs more frequently and using a great bathtub cleaner makes the job of cleaning your bathroom far easier and faster in the end. Leaving your bathtub and only cleaning in every few weeks is more time consuming and difficult than cleaning it once or twice weekly. Some of the supplies you need to clean your bathtub and bathroom are rubber gloves, mildew remover, bathroom disinfectant cleanser, old toothbrush or a grout brush, soft-bristled brush, and rags or a sponge.

You should clean the walls or surround above your bathtub before you start cleaning bathtubs Spray an all-purpose cleaning solution or your homemade solution on the walls and then leave it for five minutes, until it sinks in and loosens the dirt and grime.

While wearing rubber gloves, gently scrub any built-up dirt or soap scum and then rinse. If the grout needs cleaning, spray with a mildew remover or make your own. Scrub with either a grout brush or old toothbrush, to remove the grime and mildew.

Rinse the walls and wipe dry. When cleaning bathtubs, spray the tub with a bathtub cleaner, until you coat the tub and then let it sit for five minutes. This gives the cleanser a chance to sink in and loosen any dirt or grime. Using a soft-bristled brush, gently scrub out your tub and then rinse well. Use an old toothbrush to get at hard to reach areas, such as the corners, around the taps or the grout around the tub. Rinse well when you finish cleaning your bathtub. Here are a few suggestions and tips for cleaning the bathtub:

- After taking a bath, on a net bath puff, pour some inexpensive shampoo, wipe around the sides and bottom of the bathtub and rinse. This is an easy, quick way to keep your bathtub shining.
- Sprinkle borax in a wet bathtub and then scrub and rinse.
- Mix together 1 teaspoon of vinegar or lemon juice and a quart of warm water. Put this in a spray bottle and use to clean your tub, sink and other surfaces.
- Make a paste of vinegar and baking soda to scrub the tub and shower. This removes mildew and soap scum easily but be sure to let it sit for a few minutes to soak in. Rinse with warm water.
- Wearing rubber gloves, apply straight peroxide to light coloured grout and leave this sit for five minutes. Use a grout brush or old toothbrush to scrub the grout and then rinse with warm water.

Cleaning bathtubs more often and using the correct bathtub cleaner will keep your bathrooms will sparkling and shining.

THE EIGHT TOP BATHROOM CLEANING TIPS

Nobody likes to clean the bathroom but by following a few bathroom cleaning tips and suggestions, this job can certainly be faster and easier. A grimy bathroom is something most people cannot tolerate.

Cleaning it weekly or more frequently, if you have a large family, does not have to become an all day job. Fortunately, most of the materials and surfaces in bathrooms are not too difficult to clean. The real problems start when you neglect the bathroom for a long time and the scum and dirt have a chance to build up. That is why it is extremely important to clean your bathroom weekly at the very minimum. Here are a few great cleaning tips that will have your bathroom looking clean and fresh in no time:

- In a large spray bottle, use a mixture of 1/4 cup of rubbing alcohol, 1/3 cup of white vinegar and dilute this with water. Spray this on your bathroom mirrors and windows, wiping with a paper towel or even newspaper, and they will shine.
- Here are a couple of great bathroom cleaning tips to remove built up soap scum and grime from your glass shower doors, spray oven cleaner on the inside of the door. Leave it from half to three quarters of an hour. Scrub any built up dirt areas and then rinse with warm water. This also works fantastic on mildew. Dry the doors using a squeegee.
- A lemon cut in half and then rubbed on the glass shower doors, cuts through the dirt scum.
- To clean your tiles, mix three cups of water and three-quarters of a cup of bleach in a spray bottle. Spray, leave for a few minutes and wipe off.
- Baking soda works great for cleaning fibreglass bathtubs and shower stalls. Just sprinkle onto a damp surface, scrub and rinse. This mixture

is safe to use on your bathroom facets also. For stubborn stains, a Mr. Clean magic eraser works.

- Do not be afraid to throw your vinyl shower curtain in the washing machine on delicate or gentle, with a small amount of bleach and cool water. It controls mildew and your shower curtain lasts longer.
- Wash any throw rugs in your bathroom weekly, when you clean.
- Pour some bleach into your toilet bowl, let it sit for a while and scrub with your toilet brush. Flush and it is clean.

ELIMINATE BATHROOM ODOUR COMPLETELY

It is very upsetting to walk into your bathroom and smell an offensive bathroom odour. Some of the causes of the odour are clogged drains, mold and mildew, a kitty litter box or just a plain dirty bathroom. Here are some suggestions and tips that will have your bathroom sparkling and smelling great-quickly and inexpensively in no time.

Clogged Drains

It is no wonder that bathroom drains occasionally clog up with all the hair, dirt, soap and other gunk that goes down them. A good preventative maintenance tip is every three or four weeks, pour a cup of baking soda down your drains and then a cup of white vinegar. After an hour, turn your tap on and run some warm water through the drain. If your drain is removing the water slowly from your sink, plug the overflow openings and then use your plunger to unclog the drain. If the water is still very slow draining-there are strong chemical drain openers on the market. Be sure to protect your eyes and skin and only use this in a well-ventilated area. Follow the manufactures directions. If your drain is clear but emits an odour, pour either bleach or vinegar down the drain.

Cat Litter Box

To eliminate the odour from a cat litter box, rinse the litter box and pour some white vinegar onto the bottom. Leave for approximately fifteen minutes, rinse with cold water and then dry with paper towel. The vinegar neutralizes the smell of ammonia, from the litter. Add baking soda to the kitty litter to control the odour. There are also many litter boxes, on the market, that eliminate cat litter odour.

Mold, Mildew and Dirty Bathrooms

Instead of walking into bathroom odour when you enter the bathroom, eliminate problems such as mold, mildew and dirt. You will have it smelling fresh, and clean quickly and easily. A great all-purpose cleaner to use on most bathroom surfaces is a gallon of warm water with a half cup of bleach mixed into it. This disinfects as it cleans. NEVER mix bleach and ammonia together.

Use this on your bathroom ceiling, walls, floor, tiles, toilet, sink, and bathtub. For mold and mildew, spray one part bleach and five parts water onto the grout and repeat until the mold and mildew disappear. Putting an air freshener in your bathroom may mask the bathroom odour but you need to find the cause and eliminate it so your bathroom smells as great as it looks.

SIX GREAT SHOWER CLEANING TIPS

Shower cleaning is definitely necessary to keep this important area of your bathroom clean and sparkling. Dirty or moldy looking walls in the shower make the whole bathroom feel unsanitary. Here are some shower cleaning tips that will keep your shower and walls, sparkling and fresh looking. Always wear rubber gloves and keep the bathroom well ventilated when you clean.

Never mix chlorine bleach and ammonia, as these two products together produce very toxic fumes:

- Always wipe or squeegee your tiles or walls down after you take a shower or bath. Mold and mildew love damp, warm places so the dryer you keep your tiles, the less chance that mold and mildew will try to take over.
- Open the bathroom window slightly to circulate the air while taking a shower and turn on the bathroom fan to remove moisture. Keep a light on while taking your shower and turn it off about twenty minutes after you finish.
- Make a mixture of one part chlorine bleach to five parts warm water and wash the shower ceiling, tiles and floor with this.
- Another very good shower cleaning solution is a half-cup of ammonia and one gallon of water. Put this mixture into a spray bottle to use on your shower doors. This works great for removing soap scum. Spray the solution on your glass shower doors, scrub with a stiff-bristled brush and the rinse well with warm water.
- Shower door tracks get very dirty and need special attention occasionally. Start by removing any old hair and dirt from the shower tracks, using an old toothbrush or a small, stiff brush. Vacuum this up with a long-nosed vacuum attachment.
- Pour undiluted white vinegar into the track and leave for approximately fifteen minutes. Using a small stiff brush or old toothbrush, scrub the track and be sure to get into those hard to reach places. Rinse with warm water and repeat, if necessary.
- Use liquid car wax on clean fibreglass shower walls and glass doors to prevent alkaline deposits. It also makes cleaning the shower easier and prevents water spots. Reapply this mixture every six months.
- Wash your shower curtain in the washing machine but add one cup of bleach and one cup of vinegar to the wash water. Throw in a couple

of white towels, laundry detergent and wash in warm water. Hang the shower curtain back on the shower rod to dry. You can also substitute a cup of baking soda for the vinegar and bleach.

FIVE TIPS FOR CLEANING BATHROOM TILE

The bathroom is one room of the house that should be kept as clean as possible and using a few easy tips can help with cleaning bathroom tile. Bathroom tile that is not clean is dull and stained looking and is a breeding ground for bacteria, mold, mildew and even fungus. Keeping your bathroom tile clean is easier if it is done on a regular basis, ideally daily, instead of waiting until there is a noticeable build-up before cleaning.

For daily cleaning of bathroom tile consider these five easy tips:

- Cleaning daily is the key to making your tile sparkle. If your shower area is tiled simply mix 3/4 of a cup of bleach and 3 cups of water and keep in a spray bottle in the shower. After every shower simply spray down the walls of the shower with the mixture and wipe off with a sponge. The bleach will eliminate soap scum and will also prevent any mildew from growing on the tile or the grout.
- For heavier build up or stains mix 1 cup of salt, 1 cup of baking soda and one cup of vinegar together to form a thick paste. Apply to the stained or soiled area with a soft cloth and allow to stand for three to five minutes. Rub in a circular motion and rinse off with clean water. Be sure to use a non-abrasive sponge or cloth to avoid scratching the tile's surface.
- Keep your bathroom as dry as possible. While this is not a specific cleaning technique it will help prevent the build-up of mildew and mold. Keep lights on and run the vent fan while showering. Even using a hair dryer in the bathroom will help decrease the humidity in the air. Never leave the bathroom door closed after a shower as this will keep the humidity high and provide ideal conditions for mold and mildew growth.
- To eliminate the need for constant cleaning of white grout between tiles use a combination of one or two tablespoons of bleach to one cup of water. Spray and let stand, then wipe dry with a cloth. Once the grout is completely dry apply a grout sealer to the area between tiles. This will keep mildew from developing and keep grout looking bright and wipe. Do not use this solution on coloured grout; rather use a non-bleaching cleaner and water.
- Ammonia and water can be mixed, in a one part to three part ratio and sprayed on bathroom tile and shower doors to remove soap scum and leave a shiny surface.

Cleaning bathroom tile doesn't have to be difficult if you use a daily spray regime and keep grout and tile mold and mildew free.

CLOROX BATHROOM CLEANER TO THE RESCUE

Clorox bathroom cleaner is a versatile cleaning product that can be used to keep you bathroom looking clean, fresh and shining. In addition it will prevent the growth of mold, mildew, bacteria and fungus that can cause health problems if left unchecked.

Clorox bathroom cleaner is different from many products in that it does not contain bleach so is safe to use on most the surfaces in your bathroom. It is always recommend to test a small area of the surface you will be cleaning for the first time.

Generally test under the lip of the sink to test the countertop, or inside the cupboard to test the cabinet. Clorox bathroom is not recommended for use on varnished wood, natural marble or brass as it can cause discolorations. This cleaner works on:

- Soap scum
- Dirt
- Hard water residue
- Mold and mildew
- Bacteria

Clorox cleaner, just like all cleaners, works best on surfaces that are mildly to moderately soiled or stained. For very heavily stained or dirty bathrooms there may need to be more than one application of the cleaning product. Generally to use Clorox Bathroom cleaner simply spray the cleaner using the foam setting on the surface.

Keep the nozzle of the bottle between six to eight inches from the surface and try to avoid missing any patches. Allow the foam to sit on the surface for a few minutes and then wipe off with a wet sponge or cloth.

One of the many benefits of Clorox bathroom cleaner is that the foam is thick and sticks even to vertical surfaces in the bathroom.

This makes cleaning shower walls, doors and even the backsplash on sinks simple and easy. Using the fine sprayer adjustment is a great way to shoot the cleaner just where you need it, even around the base of toilets or behind taps and drains.

Keeping even the unseen parts of the bathroom mold and mildew free is important to prevent it from spreading. A new variety of Clorox bathroom cleaner now comes with Teflon that is designed to minimize the amount of substances that stick to the surfaces of the bathroom.

With use the Teflon does prevent mold and mildew growth as well as minimising soap residue and hard water grime that adheres to the shower surfaces. When using Clorox bathroom cleaner with Teflon be sure to have a fan circulating air and prevent using it in closed or confined spaces without appropriate ventilation.

CHOOSING THE RIGHT CLOROX TOILET BOWL CLEANER

There are several different types of Clorox toilet bowl cleaners come in many different types to allow you to choose the one that is right for your individual cleaning needs. Cleaning the toilet is usually one of the least favourite of all the bathroom cleaning chores, so using the right product is important to make the job easy and effective the first time. To understand the features of the Clorox toilet bowl cleaner family the following can be used as a guideline: Clorox toilet bowl cleaner with bleach-for that deep down clean Clorox toilet bowel cleaner with bleach provides both cleaning and disinfecting action.

Simply flush the toilet and apply about six ounces of the product under the rim of the toilet. Using a toilet brush scrub the area above and below the water line and let stand for 10 minutes. This allows time for the bleach to disinfect the toilet and kill the bacteria. Flush to rinse. Clorox toilet bowl cleaner with bleach and rain scent-provides all the benefits of the original Clorox cleaner without the harsh scent. Perfect for using to keep your bathroom smelling clean without chemical fumes or smells. Clorox toilet bowl cleaner with Teflon-provides all the cleaning power of Clorox with the added non-stick benefits of Teflon. Use this product with correct ventilation, as it is a bit stronger smelling than the original Clorox.

Clorox dual action toilet bowl cleaner-two powerful cleaners are mixed upon use and act to clean and disinfect the toilet. Use the same as the original cleaner but be sure that both openings are directed under the rim. With all Clorox products it is important to use some general safety measures when using the cleaners. Never mix Clorox cleaners with any other chemicals or cleaners including bleach. The mixture of various cleaners can cause the formation of potentially toxic gases that can be deadly. Avoid using any cleaners in closed or confined spaces, always use a circulating fan or open a window when applying cleaners. Clorox also makes other toilet cleaners such as automatic cleaners that sit in the back of the toilet tank to continually clean the toilet between scrubbings, and Clorox toilet wand systems that combine both the cleaner and the scrubbing brush, all in one easy to use and disposable package. Try experimenting with the various Clorox toilet bowl cleaner products and determine which ones best meet your needs.

TOILET CLEANERS FOR A PRETTY POTTY

The smell of a dirty toilet could be your greatest motivator for cleaning it as quickly as possible.

Here are some tips before we get started:

- Always wear rubber gloves when cleaning your toilet.
- Never combine ammonia and chlorine bleach as it produces a toxic gas.
- Always clean in a well-ventilated area.

HOMEMADE TOILET BOWL CLEANERS

- To remove hard water stains from your toilet bowl, start by turning off the water shut-off valve to the tank so when you flush the toilet you remove most of the water from the bowl.
- Fill a spray bottle with white vinegar and use this to spray the entire toilet bowl.
- Sprinkle borax in the toilet over the vinegar and then let this mixture sit for about half an hour.
- Using a stiff bristled toilet brush, scrub the inside of the toilet, adding more vinegar if necessary. Turn the water back on and flush the toilet.
- Dissolve a couple of denture-cleaning tablets in the toilet and leave this overnight to help dissolve hard watermarks and stains.
- To remove rust stains from your toilet bowl, use two tablespoons of tang and sprinkle on the rust stains. Leave on for approximately an hour and then scrub with your toilet brush. Flush and repeat if necessary.
- Two great toilet cleaners are rubbing alcohol and borax. Mix one gallon of hot water and a half cup of borax and use this solution to clean the outside of your toilet.
- It not only cleans but also deodourizes and disinfects. Put rubbing alcohol on a sponge and clean your toilet handle, lid and seat to disinfect. Allow this to dry and do not rinse off.
- Pour one-half cup of baking soda onto the sides of a wet toilet bowl. Let this sit for half and hour, brush and flush.
- Pour a half cup of bleach into the toilet bowl, leave overnight and scrub in the morning. Flush and you have a clean toilet.
- Pour one-half can of coca cola into your toilet bowl and leave it for a few hours. Relax and drink the other half can. Scrub with a toilet brush and then flush.

CLEANING MOLD TIPS

Cleaning mold needs to be done by a professional as mold is spread through tiny spores which once opened, float throughout the home. Once they get into the carpeting or even the air duct system-the spores are blown throughout the inside of the home and can cause harsh allergy symptoms. Allergists are finding more and more people who live in a damp climate are suffering from aches, pains, fatigue, and constant congestion due to the non- stop growth of mold. Today mold is considered a dirty and toxic word. No one wants to have any kind of mold in their home. Usually mold grows in dampness and common place is in the bathroom and shower. There are cleaning products on the market which claim to kill the mold by spraying it on the infected areas and let sit for a few minutes before cleaning the mold away. So-how do we actually know how to clean mold? To date, many people believe that by using straight bleach, bleach mixed with water, or a bleaching product supposedly destroys the growth of mold. Unless you know of a professional mold cleaner, always consult your town's hazmat board and ask them to come inside the home to evaluate any possible mold growth.

MAKE LIME SCALE AND WATER MARKS DISAPPEAR IN YOUR BATHROOM

Anyone that lives in an area with hard water knows how difficult it is to remove lime scale buildup and watermarks in the bathroom. Even in a clean bathroom the unsightly mineral buildup and stains in the sink, toilet, tub, shower and on the tiles and fixtures caused by hard water makes it look unkempt and dirty. If you have hard water, you know that lime scale deposits are so hard that you need a chisel to remove it. One way to eliminate this problem is by installing a water softener but that does not get rid of the lime scale buildup and watermarks that are already there.

Here are some ways to remove the lime scale from your bathroom:

- Showers and Tiles–Use a heavy-duty gel cleaner made specifically for removing lime scale buildup.
- Avoid abrasive cleaners as they can scratch tile, porcelain, and other finishes.
- Be sure to leave the window or bathroom door open for ventilation and wear rubber gloves.
- Use a damp cloth or sponge and apply the cleaner to the tiles, shower door and other surfaces. Leave it on for the length of time the manufacturer suggests and then rinse thoroughly.
- Soak the showerhead in white vinegar for a few hours to remove lime buildup.
- Sinks–You can use the same heavy-duty gel cleaner on your bathroom sink and faucet.
- Use an old, soft toothbrush to apply the cleaner behind and around the faucet. Use warm water to rinse it thoroughly.
- Toilet–There are several liquid and gel cleaners for removing lime scale made specifically for toilets.
- Put this around under the rim and on the scale, leave it for the suggested length of time, scrub with a toilet brush, and then flush a few times.
- Another solution is to use a mixture of half borax and half vinegar. Drain the toilet bowl, apply the mixture to the lime scale and leave it on for a few hours before removing.
- Another solution for removing lime scale buildup and water marks is taking an empty spray bottle and filling it with a half cup of white distilled vinegar and two cups of water.

- Spray this on all the problem areas and wait for an hour or so but be sure not to let it dry. Spray again if necessary.
- Rinse all the problem areas with warm water and repeat if necessary.
- If the lime scale buildup is very heavy, soak some extra-strength paper towels in white distilled vinegar or all-purpose bathroom cleaner.
- Drain the toilet and line the bowl with these soaked paper towels.
- Do the same with the sink and shower if necessary.
- Leave them for several hours but add more vinegar or cleaner if the paper towel starts to dry out. Remove the paper towels, discard, and scrub with a stiff brush.

METHODS OF CLEANING

The dust and dirt can be removed by dusting, mopping etc. Based on these we can describe the cleaning methods as follows.

DUSTING

You are already familiar with the term 'dust'. But how do you remove dust? When any surface is wiped with a piece of dry cloth, (duster), it carries the loose dust with it and the process is known as dusting. This should be done with a clean soft cloth.

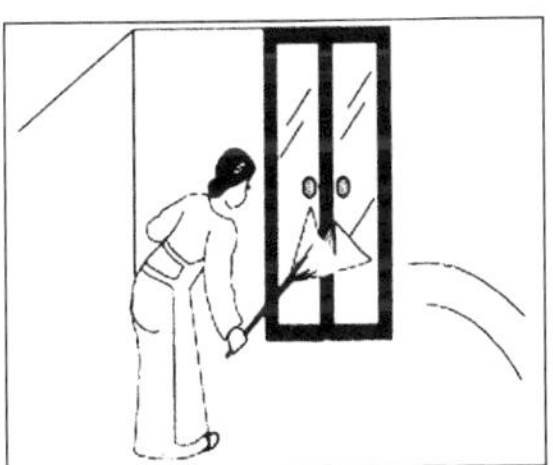

Fig. Dusting wiht a Cloth

SHAKING AND BEATING

What happens when you shake a cloth full of dust? Yes, the dust falls out. Similarly when you shake or beat any soft material, like a carpet/rug or a curtain, the dust falls out, making the article dust free to a large extent. This is mostly done in open air so that other things do not get dusty.

Fig. Carpet being beaten

SWEEPING

When a broom or a brush is used to carry the dust laterally along the room, the process is known as sweeping. While sweeping any vertical surface as walls, you should remember to start from the top and sweep downwards. Similarly for lateral sweeping as for floors, start from one end of the room and move to another, preferably a door, and carry the dust all along or collect in a dust pan. All the movable articles kept on the floor should be lifted, swept under, and kept back in place.

Fig. Sweeping the Floor

MOPPING

You have read that wiping with a dry cloth is dusting, similarly, wiping a surface with a damp cloth is called 'mopping'. The piece of cloth used is known as a 'mop' and is generally coarser than a duster. In this process, both the dust, as well as easily removable dirt, is also removed. Mopping is mostly done on floors. Extra attention should be paid to nooks and corners otherwise it gets tougher to remove fixed grime later on.

Fig. Mopping

WASHING

Fig. Floor Being Washed

Sometimes mopping alone is not sufficient to remove dirt. Such surfaces are then scrubbed with the help of a yard (bamboo) broom along with plenty of water. Eventually the dirt loosens and is carried off by water. This process is known as 'washing'. In case of tougher stains or dirt, detergent may be added to the water.

POLISHING

When some reagent is rubbed on a surface to bring out the shine, the process is known as polishing and the reagent applied is known as the 'polish'. Similarly, many other articles/decorative items made of brass, wood, marble etc, may be polished.

Fig. Polishing a statue

CLEANING EQUIPMENTS AND MATERIALS

Let us now learn about the equipment and other materials, which assist us in the process of cleaning. Can you name a few? Let us try to make a list of such equipments.

CLEANING EQUIPMENTS

Following are some of the equipments which you will come across during the process of cleaning:

- *Dusters*: These are mostly made of soft cotton, flannel or artificial feathers mounted on a stick. These are used to clean loose dust and are also used for wiping various surfaces. You should use separate dusters for dusting and wiping surfaces such as dining table, mirrors, kitchen slabs, etc. They should be washed and dried after use.
- *Dust pans*: These are made of either plastic or metal and have flat surfaces, rounded at the sides. After sweeping, dirt and dust is collected directly into these with the help of a broom and carried to a dustbin. Dustpans save sweeping the entire amount of dust from one room to another. Instead, dust can be collected from each room and disposed of simultaneously. Dust pans should be cleaned after use.
- *Mops*: Are mostly made of thick, loosely woven cotton cloth. These are used to wipe dust from the floors. These are dipped in clean water and

squeezed before wiping the floors. You should change the water after mopping each room or when it gets dirty. You should thoroughly wash the mop and spread it for drying, after use.

- *Polishing cloth*: these are made of soft absorbent cloth such as flannel. Dry polishing cloth helps to clean and shine the polished surfaces by rubbing them vigourously.
- *Brooms*: brooms are either soft or hard. The soft ones are used to sweep the floors, whereas the hard ones (yard broom) are used to wash the floors.
- *Brushes*: Are available in various sizes and shapes and are made of different materials. Different brushes are used for specific jobs. Brushes with nylon or plastic bristles are used for cleaning carpets or furniture, round feather brushes are used to remove cobwebs, metal brushes are used to clean wire mesh in the windows. You have special nylon brushes to clean the toilets.
- *Buckets or basins*: metal or plastic buckets/basins of suitable sizes are used to carry water, detergents and chemicals so that there are no spills.
- *Dust bins*: These are available in plastic with a lid. These should be lined with paper so that the garbage does not stick to the surface. They should be emptied and washed daily.
- *Vacuum cleaner*: It works on electricity and has a fan. This sucks in the dirt and dust from the surfaces and stores it in a disposable bag inside. This bag should be emptied regularly.

CLEANING MATERIALS

There are many materials and reagents, which help in cleaning, scrubbing and polishing surfaces. Some of these are commercial preparations for cleaning and you may be already familiar with some of them.

- *Water*: Water is the simplest cleaning reagent available to us. Some dirt may be loosened and dissolved in it. Although most of the time, some other cleaning agent is also used along with it.
- *Detergents*: Detergents are available in powder, solid (soap, soap flakes etc.) and liquid form.These are used with water to clean various surfaces. The basic ingredients in a detergent are surface active agents, known as surfactants. A detergent may have more ingredients to make it more effective, like alkaline salts, bleaches, foam boosters, germicides and perfumes. The exact nature and use of a detergent will actually vary just as to its ingredients. However, there are a few points which should be kept in mind while choosing a detergent.
  It should–
  - Be readily soluble in water
  - Be effective in all types of water and produce no scum

- Have good wetting powers so that the solution penetrates between the article and the dirt particles
- Have good suspending powers to suspend dislocated dirt and not allow it to settle back
- Be effective over a wide range of temperatures
- Be harmless to the article and the skin.
- Clean quickly
- Be easily rinsed away

Furniture Cream		
Ingredients	**Method**	**Use**
1. Bees wax 50gm	1. Shred wax and put in a pan. Cover with turpentine.	1.Use to polish light coloured furniture.
2. Turpentine 30ml	2. Heat in a double boiler till wax melts.	
	3. Cool and allow it to set.	
Furniture Polish		
Ingredients	**Method**	**Use**
1.Linseed oil 50 gm	1.Mix all ingredients together in a clean bottle and store	1.This can be applied on furniture with a pad of old cloth
2.Turpentine 30 ml		
3.Vinegar 30 ml		
4.Methylated spirit 30 ml		

- *Abrasives*: Some of the common abrasives are sand, finely powdered brick, saw dust, wheat bran, emery paper, fine ash, filtered chalk etc. Besides these, steel wool, nylon mesh, coconut fibres are also used to scrub dirt. Their use depends on the surface to be cleaned and the type of dirt to be removed. The extent of cleaning will depend upon the nature of the abrasive used and on the scrubbing action.
- *Acids*: Strong acids are used to clean toilets (water closet and sinks) and are available in crystals or liquid form. Milder forms of acids are also used to clean very dirty tiles. Acids should be rinsed off as soon as possible after use and should be stored away from children. Vinegar and lemon are used to clean stains on metals like brass and copper.

- *Alkalis*: Baking soda and ammonia are used as grease emulsifiers and stain removing agents.
- *Bleaches*: Stains on fabrics are removed by bleaches such as sodium hypochlorite, sodium perborate, hydrogen peroxide, sodium hydrosulphite etc.
- *Solvents*: Solvents such as methylated spirit, carbon tetrachloride, kerosene, petrol etc; are used to remove grease, wax and other stains from the surfaces. You should keep methylated spirit, kerosene, petrol, away from fire as they are inflammable. Carbon tetrachloride is harmful if inhaled.
- *Polishes*: Polishes are used on surfaces such as floors, furniture, leather and even metals. When rubbed on a surface, they provide a protective covering to the surface and produce shine. The article also gets cleaned in the process.

Metal Polish		
Ingredients	**Method**	**Use**
1.Soap-2 tbs	1.Dissolve soap in boiling water	1. Shake well before use.
2.Ammonia-1 tbs	2.Mix with bath brick and ammonia.	2. Soak soft toweling in the mixture, let it drip dry.
3.Boiling water-2½ cup	3.Cool and store in air tight bottle.	3.Wipe and rub with this toweling.
4.Bath brick-50		
Copper Cleaner		
Ingredients	**Method**	**Use**
1.Fine sand-4 tsp	1.Mix all ingredients and keep in jar.	1.Rub well into brass or copper surfaces to remove stains.
2.Flour-2 tsp	2.Moisten a small amount of above mixture to a paste by using equal amounts of vinegar and water.	
3.Salt-1 tsp		

Note:

Tbs-table spoon; tsp-tea spoon.

Ready-made polishes are expensive as compared to home-made ones. Recipes of some commonly used polishes are given below. You can easily make them at home. But before you use polishes, you should keep the following basic principles in mind:

- Remove dust and dirt thoroughly before polishing a surface.
- Use small quantities of polish as extra polish could be harmful to the surface, besides being uneconomical.
- Rub off polishes thoroughly as surfaces could otherwise become greasy and sticky.
- Surfaces already provided with permanent or semi-permanent polishes should be polished very carefully, so as not to destroy the original shine.

Apart from these equipments and cleaning agents, there are other materials which are used in a cleaning process, such as disinfectants, deodourants, antiseptics, etc. Can you tell where these are used?

SCHEDULE OF CLEANING

Now the important question is how to do cleaning? You must have observed the cleaning process at your own house. Do you clean your rooms completely by removing all the furniture etc, every day? No, because that would require a lot of time and labour which can not be devoted everyday. Then how to do the cleaning? For this, it is important to follow a certain schedule of cleaning. Everyday, a general cleaning of the open surfaces like floors, furniture and other such surfaces is required. Once in a while some more time is given to cleaning and you probably move heavy furniture and clean beneath it or beneath the carpets. Maybe once in six months or a year you empty the room completely and give it a complete wash, polish the floors, whitewash the walls, ceiling etc.

Thus we can basically divide cleaning into three types of schedules:

- Daily clean
- A weekly clean
- A spring clean

A daily cleaning would be a general cleaning done every day; a weekly cleaning would be a more thorough cleaning done periodically, depending on the frequency of use. In a guest house, hotel, or a hospital, it may be done once a week or even earlier. Spring cleaning is usually done once a year or when particularly needed. It may be earlier in the case of a hospital.

GENERAL PROCEDURE FOR DAILY CLEANING

Let us now see how a room is cleaned daily. Can you suggest in what order the work should be carried on?

- Once you enter the room, open all windows in order to let the fresh air come in.

- Remove all unwanted articles like tea cups etc., and empty ash trays and dust bins.
- Sweep the floor.
- Dust all surfaces including furniture and fixtures.
- Brush or vacuum clean the carpet.
- Mop the whole area.
- Replace linen wherever required, like in a bedroom, make the bed, in a restaurant cover the tables, in bathrooms, check for towels, soaps etc.
- In the end, adjust windows, do a general survey to see that everything is in order and to your satisfaction.

Similarly the kitchen can also be cleaned in the same way:

- Collect all used utensils from the counters.
- Wipe and clean the gas stove, electrical appliances and the counters.
- Wash all utensils. Drain and store.
- Sweep the floor.
- Empty the dustbin, wash, wipe and line it with newspaper.
- Mop or wash the kitchen with a mild disinfectant.

GENERAL PROCEDURE FOR WEEKLY CLEANING

You now know that special cleaning is more thorough than daily cleaning. *Let us now see in what order should one work for special cleaning of a room*:

- Start in the same way as in a daily clean–that is, first open all the windows for fresh air.
- Remove all unwanted articles like trays, teacups, bottles etc. Empty the ash tray and dust bins.
- Remove all dirty linen.
- Remove stains from walls, doors, windows and furniture.
- Check and clean thoroughly, all the drawers, furniture, fittings, all hangings or pictures, lights, etc.
- Wipe, dust or polish table lamps, accessories, telephone, if needed.
- Vacuum clean the carpets and other upholstery. If vacuum cleaner is not available, use a brush.
- Sweep, dust and mop the surfaces.
- Replace linen with clean linen
- Survey the room for any discrepancy and adjust windows as desired.

In the case of kitchen:

- You can empty out the shelves.
- Clean the jars and bins.
- Change the newspapers.
- Rearrange the cupboards.
- Clean the sunmica on the cupboard door panels with a wet cloth.
- Clean the tiles.

GENERAL PROCEDURE FOR SPRING CLEANING

Spring cleaning is done after long intervals, the frequency being as less as once a year. Thus, it may also be called annual cleaning. It is the most thorough cleaning of a room.

Let us now see how a spring cleaning should be done:

- Ventilate the room.
- Take off all linen, including curtains and remove them from the room.
- Remove all the movable articles including lamp shades, pictures, wall hangings etc., wipe and clean everything.
- If necessary, remove all furniture and furnishings from the room. At least remove soft furnishings like carpets. Clean the cobwebs.
- Sweep the floors.
- If any maintenance work is required, this is the right time to do it.
- Polish the furniture, decorative articles and floors.
- Clean carpets thoroughly in the sun or send for dry cleaning. Re-lay it.
- Replace everything at the predetermined place, including all furniture and fixtures.
- If desired, rearrange the heavy furniture to give a new look.
- Dust and mop.
- Adjust windows, survey the room to satisfaction.

In the case of kitchen:

- Empty out the kitchen.
- Spread the pulses, spices, etc out in the sun.
- Clean the cobwebs.
- Clean exhaust fan and light switches.
- Clean tiles with detergent.
- Spray insecticides in corners.
- Wash kitchen counters with hot soapy solution and if needed, polish them.
- Wipe stains on cupboard doors.
- Tighten any loose screws.
- Replace newspaper lining in cupboards.
- Label and arrange all boxes back in place.
- Wash the floor.

CLEANING AGENTS

Cleaning agent in general can be defined as natural or synthetic substances that are used to assist the cleaning process-that is, the removal of dirt and dust and the maintenance of a clean appearance on the surface.

WATER

Water is the probably the most common and widely used cleaning agent as it is easily available. It is useful in rinsing and finishing of cleaning processes. Precaution must be taken to change dirty water with fresh water because it could leave a film of dirt instead of removing it.

Warm water dissolves soap more readily than cold water; hence it must be used to remove dirty soap leather. Water is of two types, hard water and soft water.soft water is best for cleaning.Hardness in water is caused by the presence of mineral salts-mostly calcium (Ca) and magnesium (mg), iron(Fe) and manganese(Mn).the mineral salts reach with soap to form an insoluble precipitate known as soap film or scum.

The result is that the soap film does not rise away easily/it tends to remain behind and produces visible deposits on clothing making it stiff. It attaches to the insides of bathtubs and sinks. Caution must be taken that water is soft as no detergent is effective with hard water.Moreover, hard water does not wet the surface well as a precondition for good cleaning action.

DETERGENTS

These are the cleaning agents that, when used in conjunction with water loosen and remove dirt and then hold it in suspension so that the dirt is not re-deposited on the cleaned surface. They can be of two types. Soapy detergents and synthetic detergents.

The three basic properties of a good detergent are:

- Good wetting power-to lower the surface tension of water and enable the surface of the articles to be thoroughly wet.
- Good emulsifying power-to break up the grease and enable the dirt to be loosened.
- Good suspending power-to suspend the dirt in solution, thus preventing its re-deposition.
- Readily dissolve in water
- Cleanse quickly wit minimum agitation.
- Be effective in all rabges of hard water, without producing scum.
- Be effective over a wide range of temperatures.
- Be harmless to the skin and surface to be cleaned.
- Be easy to rinse away and be biodegerable.

THE CORRECT USE OF DETERGENTS

- Dilute as per the manufacturer's recommendations, using the measuring scoops use the right detergent for the surface to be cleaned.
- Use protective gloves when using strong detergents.
- Dissolve the detergent thoroughly before use.

- Rinse away all traces of detergent from the surface and any cleaning equipment employed.
- Label detergent containers neatly.
- Store detergent containers in a dry, well-ventilated storage area.
- Wipe up any spilled detergent, as it may be a safety hazard.

ABRASIVES

These are substances or chemicals that depend on their rubbing or scratching action to clean dirt and dust from the hard surfaces. They are used to remove very stubborn stains on various surfaces.

TYPES OF ABRASIVES

Based on the scale of hardness for various substances abrasives are classified as;

Table. The Scale of Hardness of Abrasives.

1	2	3	4	5	6	7	8	9	10
Talc		Calcite	Flourite						Diamond

Fine Abrasives: these include precipitated whiting (filtered chalk) and jeweler's rouge (a pink oxide of iron) used for shining silver. They are also constituents of commercial silver polishes.

Medium abrasives: these include rotten stone, salt, scouring powder and scouring paste. Scouring powders are made up of fine particles of pumice mixed with soap/detergent, and alkali and a little bleach. Hard/coarse abrasives: these include bath bricks, sandpaper, pumice, steel wool, and emery paper.

Glass paper, calcite, sandpaper, fine ash, emery powder and paper, jeweler's rouge, powdered pumice, precipitated whiting (filtered chalk). Ground limestone, sand, steel wool and nylon scourers are some commonly used abrasives. Abrasives are usually not used alone in cleaning agents. For example, a cream or paste meant for cleaning utensils contain about 80per cent of finely ground limestone, along with other substances such as bleaches, anionic surfactants, alkaline builders, and perfumes.

REAGENTS

These bring about cleaning be a chemical reaction requiring a distinctly low or high pH.pH is a measurement of the level of acid or alkali in solution or substance. In the pH range of 0 to 14 a reading below 7 shows an acid and one above 7 shows an alkali. A pH

Table. pH Scale.

1	2	3	4	5	6	7	8	9	10	11	12	13	14
			Alkaline							Acidic		Neutral	

TYPES OF REAGENTS

Acids

Acids used as cleaning agents may vary from mild acids with a pH of 3 to strong acids with a pH of 1.mildly acidic substances used commonly in cleaning include lime, vinegar, tamarind and buttermilk. acids dissolves metal stains, such as water stains in bath tub, hard water around taps and tarnish o silver, copper and brass articles.

- Acids may be used in solution alone or may be part of some special formulations as in toilet cleaners.
- Housekeeping staff need to be trained in the safe handling of strong acids, as they are highly corrosive. They literally'eat away' dirt.
- Rubber gloves should be used while handling them. They should be used in very small quantities as they emit toxic fumes as well.
- Strong acids should be thoroughly rinsed away after the cleaning process.
- Some common acids are: Dilute HCL, Acetic acid, Concentrated HCL, Sodium acid sulphate.
- Acids and their use in cleaning

Acid	pH	Uses
Concentrated HCL	1	Removing stubborn hard-water deposits.
Dilute HCL	1	Removing stubborn scales and deposits from sanitary ware. Removing excess cement from newly cemented tiled areas.
Oxalic	2	Removing stubborn hard-water deposits
Acetic acid	3	Removing tarnish and stains from metals such as copper and brass. Neutralising alkalis are used in cleaning for preventing colours from running during washing.
Sodium and sulphate	5	Removing hard-water deposits and scales from toilets.

Alkalis

These are used as cleaning agents in the form of liquids and powders. They are particularly useful in the laundry.

Very strong alkalis should be used with utmost caution as they are corrosive and toxic. These are called caustic alkalis.

Many alkalis at as bleaches. Caustic soda-based cleaning agents are used to clear blocked drains and to clean ovens and other industrial equipment. Alkalis and their use:

Alkalis	pH	Uses
Sodium hydroxide(caustic soda).	14	Removing stubborn grease from ovens and equipments
Ammonia	11	Removing stubborn grease
Sodium carbonate	10	Used as an alkalis builder in synthetic and soapy detergents. Clearing blocked drains.
Sodium Perborate	10	Removing stains and whitening due to bleaching action at higher temperature (above 40°C)
Sodium Hypocholorite	9	Removing stains and whitening due to bleaching action on various types of surfaces. Acts as disinfectant.
Sodium Bicorbonate	8	Removing stubborn grease from smooth, delicate surfaces. Removing stains such s tea, coffee and fruit juice.
Sodium Pyroborate (borax)	8	Removing stubborn grease from smooth, delicate surfaces. Removing stains such s tea, coffee and fruit juice.
Sodium Thiosulphite	7	Removing iodine stains.

ORGANIC SOLVENTS

Grease is soluble in organic solvents such as carbon tetrachloride, acetone, turpentine and methylated spirit.

Thus, these organic solvents are used extensively in the removal of grease, dry-cleaning of fabrics and stain removal.Solvents are also useful in cleaning surfaces that may be harmed by water.

Organic solvents evaporates rapidly from a surface and are therefore ideal for cleaning glass surfaces such s mirrors and windows. Organic solvents should be handled with care as they are harmful to the skin, flammable and poisonous.

DISINFECTANT S AND BLEACHES

Disinfectants aid in the cleaning process by bringing about varying ranges of microbial control. The term' disinfectant' is now used as a general term that covers all kinds of agents that bring about germ control. Most disinfectants have a strong smell and therefore should be used only in recommended amounts in areas where germ control is required.

TYPES OF DISINFECTANTS

Disinfectants can be categorized in terms of their chemical action and compositions

Phenols

These are hydroxyl derivatives of the aromatic hydrocarbon benzene. They are used in dilute or high concentrations to disinfect surfaces in hospitals especially.in hotels, diluted phenols are used with their sharp smell masked by other additives.

Halogens

The elements chlorine and iodine may be used as disinfectants.Chlorine is used both as bleach and as a disinfectant on many surfaces.Iodine is not often used to disinfectant surfaces because it tends to leave brown stains.

Quaternary Ammonium Compounds

These are cationic surfactants useful as bacteriocides. Natural pine oils: pine oils are obtained from pine trees. They are germicidal to some extent, but are mainly added changing formulation for their pleasant smell.

Guidelines for using disinfectants:

- Clean the surface first with detergent and rinse with soft water only
- Rinse away the detergent solution thoroughly before using disinfectants on the surface
- Use the correct disinfectant for the range of disinfection required.
- Use the disinfectant at the correct dilution for it to be effective. Different surfaces may require different dilutions of the disinfectants to act.
- Allow the recommended time for the disinfectant to act.

Glass Cleaners

These are composed of organic, water-miscible solvent such as isopropyl alcohol and an alkaline detergent. Some glass cleaners also contain a fine, mid abrasive. Most glass cleaners are available as sprays or liquid. They are sprayed directly onto windows, mirrors and other glass surfaces or applied on with a soft cloth and rubbed off using a soft, lint-free duster. A glass cloth ideal for the purpose.soft water to which some mathylated spirit or vinegar is added is an inexpensive glass cleaner that can be readily made in the housekeeping department.

Deodourizers

Deodourizers aid in the cleaning process by concentrating stale odours and sometimes also introducing a fragrance to mask them. They are used in restrooms, guestrooms, guest bathrooms, cloakrooms and public areas such as lobbies. Some deodourizers leave no trace of a perfume cover-up. They are usually available as aerosol sprays. Liquids, powders and crystalline blocks. the crystalline blocks are effervescent and manufactured using the principle of time0 released aromatic chemicals. Naphthalene ball also serve as effective deodourize the crystalline blocks are effervescent and manufactured using the principle of time0 released aromatic chemicals. Naphthalene ball also serve as effective deodourizers. If through cleaning and good ventilation are provided, money need not to be spent on expensive deodourants.

LAUNDRY AIDS

Laundry'aids' are the materials used to improve laundering results(bleaches, optical whiteners) or to accomplish specific functions or effects (soaks, stain removers, softeners, stiffeners. the important laundry agents or acids are water, laundry soaps and detergents, stiffening agents, bleaches, alkaline agents, acid agents, organic solvents, and absorbents.

TOILET CLEANERS

These are strong, concentrated cleaning agents designed to clean and disinfect WCs and urinals. They are available in liquid, powder and crystalline forms. They are acidic in nature as their main function is to remove stubborn stains and limescale.

They all contains some form of disinfectant:

- *Liquid toilet cleaners*: These contain dilute hydrochloric acid, bleach and pine oil. Adequate protective gear should be worn by the user while using such a toilet cleaner.
- *Crystalline toilet cleaners*: These contain sodium acid sulphate, anionic surfactants, and pine oil.
- *Powdered toilet cleaners*: These cleaners contain a soluble acidic powder, chlorinated bleach, a fine abrasive and an effervescing agent to help the active ingredient spread in water.

Whatever the from of toilet cleaner used, they should never be mixed with other cleaning agents since harmful gases may be produced in the resulting reaction.

POLISHES

These chemicals produce a shine by providing a smooth surface from which light is reflected evenly.

Polishes are primarily applied to a surface to form a hard, protective layer and thus guard against finger marks, stains and scratches. They also create attractive sheen on the hard surfaces.

CLASSIFICATION OF POLISHES

Polishes are used on metal, furniture and floorings and are classified just as to the type of surface they are used on. On metals they also smooth out any unevenness on the surface of the articles and in case of flooring and furniture they provide a smooth protective layer.

Metal Polishes

These remove the superficial tarnish that forms on metal surfaces due to the attack of certain compounds in the air and some foodstuffs. These polishes also eliminate May scratches on the metal.

They consist mainly of a very fine, mildabrasive.in hotels; hard surfaces where metal polishes are used include door-plates and handles, foot rails in bars, staircase banisters, ashtrays, bathroom fittings, tableware and cutlery. In metal polishes such as Brasso, and Silvo, the grease solvent or acid mixed with the abrasive powder aids in the removal of tarnish.

Certain recommendations on the use pf metal polishes are given below:

- Cover the surroundings area with newspaper or protective sheets.
- Carry out any polishing work in a well-ventilated room.
- Use an appropriate polish applicator or disposable rags.
- Use a cocktail stick covered with a rag to apply polish in narrow, hard-to reach nooks and corners.
- Remove polish with cotton or soft, dry cloth.
- Buff the polish with rags and dusters.
- Wash any polish cutlery in warm detergent solution before use.
- Leave the area and equipment clean and tidy after polishing work is complete.
- Dispose of the rags and newspaper used.

Furniture Polishes

These contain a wax or resin, solvent water and a silicone. The main role of wax is to provide a smooth surface from which light is reflected evenly, producing an attractive shine the types of waxes commonly used are carnauba, beeswax, ozokerite, paraffin wax.

Types of furniture polishes:

- *Paste polishes*: these are ideal for use on antique wooden furniture.
- *Cream polishes*: they are used on furniture to give a gloss finish
- *Liquid polishes*: they are used on glossy furniture to remove grease marks and other stains.
- *Spray-on polishes*: they are ideal for use on non-porous surfaces such as glass, chromium, plastic, and varnished or gloss-painted wood.

Considerations for the use of furniture polishes are as listed below:

- Apply the polish on a clean surface.
- Use the least quantity required to accomplish a good polishing of the surface, else the solvent will evaporate and the polish will dry out.
- Always keep the polish container closed when not in use, else the solvent will evaporate and the polish will dry out.
- Use soft, disposable rags, for applying polish to the surface, except in the case of spray-on-polish.

- Use polishes undiluted, unless it is specified otherwise by the manufacturer.
- Be careful while using polishes with a high solvent content since they are flammable.

Floor Polishes

These have a two-folded function. They not only lens an attractive sheen to the surface, but also provide a protective coat on it. The right kind of polish should be used along with the right equipment.

Types of Floor Polishes

Spirit/Solvent-based Polishes

These polishes are used on the porous floor such as wood, wood composition, cork, magnetite and linoleum.

Water-based Polishes

Theses polishes are used on semi-porous surfaces such as thermoplastics, PVC, rubber, asphalt, terrazzo, marble, and natural materials such as Cuddapah tiles and so on.

Considerations for the use of furniture polishes are as listed below:

- Use an appropriate sign to warn people walking along that area of the fact that floor polishing is being carried out.
- ventilate the area well before starting
- Apply the polish to clean, dry floor.
- Rinse the floor thoroughly using a neutralising agent such as diluted vinegar after stripping the old polish.
- Apply several thin coats of polish rather that a few thick coats.
- Work systematically to ensure that all areas are covered.
- Allow sufficient drying time before applying a second coating.
- Buff thoroughly to reduce the slipping hazard.
- Remove any extra build-up of polish with an appropriate abrasive pad.
- Leave all polishing equipment clean and store them properly.

Leather Polishes

Theses contain a special blend of waxes, a spirit solvent, and occasionally a dye. They are available in the form of creams and liquids. They help to keep the leather supple and impart a shine to it.they also prevent deterioration of old leather articles.

FLOOR SEALERS

These are applied to flooring surfaces as a semi-permanent finish that acts as a protective barrier by preventing the entry of dirt, gems and liquid, grease, stains and bacteria. They prevent scratching and provide an easily maintainable surface. The right type of seal should be applied to each type of floor for effective protection and an attractive appearance. Their functions, floor sealers can be finishing protective or combination of both.

TYPES OF FLOOR SEALERS

- *Oleo-resinous sealers*: they are used for imparting an attractive surface gloss penetrating the floor darkening the colour and highlighting the grain of wood floors.
- *One-pot plastic sealers*: they are used on wood, wood-composition, cork and magnesite floors.
- *Two-pot plastic sealers*: they are also used on wood, wood-composition, cork and magnesite floors.
- *Pigmented sealers*: these may be used on concrete, wood, wood-composition, magnesite, asphalt, and stone floors.

Water-based seals: these may used on marble, terrazzo, magnesite, linoleum, rubber, thermoplastic tiles, PVCs, asphalt, concrete, stone-, and quarry tiles.

Considerations for the use of furniture polishes are as listed below:

- Use appropriate signs to warn passers-by that sealing is being carried out; else it may be a safety hazard.
- Ensure the floor surface is clean, chemically neutral, and dry before applying the sealer. otherwise the seal will not'key' to the floor surface.
- Maintain an ideal room temperature of 21.C
- Keep the room well ventilated.
- Protect the area from flies and pests until the sealer is dry.
- Keep on hand only the required amount of sealer and store the rest tightly lidded, else the whole bulk may deteriorate.
- Apply several thin coats rather than a few thick ones.
- Allow the recommended drying time between coats.
- Clean and store all equipment, such as sealer applicators, neatly after use.

FLOOR STIPPERS

These are uses to remove a worn-out floor finish so that a new sealer or polish can be applied.most are based on alkalis with a high pH.there are two main types available. One is based on ammonia and the other is non-ammoniated product. Ammonia has an intense odour and therefore the area should be well ventilated for many days to get rid of the smell.

CARPET CLEANERS

These are composed of neutral water-soluble solvents, emulsifiers, de-foamers, sanitizers, optical brighteners and deodourizers. They are available as sprays, powders, foams, and liquid shampoos. Whichever they selected it is essential that they are used in correct dilutions.

Some common cleaning agents used in professional housekeeping are:

- *Ammonia*: Liquid ammonia is a solution of ammonia gas in water, held as ammonium hydrxide.it is a strong alkali used for softening water, cleaning window panes, and emulsifying grease.
- *Bath brick*: This is a reddish-brown powder, also obtained in a brick form. it is used fro scouring and polishing metals such as Brass and Copper. In powdered form, it is used for cleaning earthenware.
- *Benzene*: obtained from the distillation of coat tar, benzene is used as a grease solvent and for removing paint and tar stains.
- *Borax*: chemically sodium borate, this white crystalline powder is used to soften hard water to remove coffee and tea stains.
- *Bran*: the husk of wheat grain. It is used in dry-cleaning as grease absorbent.
- *Fuller's earth*: this is ash-white clay that readily absorbs grease. it is used on coloured wood surfaces.
- *Hydrochloric acid*: this is a corrosive and poisonous mineral acid, used diluted for removing stains in bathrooms.
- *Jeweler's rouge*: chemically this is fabric tetroxide, a pinkish powder used for polishing silver. It is a constituent of commercial silver polishes too.
- *Lemon*: lemon is used for removing ink stains from wooden surfaces.
- *Linseed oil*: this is obtained from the crushed seeds of the flax plant. It is a constituent of furniture polishes and paints. It darkens unpainted wood slightly.
- *Magnesia*: chemically magnesium carbonate, this fine white powder is used for dry-cleaning felt, fur and woolen articles.
- *Methylated spirits*: this is used for cleaning window panes and mirrors to a shine. It is a constituent of varnishes and lacquers.
- *Oxalic acid*: this is an organic acid used for the removal of stains from fabrics and bath fittings. It is also used for cleaning porcelain.
- *Paraffin oil*: this is a liquid product of distillation of crude petroleum and is used for cleaning greasy iron and steel articles. It also cleans greasy earthenware when used in combinations with bath brick.
- *Petrol*: This too is obtained from petroleum distillation. It is highly inflammable and is use for dry-cleaning and for removing grease stains.
- *Pumice*: this is a light; porous rock of volcanic origin. It is used as an abrasive for hard metals, earthenware and enamel.
- *Rottenstone*: this is a decomposed siliceous limestone and is used for cleaning copper, brass and earthenware.

- *Common salt*: chemically sodium chloride, this is used as a medium-grade abrasive. It is used for stiffening the bristles of brushes and stiff brooms. Salt is added as a mordant while washing coloured clothes. (A mordant is a substance that prevents undue loss of colour while washing clothes.
- *Sand*: this hard compound of silica is used as a hard abrasive on stone floors and hard, coarse wood.
- *Sikakai*: sometimes called soap-nut or soapberry, but more accurately soap-pod (to distinguish from the fruit of reetha).this is used for non-abrasive cleaning of tarnished metals.
- *Soda*: It emulsifies grease and aids in the cleaning of dirty pans.
- *Steel wool*: this is steel manufactured into long filaments, in varying grades of fitness it is used for scouring hard metals and dirty pans.
- *Turpentine*: this is a constituent of paints.it is also a diluent for paints and removes tar stains.
- *Vaseline*: this is obtained as a residue in petroleum distillation.it prevents rust formation on metals, act as a lubricant, and may be applied on leather to make it soft and supple.
- *Vinegar*: chemically this is 4per cent acetic acid. It is used to remove stains and tarnish from metals such as copper. It is also effective in removing streaks from glass surfaces such as window panes and mirrors.
- *Whiting/precipitated whiting*: chemically this is calcium carbonate.in pure form. It is used as a mild abrasive on soft metals and in cleaning white-painted articles.

SELECTION OF CLEANING AGENTS

The use of cleaning agent is meant to save time, effort and money. if selected well, all the three objective may be fulfilled. The following points need to be considered when selecting cleaning agents:

- The type of spoilage
- The type of surface
- Odour
- Range of action or versatility
- Composition of the cleaning agents
- Ease of use, saving of effort and time.
- Toxicity or side-effects.
- Shelf life
- Packing volume and quantities.
- Cost effectiveness.

STORAGE OF CLEANING AGENTS

Cleaning agents with a longer shelf life are usually bought in bulk because of the reduced costs that accrue from the economics of scale. other agents are bought and replenished periodically.storage of cleaning agents is crucial and the various points to be kept in mind.

The points are listed below:

- Ensure that the storage racks are strong and with selves. Heavier containers must be kept on the bottom shelf.
- The store should be kept clean and well-ventilated at all times.
- Ensure that the lids are tightly fitted.
- When issuing cleaning agents use appropriate dispensers and measuring apparatus.
- Ensure that no residual deposits of cleaning agent are left around the rims of the containers.
- Avoid spillage, if a spill occurs, clean it up immediately.
- Follow a systematic procedure for rotating stocks.
- Organic solvents, strong reagents, polishes should be kept away from heat sources.
- Check stock regularly the store should be locked when not in use.

Table. Store Stock Statement.

Store Stock Sheet									
S.NO	**Name of the Item**	**Unit**	**Stock in Hand**	**Stock Received**	**Total Stock**	**Less Issue**	**Book Stock**	**Actual Stock**	**Difference in Stock**
1	All purpose detergent	500ml. Bottles.							
2	Mansion polish	1 litre tins							
3	Floor cleaner-soap oil	5 litre cans							
4	Air freshener	20 blocks per carton							
Signature of housekeeper..........................					Signature of storekeeper				

DISTRIBUTION OF CLEANING AGENTS

The housekeeper should implement proper system for the methodical issuing of cleaning agents from the housekeeping stores.

REQUISITIONING

This system of issuing is followed in large hotels. The floor supervisor maintains a requisition book with requisition slips in triplicate. a requisition slip is filled out by a GRA whenever supplies are diminishing. This is signed by the floor supervisor and the book is then sent to the housekeeping stores.

The store keeper collects the requisitioned items and signs the triplicate copies of the requisition slip. The storekeeper then issues the requisitioned items which are collected by a porter and transported to the floor to the room attendant and they should sign in the requisition slip after receiving it.thesecond copy is sent to the executive housekeeper and the third copy remains in the requisition book. Which too is returned with the fresh supplies.

FULL OR EMPTY

This system of issuing is followed in smaller hotels. Empty containers of used-up cleaning supplies are taken to the housekeeping stores by individual GRAs.the store assistant then replaces the empty containers whit full ones.

The disadvantage in this system are that it works well only when the housekeeping stores are open round the clock and that constant supervision is required. The topping-up method is an improvement on this system of issuing.

TOPPING-UP

The difference between this method and full for empty method is that here the GRAs approach the housekeeping stores only at a fixed time each week for getting their supplies toped up. An even better system is having GRAs deposit their hand caddied in the housekeeping stores at the end of the shift, so that the store assistant may replenish or top up the cleaning agents and keep them ready for the staff on the next shift.

9

Staffing

INTRODUCTION

Staffing, which is one of a hotel's most important management functions, is an ongoing challenge because of the high rate of employee and manager turnover. Full-service hotels can experience annual turnover rates in excess of 100 per cent in certain employee classifications. Some managers consider an annual employee turnover rate of 33 per cent low. At this rate, the entire hotel must be completely restaffed every three years. The higher the turnover rate, the larger the number of employees who must be replaced. For example, if a hotel with 450 employees has a 75 per cent annual turnover rate, it will be completely restaffed every 16 months.

Staffing is the responsibility of the human resources department, which is considered in more detail in chapter 5. In an attempt to reduce employee turnover, hotel and lodging businesses are giving increasing attention to job design, seeking to enhance those job characteristics that give the employee the greatest satisfaction and motivation.

Good job design must take into account the needs of employees as well as the demands of the job. Well-thought-out job design begins when management conducts a job analysis—that is, a thorough evaluation of the specific tasks performed for a particular job and the time required to perform them. Job analysis is an ongoing process, as many jobs change with improvements in technology and pressure to improve product quality. The job analysis is the basis for the job description and job specification.

A job description includes the job title, pay, a brief statement of duties and procedures, working conditions, and hours. The job specification is an outline of the qualifications necessary for a particular job. In response to the limits of specialization, organizations can redesign jobs to improve coordination, productivity, and product quality while responding to an employee's needs for learning, challenge, variety, increased responsibility, and achievement.

Such job redesign often involves job rotation, the systematic movement of employees from one job to another; job enlargement, an increase in the number of tasks an employee will do in the job; job enrichment, the attempt to give the employee more control over job-related activities; and flextime, a flexible work schedule that permits employee input in establishing work schedules. In team-driven job redesign, a concept similar to job rotation, employees can transfer back and forth among teams that provide different services or products. Hotels recruit employees from a variety of sources.

Newspapers and employee referrals are used to recruit nonskilled hourly employees. Supervisory and management employees generally are recruited through colleges and universities, promotions from within, professional associations, and management recruiters.

Hotels that take more time in making their selections are more successful in retaining employees. Discussions of employee training and development often concentrate on training techniques without giving a full explanation of what a hotel is trying to accomplish. As training and development impart job skills and educate employees, supervisors, and managers, they also improve current and future employee performance, which affects the bottom line. Effective training includes problem solving, problem analysis, quality measurement and feedback, and team building.

Performance evaluation, also called performance appraisal, is the systematic review of the strengths and weaknesses of an employee's performance. The major difficulty in a performance appraisal is quantifying those strengths and weaknesses. The performance of some jobs is easy to quantify, while for others it is more difficult. An important part of the appraisal process is a well-established job description, so that the employee and the supervisor have similar expectations.

Compensation includes the monetary and nonmonetary rewards that managers, supervisors, and employees receive for performing their jobs. In order to set compensation levels, the human resources department must periodically conduct job evaluations, which determine the value of the job to the hotel. Knowledge of the value of the job to the organization and of wage rates for each job classification allows the hotel to establish a fair compensation policy.

ATTRIBUTES AND QUALITIES OF HOUSEKEEPING STAFF

Most essential especially for floor and public area supervisors, room attendants and housemen who are in guest contact, such staff would be normally uniformed. Hence each staff member must ensure that his/her uniform crisp, clean and well pressed.

Lady staff must wear light make-up and restrict their jewellery to the minimum such as wedding bands and ear tops. Hair must be tied in a burn or worn short. Shoes worn must be low heeled and sturdy as housekeeping staff work long hours on their feet.

Grooming and Personal Hygiene:

- Gentlemen should shave every day.
- Trim moustaches daily.
- Trim nails twice a week-once On Wednesday and on Sunday
- There should be no hair covering any part of the ear, collar. Staff look smarter when hair doesn't cover the forehead. Staffs are advised to trim their hair once every three weeks.
- Shirt cuffs and collars lllust always be clean.
- Bath everyday. Use soap and Shampoo to prevent skin infections and body odour due to unclean hail'.
- Cloths should be pressed every day and have a freshly laundered look.
- Brush the teeth at least twice every day, gargle after smoking or eating to prevent bad breath.
- Wash the hands as often as necessary especially after any other activity where hands may get unclean.

HONESTY

This is a very essential attribute for housekeeping staff, especially Room Attendants, who have access to all guest rooms. Guest belongings, sometimes invaluable are often found lying around in the room. The temptations to thieve are great.

It is only the personal quality of discipline and integrity that checks these temptations:

- *Eye for Detail*: It is one of the greatest qualities that house keeping staff must have. It is with this quality that the finer aspects of housekeeping are taken care of and it is what determines a good service from an average one. This quality enables housekeeping staff to take into consideration the minutest details.
- *Co-Cooperativeness*: Housekeeping staff needs to be co-operating with other departments to achieve more efficiency.
- *Briefing and Scheduling of Staff*: Briefing is that process at the beginning of a work shift which is provided by management to facilitate a two-way communication between management and staff. It is the one time during a shift that all housekeeping staff are together to share information and feelings before they disperse to their work areas.
  - *Briefing Schedule*:
    i. Personal hygiene and grooming.
    ii. Any new policies and procedures introduced by managcl1lenL must be made out and explained to the staff.
    iii. At n briefing the duties or each staff member and the areas of accountability are explained. This would mean that staffs

are assigned a floor and allotted their number of rooms. The staffs likewise, are told which floors or public areas they are assigned to for cleaning. They are also told which supervisor would be in charge.

iv. Briefing is a time which can be used as a training opportunity. Simple tasks may be demonstrated so that they can be practiced under supervision at their work place.

RULES ON GUEST FLOORS

Prior to commencing work, all house keeping staff must follow some floor rules that lend an air of efficiency and least inconvenience to guests.

- Speech amongst the floor staff must be restricted to a minimum. In case communication is necessary, this must be done in low tones even when guests are not in sight.
- Unnecessary movements like running or jumping must be avoided.
- The passageways must be kept free of equipments, trays or trolleys.
- Room attendants must greet all guests just as to The Time of the day.
- Staff must be helpful and readily give required information.
- Remember the guest is always right. Arguing with a guest is prohibited.
- The door of the room in which the attendant is cleaning should always be kept wide open.
- If the guest returns when the room is being cleaned the room attendant may ask the guest if they can continue or come later.
- Always follow the procedure of entering a room even if the room is seemingly vacant.

CLEANING A ROOM

Prior to reporting on a 1loor the room attendant already knows the status of a room in her given lot of rooms. The room attendant can prioritize room to be attended to first on the basis of immediate needs. Before entering the room knock at the door firmly with the index finger knuckle announcing clearly" Housekeeping". When there is no answer, repeat the knock after ten seconds announcing yourself as before. If there is still no answer open the door and knock announcing inside the room "Housekeeping". When there is no reply and one is relatively sure that there is no one in, open the door wide and keep it that way till the entire cleaning cycle in the room is complete.

ROOM CLEANING PROCEDURE

- Switch off the room air-conditioner. Draw all curtains and open the windows for airing the room.

- Check the maintenance requirements and report to the department head.
- Turn the mattress side-to-side on succeeding days followed by end-to-end turning. Smooth out mattress to air it.
- Clean the bath room.
- Clean the ceiling and air-conditioning vents for cobwebs.
- Collect all loose papers or magazines and stack them neatly on the desk.
- Clean all the surfaces in single circular motions with a dry cloth. Use a hand dust pan to collect any unwanted matter on the surface without lifting dust in the air Ensure that all surfaces are spotlessly clean. Pay special attention to nooks and corners especially those points that may not obviously be visible to the guests eye.
- Use a stiff upholstery brush or vacuum cleaner on upholstered furniture arms, backs and seats.
- Clean lamp shades with a clean dry duster.
- Disinfect telephone mouthpiece with Dettol. Wipe balance of the telephone with a damp cloth, check phone for the dial tone.
- Clean mirror with a dry cloth.
- Dust closet, shelves, hangers and rods. Brush the closet floor.
- Dust both sides of all room doors, baseboards, window sills, inside and out, bottom
- And centre sashes or windows, close windows.
- Wash the floors.
- Arrange furniture if necessary
- Switch on the air-conditioning.
- Have a last look at the room referring to the checklist for completion of work.

CLEANING A BATHROOM

- Cleaning activity starts from the ceiling downwards to the floor.
- Floors are cleaned from the wall farthest to the door to the exit.
- Open all exhaust vents.
- Collect all trash in bathroom waste basket and deposit in trash hamper of the maids-cart.
- Clean the ceiling and air-conditioning vents for cobwebs.
- Wipe off light bulbs and shades with dry cloth. Check that all bulbs are working.
- Wipe down tile walls using a sponge or damp cloth. Follow with a dry cloth ensuring that tiles are free of water marks.
- Clean mirror first with dry cloth then with glass cloth and finally with dry cloth.

- Wipe dry the shower curtain with a sponge.
- Scrub to dry the area next to the wash basin.
- Scrub the toilet bowl and bidet using the special brush or mop and the prescribed sanitizer. The inner rim should be cleaned. Ensure it is dry and spotless inside. Clean the WC from the outside with a sponge till it is sparkling find dry. Clean the lid and toilet seat of the toilet bowl dry and close them.
- Scrub the floor with the prescribed mop and ensure it is dry
- Finally close the windows shut all lights and close the bathroom doors.

DIRTY DOZEN

- Top of the door edges and ceiling.
- Air-conditioning ducts and diffuser grills. Under bathroom counters.
- Behind the WC bowl-the s-trap.
- In the toilet roll niche
- Faucet nozzle filter
- Top of the picture frames
- Area above racks
- Toilet vents
- Rear surface of doors
- Interior surface of drawers
- Beneath the table

ROOM MAINTENANCE PROCEDURE

As hose keeping has contact with all rooms and public areas practically in every shift, it is they who detect report and ensure the completion of all maintenance work. This requires close co-ordination with the engineering department.

WEEKLY CLEANING PROCEDURE

In addition to daily cleaning routine, a room attendant normally has some cleaning chores that are of a time-consuming nature. Such items may sometimes be beyond the physical capacity and need the assistance of a skill worker.

Such tasks are:

- Polishing of brassware
- Scrubbing of bathroom tiles
- Cleaning of window panes
- Scrubbing of balconies and terraces
- Vacuuming of under heavy furniture.

PUBLIC AREA CLEANING

A house maid is assigned to do this task and is responsible for the cleanliness of ceilings, walls and floors, carpeted floors should be vacuum cleaned daily, tile floors to be brushed clean and then wet mopped. They should also remove stains. Floor tile edges, corners, baseboards and the immediate wall area above are to be inspected to ensure that there are no water marks. Wooden railings and-skirtings has to clean with dry clothes.

All corridor lighting fixtures are to be cleaned as often as required. It is also the responsibility of a houseman to clean fire extinguishers and fire extinguisher recesses including glass door and metal paneling. Metal railing and paneling to be polished weekly using min cream so that the shine remains. The house keeping department is responsible for the cleanliness of the interior of elevator cars.

A thorough cleaning of walls, ceilings, and floors should be carried out at least once daily. The volume of traffic may require more frequent cleaning of elevator floors. The Door houseman is assigned the task of cleaning the stairways on a daily or more frequent schedule depending up on traffic requirements. Floor terraces, balconies, shopping arcade and offices are also to be cleaned.

While cleaning the offices should be scheduled at times when the offices are not in service:

- Carpet cleaning can be done by electrical method *e.g.* vacuum cleaner
- *Manual method ex*: carpet brush.
- Cleaning of ceramic tiles marble can sweep, wash, use electric scrubber with prescribed liquid cleaning agents and solutions. It is as a daily cleaning procedure.
- Cleaning Methods
- Cleaning basically involves the removal of dust and other foreign matter from surfaces. The choice of a cleaning method depends on various factors. They are.
  - The nature of soiling.
  - The nature of surface soiled.
  - The properties of cleaning agents suitable for the surface.
  - The best way to clean without disposing dust to other areas.
  - The method should restore the surface to its original colour.

GENERAL PRINCIPLES THAT CAN BE APPLIED TO ALL CLEANING

- All loose dust and litter should be removed before dealing with any stubborn stains/dirt.
- Use lighter cleaning methods first before attempting stronger methods
- Before any implement or cloths are used, they should be made clean and dry.
- Abrasives should be used as a last resort as they can damage the surface.

- Use all agents that is least offensive in smell if alternatives are available.
- When cleaning a surface, be cautions of marring the surrounding area *e. g.* finger prints on wall, grasing other article etc.
- Be sure that during the process of cleaning areas do not become accident prone *e.g.* wet, slippery floor etc.

CLEANINGAGENTS

One of the basic methods used is cleaning with water. The role of water is to hold the dirt and remove it away as in rinsing. This is done with the aid of detergents.

Multipurpose liquid Cleaning agents are available that can either diluted in water or used directly with a dry cloth. For glasses liquid glass cleaning agents are used.

CLEANING EQUIPMENTS

- Mechanical equipments.
  - Electric vacuum cleaner with full range of nozzles and attachments for all types of surfaces.
  - Electric polishers and scrubbers
  - Shampoo machines.
- Containers
- Brushes
  - Toilet Brush
  - Sink Brush Scrubbing Brush
  - Carpet hand brush
  - Soft hand brush
- Brooms: Yard Brooms
- Mops
- Bath room wipers
- Cleaning cloths

JOB DESCRIPTION OF HOUSEKEEPING STAFF

MAIN HOSPITAL

Duties and Responsibilities:

- 'A' for each type of linen to be maintained.
- All Ledgers are to be put up for Joint Directors signature through housekeeping Manager on a quarterly basis.
- Maintain a sepearate Indent for the cleaning agents used in Laundry and the Indent should be signed by the housekeeping Manager.
- Daily use of cleaning agents are to be recorded and the records to be put up for housekeeping managers signature monthly.
- Linen and curtains are to be checked for wear and tear quarterly.

- Torn or faded linen is to be segregated and to be shown to joint director quarterly. If any item is found unserviceable the same should be written off the ledger getting after the approval of Jt.Director.
- Torn or faded linen is to be used for cleaning purposes.
- Periodical Maintenance of washing Machine, Ironing Machine, Iron Box, Sewing Machine, and floor scrubbing Machine to be carried out and the record to be maintained.
- Floor scrubbing Machine is to be taken by other housekeeper only with the permission of the linen housekeeper.
- Washing charges for various linen are to be fixed and approval. For any change in the charges, prior approval to be taken from secretary.
- Tailoring rates for various items of stitched materials are to be maintained. For any revision in charges prior approval to be taken from secretary.
- Planning and scheduling the standard procedure for cleaning all types of linen to be displayed in laundry and to be followed strictly.
- Time schedule to be prepared for collection of clean/soiled linen and to be followed strictly.
- Ensure proper discipline among Housekeepers, Sweepers, Dhobi, and Tailor working in linen department. Make sure that they wear name badges.
- Floor scrubbing machines are to be chain locked when not in use.
- Training classes are to be taken for junior housekeepers when required.
- Train and Guide the trainees housekeeper posted in linen department.
- Sell all waste materials and deposit the sale proceeds to secretary.
- Supervision and checking the cleanliness of the surrounding area of main hospital.
- Responsible for the cleanliness of sweepers uniform.
- Any other job given by the housekeeping manager or the senior management staff from time to time.

DESIGNATION–FLOOR EXECUTIVE: HOUSEKEEPING (OUT PATIENT DEPARTMENTS AND BASEMENT AREA)

- Supervision and checking the cleanliness of out patient departments and Basement area.
- Maintenance of sweepers attendance Register, wage sheets, deployment, control and details for continuous duties.
- Control over all keys of all departments in OPDS.
- Preparing inventories for furniture and keeping records for their maintenance.
- Indenting cleaning agents and equipments and ensure their proper use and keeping records.

- To develop proper use of cleaning procedures.
- Reporting and checking of all maintenance work.
- Supervision of quality maintenance and infection control.
- Ensure proper discipline of Housekeepers and sweepers working in out patient department and make sure that they wear name badge.
- Planning and scheduling the standard procedures in writing for the proper care of all types of floors, walls, windows, furniture, bathrooms, Lavatories and other equipments to be prepared and follows trictly.
- Maintenance of House Keeping department room and attending to phone calls promptly.
- Make sure the tyre cart is secured and locked after working hours.
- Disposal of refuse is to be monitored.
- Training and taking classes for juniors
- Experimenting new techniques and equipments for cleaning.
- Maintenance details of continuous duties of housekeepers.
- Maintenance responsible for the sweepers uniform collected after working hours from the sweepers.
- Responsible for the cleaning schedule of freshwater tank, filters, coolers and septic Tanks and the cleaning and due dates are to be displayed in the boards as well as in the Register. The register shall be put up for Housekeeping managers signature every month.
- Maintain the Leave list of all sweepers working in main hospital, free hospital, Laico and other supporting areas and day off Roster of sweepers working in OPDs.
- Maintaining the checklist of furniture, electrical plumbing, carpentry and mason work in the OPDs.
- Any other job given by the housekeeping manager or the senior management staff from time to time.

DESIGNATION–WARD EXECUTIVE: HOUSEKEEPING (1ST AND 2ND FLOOR OF MAIN HOSPITAL.)

- Supervision and checking the cleanliness of 1st and 2nd floor.
- Control of all keys of 1st and 2nd Floor
- Preparing inventories for 1st and 2nd floor furniture and keeping records for their maintenance.
- Indenting cleaning agents and equipments and ensure their proper use and keeping necessary records.
- Supervision for quality maintenance and infection control.
- Ensure proper discipline of housekeepers and sweepers in 1st and 2nd floor and make sure the wear name badges.
- Planning and scheduling the standard procedures in writing for the proper care of all types of floors, walls, windows, furniture, bathrooms,

lavatories and other equipments to be placed and to be followed strictly.
- Attending to patients complaints
- Development and standardization of newer and improved method of cleaning for better results at lower costs.
- Take adequate precautions for controlling cross infections.
- To assist in quality health care and patient care programme.
- Ensure up keep and maintenance of hospital property.
- Training and taking classes for juniors
- Maintain day off roaster of sweepers in 1st and 2nd floor.
- Responsible for the sweepers uniform collected after working hours from the sweepers of 1st and 2nd floor.
- Any other job that may be assigned by the housekeeping Manager or the senior management staff from time to time.

DESIGNATION–WARD EXECUTIVE:HOUSEKEEPING (3RD AND 4TH FLOOR MAIN HOSPITAL)

- Supervision and checking the cleanliness of 3rd and 4th floor.
- Control of all keys of 3rd and 4th floor.
- Preparing inventories for 3rd and 4th floor furniture and keeping records for their maintenance.
- Indenting cleaning agents and equipments and ensure their proper use and keeping records.
- Supervision for quality maintenance and infection control.
- Ensure proper discipline of Housekeepers and sweepers in 3rd and 4th floor and make sure they wear name badges.
- Planning and scheduling the standard procedures in writing for the proper care of all types of floors walls, windows, furniture, bathrooms lavatories and other equipments to be placed and to be followed strictly.
- Attending to patient's complaints.
- Development and standardization of newer and improved method of cleaning for better results at lower costs.
- Take adequate precautions in controlling cross infections.
- To assist in quality health care and patient care programme
- Ensure upkeep and maintenance of hospital property
- Training and taking classes for juniors.
- Maintain day off roster for sweepers in 3rd and 4th floor.
- Responsible for the sweepers uniform collected after working hours from the sweepers of 3rd and 4th floor.
- Maintaining the checklist of furniture, Electrical, plumbing, Carpenting and Mason works in 3rd and 4th floor.

- Any other job that may be assigned by the housekeeping manager or the senior management staff from time to time.

DESIGNATION–SENIOR TRAINEES: HOUSEKEEPING (COMPASSION 503, SINCERITY 143, GRACE 140)

- Work under the supervision of executive Linen housekeeper.
- Planning and scheduling the standard procedures for cleaning in writing and follow strictly.
- Indenting cleaning agents, equipments and ensure the proper use and maintain their records.
- Preparing inventories for furniture and keeping records for their maintenance.
- Attend all theory and practical classes as per the programme.

JOB SPECIFICATIONS OF HOUSEKEEPING STAFF

Job specifications should be written as job descriptions are prepared. Job specifications are simple statements of what the various incumbents to positions will be expected to do.

JOB SPECIFICATION—EXAMPLE

The incumbent will work as a member of a housekeeping team, cleaning and servicing for occupancy of approximately 18 hotel guestrooms each day. Work will generally include the tasks of bed making, vacuuming, dusting, and bathroom cleaning.

Incumbent will also be expected to maintain equipment provided for work and load housekeeper's cart before the end of each day's operation. Housekeepers must be willing to work their share of weekends and be dependable in coming to work each day scheduled.

EMPLOYEE REQUISITION

Once job specifications have been developed for every position, employee requisitions are prepared for first hirings. Note the designation as to whether the requisition is for a new or a replacement position and the number of employees required for a specific requisition number.

The human resources department will advertise, take applications, and screen to fill each requisition by number until all positions are filled. For example, the first requisition for GRAs may be for 20 GRAs.

The human resources department will continue to advertise for, take applications, and screen employees for the housekeeping department and will provide candidates for interview by department managers until 20 GRAs are hired. Should any be hired and require replacing, a new employee requisition will be required.

STAFFING HOUSEKEEPING POSITIONS

There are several activities involved in staffing a housekeeping operation. Executive housekeepers must select and interview employees, participate in an orientation programme, train newly hired employees, and develop employees for future growth. Each of these activities will now be discussed.

Selecting Employees

Sources of Employees

Each area of the United States has its own demographic situations that affect the availability of suitable employees for involvement in housekeeping or environmental service operations.

For example, in one area, an exceptionally high response rate from people seeking food service work may occur and a low response rate from people seeking housekeeping positions may occur.

In another area, the reverse may be true, and people interested in housekeeping work may far outnumber those interested in food service. Surveys among hotels or hospitals in your area will indicate the best source for various classifications of employees.

Advertising campaigns that will reach these employees are the best method of locating suitable people. Major classified ads associated with mass hirings will specify the need for food service personnel, front desk clerks, food servers, housekeeping personnel, and maintenance people.

Such ads may yield surprising results. If the volume of response for housekeeping personnel is insufficient to provide a suitable hiring base, the following sources may be investigated:

- Local employment agencies
- Flyers posted on community bulletin boards
- Local church organizations
- Neighbourhood canvass for friends of recently hired employees
- Direct radio appeals to local homemakers
- Organizations for underprivileged ethnic minorities, and mentally disabled people

If these sources do not produce the volume of applicants necessary to develop a staff, it may become necessary to search for employees in distant areas and to provide regular transportation for them to and from work. If aliens are hired, the department manager must take great care to ensure that they are legal residents of this country and that their green cards are valid.

More than one hotel department manager has had an entire staff swept away by the Department of Immigration after hiring people who were illegal aliens. Such unfortunate action has required the immediate assistance of all available employees to fill in.

Processing Applicants

Whether you are involved in a mass hiring or in the recruiting of a single employee, a systematic and courteous procedure for processing applicants is essential. For example, in the opening of the Los Angeles Airport Marriott, 11,000 applicants were processed to fill approximately 850 positions in a period of about two weeks. The magnitude of such an operation required a near assembly-line technique, but a personable and positive experience for the applicants still had to be maintained. The efficient handling of lines of employees, courteous attendance, personal concern for employee desires, and reference to suitable departments for those unfamiliar with what the hotel or hospital has to offer all become earmarks for how the company will treat its employees. The key to proper handling of applicants is the use of a control system whereby employees are conducted through the steps of application, prescreening, and if qualified, reference to a department for interview.

The opportunity for employees to express their desires for a specific type of employment. Even though an employee may desire involvement in one classification of work, he or she may be hired for employment in a different department. Also, employees might not be aware of the possibilities available in a particular department at the time of application or may be unable to locate in desired departments at the time of mass hiring. Employees who perform well should therefore be given the opportunity to transfer to other departments when the opportunities arise. The laws regulated by federal and state Fair Employment Practices Agencies no person may be denied the opportunity to submit application for employment for a position of his or her choosing. Not only is the law strict on this point, but companies in any way benefiting from interstate commerce may not discriminate in the hiring of people based on race, colour, national origin, or religious preference. Although specific hours and days of the week may be specified, it is a generally accepted fact that hotels and hospitals must maintain personnel operations that provide the opportunity for people to submit applications without prejudice.

Prescreening Applicants

The prescreening interview is a staff function normally provided to all hotel or hospital departments by the human resources section of the organization. Prescreening is a preliminary interview process in which unqualified applicants—those applicants who do not meet the criteria for a job as specified in the job specification–special qualifications—are selected out. For example, an applicant for a secretarial job that requires the incumbent to take shorthand and be able to type 60 words a minute may be screened out if the applicant is not able to pass a relevant typing and shorthand test. The results of prescreening are usually coded for internal use and are indicated on the Applicant Processing Record.

If a candidate is screened out by the personnel section, he or she should be told the reason immediately and thanked for applying for employment. Applicants who are not screened out should either be referred to a specific department for interview or, if all immediate positions are filled, have their applications placed in a department pending file for future reference. All applicants should be told that hiring decisions will be made by individual department managers based on the best qualifications from among those interviewed. A suggested agenda for a prescreening interview is as follows:

- The initial contact should be cordial and helpful. Many employees are lost at this stage because of inefficient systems established for handling applicants.
- During the prescreening interview, try to determine what the employee is seeking, whether such a position is available, or, if not, when such a position might become available.
- Review the work history as stated on the application to determine whether the applicant meets the obvious physical and mental qualifications, as well as important human qualifications such as emotional stability, personality, honesty, integrity, and reliability.
- Do not waste time if the applicant is obviously not qualified or if no immediate position is available. When potential vacancies or a backlog of applicants exists, inform the candidate. Be efficient in stating this to the applicant. Always make sure that the applicant gives you a phone number in order that he or she may be called at some future date. Because most applicants seeking employment are actively seeking immediate work, applications more than 30 days old are usually worthless.
- If at all possible, an immediate interview by the department manager should be held after screening. If this is not possible, a definite appointment should be made for the candidate's interview as soon as possible.

THE INTERVIEW

An interview should be conducted by a manager of the department to which the applicant has been referred. In ongoing operations, it is often wise to also allow the supervisor for whom the new employee will work to visit with the candidate in order that the supervisor may gain a feel for how it would be to work together. The supervisor's view should be considered, since a harmonious relationship at the working level is important. Although the acceptance of an employee remains a prerogative of management, it would be unwise to accept an employee into a position when the supervisor has reservations about the applicant. Certain personal characteristics should be explored when interviewing an employee. Some of these characteristics are native skills, stability, reliability, experience, attitude towards employment, personality, physical traits, stamina, age, sex, education, previous training, initiative, alertness, appearance, and personal cleanliness. Although employers may not discriminate against race, sex, age, religion, and nationality, overall considerations may involve the capability to lift heavy objects, enter men's or women's restrooms, and so on.

In a housekeeping department, people should be employed who find enjoyment in housework at home. Remember that character and personality cannot be completely judged from a person's appearance. Also, it should be expected that a person's appearance will never be better than when that person is applying for a job. Letters of recommendation and references should be carefully considered. Seldom will a letter of recommendation be adverse, whereas a telephone call might be most revealing.

If it were necessary to select the most important step in the selection process, interviewing would be it. Interviewing is the step that separates those who will be employed from those who will not. Poor interviewing techniques can make the process more difficult and may produce a result that can be both frustrating and damaging for both parties. In addition, inadequate interviewing will result in gaining incorrect information, being confused about what has been said, suppression of information, and, in some circumstances, complete withdrawal from the process by the candidate. The following is a well-accepted list of the steps for a successful interview process.

- Be prepared. Have a checklist of significant questions ready to ask the candidate. Such questions may be prepared from the body of the job description. This preparation will allow the interviewer to assume the initiative in the interview.
- Find a proper place to conduct the interview. The applicant should be made to feel comfortable. The interview should be conducted in a quiet, relaxing atmosphere where there is privacy that will bring about a confidential conversation.
- Practice. People who conduct interviews should practice interviewing skills periodically. Several managers may get together and discuss interviewing techniques that are to be used.
- Be tactful and courteous. Put the applicant at ease, but also control the discussion and lead to important questions.
- Be knowledgeable. Be thoroughly familiar with the position for which the applicant is interviewing in order that all of the applicant's questions may be answered. Also, have a significant background knowledge in order that general information about the company may be given.
- Listen. Encourage the applicant to talk. This may be done by asking questions that are not likely to be answered by a yes or no. If people are comfortable and are asked questions about themselves, they will

usually speak freely and give information that specific questions will not always bring out. Applicants will usually talk if there is a feeling that they are not being misunderstood.

- Observe. Much can be learned about an applicant just by observing reactions to questions, attitudes about work, and, specifically, attitudes about providing service to others. Observation is a vital step in the interviewing process.

Interview Pitfills

Perhaps of equal importance to the interviewing technique are the following pitfalls, which should be avoided while interviewing.

- Having a feeling that the employee will be just right based on a few outstanding characteristics rather than on the sum of all characteristics noted.
- Being influenced by neatness, grooming, expensive clothes, and an extroverted personality—none of which has much to do with housekeeping competency.
- Over generalising, whereby interviewers assume too much from a single remark.
- Hiring the "boomer," that is, the person who always wants to work in a new property; unfortunately, this type of person changes jobs whcncvcr a new property opens.
- Projecting your own background and social status into the job requirement. Which school the applicant attended or whether the applicant has the "proper look" is beside the point. It is job performance that is going to count.
- Confusing strengths with weaknesses, and vice versa. What is construed by one person to be over aggressiveness might be interpreted by another as confidence, ambition, and potential for leadership, the last two traits being in chronic short supply in most housekeeping departments. These are the very characteristics that make it possible for management to promote from within and develop new supervisors and managers.
- Being impressed by a smooth talker—or the reverse: assuming that silence reflects strength and wisdom. The interviewer should concentrate on what the applicant is saying rather than on how it is being said, then decide whether his or her personality will fit into the organization.
- Being tempted by overqualified applicants. People with experience and education that far exceed the job requirements may be unable for some reason to get jobs commensurate with their backgrounds. Even if such applicants are not concealing skeletons in the closet,

they still tend to become frustrated and dissatisfied with jobs far below their level of abilities.

The application of the techniques and avoidance of the pitfalls will be valuable tools in the selection of competent personnel for the housekeeping and environmental service departments. For many years, the approach of many managers was to write a job description and then fill it by attempting to find the perfect person. This approach may overlook many qualified people, such as disadvantaged people or slow learners.

Job descriptions may be analysed in two ways when filling positions:

- What is actually required to do the work, and
- What is desirable.

Is the ability to read or write really necessary for the job? Is the ability to learn quickly really necessary? A person who does not read or write or who is a slow learner can be trained and can make an excellent employee. True, it may take additional time, but the reward will be a loyal employee as well as less turnover. It has been proven many times that those who are disadvantaged or slightly retarded, once trained, will perform consistently well for longer periods. There are agencies who seek out companies that will try to hire such people.

Results of the Interview

If the results of an interview are negative and rejection is indicated, the candidate should be informed as soon as possible. A pleasant statement, such as "Others interviewed appear to be more qualified," is usually sufficient. This information can be handled in a straightforward and courteous manner and in such a way that the candidate will appreciate the time that has been taken during the interview. When the results of the interview are positive, a statement indicating a favourable impression is most encouraging. However, no commitment should be made until a reference check has been conducted.

Reference Checks

In many cases, reference checks are made only to verify that what has been said in the application and interview is in fact true. Many times applicants are reluctant to explain in detail why previous employment situations have come to an end. It is more important to hear the actual truth about a prior termination from the applicant than it is to hear that they simply have been terminated.

Reference checks, in order of desirability, are as follows:

- Personal (face-to-face) meetings with previous employers are the least available but provide the most accurate information when they can be arranged.
- Telephone discussions are the next best and most often used approach. For all positions, an in-depth conversation by telephone

between the potential new manager and the prior manager is most desirable; otherwise a simple verification of data is sufficient to ensure honesty.

- The least desirable reference is the written recommendation, because managers are extremely reluctant to state a frank and honest opinion that may later be used against them in court.

Applicants who are rated successful at an interview should be told that a check of their references will be conducted, and, pending favourable responses, they will be contacted by the personnel department within two days. Applicants who are currently employed normally ask that their current employer not be contacted for a reference check. This request should be honoured at all times. Applicants who are currently working usually want to give proper notice to their current employers. If the applicant chooses not to give notice, chances are no notice will be given at the time he or she leaves your hotel. In some cases, the applicant gives notice and, upon doing so, is "cut loose" immediately. If such is the case, the applicant should be told to contact the department manager immediately in order that the employee may be put to work as soon as possible.

Interview Skills versus Turnover

There is no perfect interviewer, interviewee, or resultant hiring or rejection decision in regard to an applicant. We can only hope to improve our interviewing skills in order that the greatest degree of success in employee retention can be obtained. The executive housekeeper should expect that 25 per cent of initial hires into a housekeeping department will not be employed for more than three months. Some new housekeeping departments have as much as a 75 per cent turnover rate in the first three months of operation. However, regardless of the outcome of the interview, the processing record should be properly endorsed and returned to the personnel department for processing.

ORIENTATION

A carefully planned, concerned, and informational orientation programme is significant to the first impressions that a new employee will have about the hospital or hotel in general and the housekeeping department in particular. Too often, a new employee is told where the work area and restroom are, given a cursory explanation of the job, then put to work. It is not uncommon to find managers putting employees to work who have not even been processed into the organization, an unfortunate situation that is usually discovered on payday when there is no paycheck for the new employee.

Such blatant disregard for the concerns of the employee can only lead to a poor perception of the company. A planned orientation programme will eliminate this type of activity and will bring the employee into the company with personal concern and with a greater possibility for a successful relationship. A good orientation programme is usually made up of four phases: employee acquisition, receipt of an employee's handbook, tour of the facility, and an orientation meeting.

Employee Acquisition

Once a person is accepted for employment, the applicant is told to report for work at a given time and place, and that place should be the personnel department. Pre-employment procedures can take as much as one-half day, and department managers eager to start new employees to work should allow time for a proper employee acquisition into the organization. At this time it should be ensured that the application is complete and any additional information pertaining to employment history that may be necessary to obtain the necessary work permits and credentials is on hand. Usually the security department records the entry of a new employee into the staff and provides instructions regarding use of employee entrances, removing parcels from the premises, and employee parking areas.

Application for work permits, and drug testing, will be scheduled where applicable. All documents required by the hotel's health and welfare insurer should be completed, and instructions should be given about immediately reporting accidents, no matter how slight, to supervisors. The federal government requires that every employer submit a W-4 for each employee on the payroll. The employee must complete this document and give it to the company. Mandatory deductions from pay should be explained, as should other deductions that may be required or desired. At this time, some form of personal action document is usually initiated for the new employee and is placed in the employee's permanent record. The permanent information that will be carried on file. The PAF is serially numbered, is created from data stored on magnetic discs, and is maintained in the employee's personnel file.

When a change has to be made, such as job title, marital status, or rate of pay, the PAF is retrieved from the employee's record, changes are made under the item to be changed, and the corrected PAF is used to change the data in the computer storage. Once new information is stored, a new PAF is created and placed in the employee's record to await the next need for processing. A long-time employee might have many PAFs stored in the personnel file. When either regular or special performance appraisals are given, the last PAF will be used to record the appraisal.

These forms are usually found on the reverse side of the PAF. Since performance appraisals may signify a raise in pay, the appropriate pay increase information would be indicated on the front side of the PAF. All recordings on PAFs, whether on one side or both, require the submission of data, storage of information, and creation of a new PAF to be stored in the employee's record. The PAF and performance appraisal system should be thoroughly explained to the new employee, along with assignment of a payroll number. The employer should also explain how and when the staff is paid and when the first paycheck may be expected.

The Employee Handbook

The new employee should be provided with a copy of the hotel or hospital employee's handbook and should be told to read it thoroughly. Since the new housekeeping employee is not working just for the housekeeping department but is to become integrated as a member of the entire staff, reading this handbook is extremely important to ensure that proper instructions in the rules and regulations of the hotel are presented. The handbook should be developed in such a way as to inspire the new employee to become a fully participating member of the organization. Note the tone of the welcoming letter and the manner in which the rules and regulations are presented.

Familiarization Tour of the Facilities

Upon completion of the acquisition phase, a facility tour should be conducted for one or all new employees. For new facilities, access to the property should be gained within about one week before opening, and many new employees can be taken on a tour simultaneously. It is possible for employees to work in the hotel housekeeping department for years and never to have visited the showroom, dining rooms, ballrooms, or even the executive office areas. A tour of the complete facility melds employees into the total organization, and a complete informative tour should never be neglected. For ongoing operations, after acquisition, the new employee may be turned over to a department supervisor, who becomes the tour director. An appreciation of the total involvement of each employee is strengthened when a facilities tour is complete and thorough. If necessary, the property tour might be postponed until after the orientation meeting; however, the orientation activity of staffing is not complete until a property tour is conducted.

Orientation Meeting

The orientation meeting should not be conducted until the employee has had an opportunity to become at least partially familiar with the surroundings. After approximately two weeks, the employee will have many questions about experiences, the new job, training, and the rules and regulations listed in the Property and Department Handbooks. Employee orientation meetings that are scheduled too soon fail to answer many questions that will develop within the first two weeks of employment. The meeting should be held in a comfortable setting, with refreshments provided. It is usually conducted by the director of human resources and is attended by as many of the facility managers as possible. Most certainly, the general manager or hospital administration members of the executive committee, the security director, and the new employees' department heads should attend. Each of these managers should have an opportunity to welcome the new employees and give them a chance to associate names with faces.

All managers and new employees should wear name tags. In orientation meetings, a brief history of the company and company goals should be presented. A planned orientation meeting should not be concluded without someone stressing the importance of each position.

Every position must have a purpose behind it and is therefore important to the overall functioning of the facility. An excellent statement of this philosophy was once offered by a general manager who said, "The person mopping a floor in the kitchen at 3:00 A.M.

is just as valuable to this operation as I am—we just do different things." The orientation meeting should be scheduled to allow for many questions. And there should be someone in attendance who can answer all of them. Although the new employee will be gaining confidence and security in the position as training ends and work is actually performed, informal orientation may continue for quite some time. The formal orientation, however, ends with the orientation meeting. Finally, it should be remembered that good orientation procedures lead to worker satisfaction and help quiet the anxieties and fears that a new employee may have. When a good orientation is neglected, the seeds of dissatisfaction are planted.

TRAINING

General

The efficiency and economy with which any department will operate will depend on the ability of each member of the organization to do his or her job. Such ability will depend in part on past experiences, but more commonly it can be credited to the type and quality of training offered.

Employees, regardless of past experiences, always need some degree of training before starting a new job. Small institutions may try to avoid training by hiring people who are already trained in the general functions with which they will be involved. However, most institutions recognize the need for training that is specifically oriented towards the new experience, and will have a documented training programme.

Some employers of housekeeping personnel find it easier to train completely unskilled and untrained personnel. In such cases, bad or undesirable practices do not have to be trained out of an employee. Previous experience and education should, however, be analysed and considered in the training of each new employee in order that efficiencies in training can be recognized.

If an understanding of department standards and policies can be demonstrated by a new employee, that portion of training may be shortened or modified. However, skill and ability must be demonstrated before training can be altered.

Finally, training is the best method to communicate the company's way of doing things, without which the new employee may do work contrary to company policy.

First Training

First training of a new employee actually starts with a continuation of department orientation. When a new employee is turned over to the housekeeping or environmental services department, orientation usually continues by familiarising the employee with department rules and regulations. Many housekeeping departments have their own department employee handbooks. For an example, which contains the housekeeping department rules and regulations for Bally's Casino Resort in Las Vegas, Nevada. Compare this handbook with that of the generic handbook. Although these handbooks are for completely different types of organizations, the substance of their publications is essentially the same; both are designed to familiarize each new employee with his or her surroundings. Handbooks should be written in such a way as to inspire employees to become team members, committed to company objectives.

A Systematic Approach to Training

Training may be defined as those activities that are designed to help an employee begin performing tasks for which he or she is hired or to help the employee improve performance in a job already assigned. The purpose of training is to enable an employee to begin an assigned job or to improve upon techniques already in use. In hotel or hospital housekeeping operations, there are three basic areas in which training activity should take place: skills, attitudes, and knowledge.

Skills Training

A sample list of skills in which a basic housekeeping employee must be trained follows:

- *Bed making*: Specific techniques; company policy
- *Vacuuming*: Techniques; use and care of equipment
- *Dusting*: Techniques; use of products
- *Window and mirror cleaning*: Techniques and products
- *Setup awareness*: Room setups; what a properly serviced room should look like
- *Bathroom cleaning*: Tub and toilet sanitation; appearance; methods of cleaning and results desired
- *Daily routine*: An orderly procedure for the conduct of the day's work; daily communications
- *Caring for and using equipment*: Housekeeper cart; loading
- *Industrial safety*: Product use; guest safety; fire and other emergencies

The best reference for the skills that require training is the job description for which the person is being trained.

Attitude Guidance

Employees need guidance in their attitudes about the work that must be done. They need to be guided in their thinking about rooms that may present a unique problem in cleaning.

Attitudes among section housekeepers need to be such that, occasionally, when rooms require extra effort to be brought back to standard, it is viewed as being a part of rendering service to the guest who paid to enjoy the room. Carol Mondesir,1 director of housekeeping, Sheraton Centre, Toronto, states that:

- A hotel is meant to be enjoyed and, occasionally, the rooms are left quite messed up. However, as long as they're not vandalized, it's part of the territory. The whole idea of being in the hospitality business is to make the guest's stay as pleasant as possible. The rooms are there to be enjoyed.

Positive relationships with various agencies and people also need to be developed.

The following is a list of areas in which attitude guidance is important:

- The guest/patient
- The department manager and immediate supervisor
- A guestroom that is in a state of great disarray
- The hotel and company
- The uniform
- Appearance
- Personal hygiene

Meeting Standards

The most important task of the trainer is to prepare new employees to meet standards. With this aim in mind, sequence of performance in cleaning a guestroom is most important in order that efficiency in accomplishing day-to-day tasks may be developed.

In addition, the best method of accomplishing a task should be presented to the new trainee.

Once the task has been learned, the next thing is to meet standards, which may not necessarily mean doing the job the way the person has been trained. Setting standards of performance is discussed in Chapter under "Operational Controls."

Knowledge Training

Areas of knowledge in which the employee needs to be trained are as follows:

- Thorough knowledge of the hotel layout; employee must be able to give directions and to tell the guest about the hotel, restaurants, and other facilities
- Knowledge of employee rights and benefits

- Understanding of grievance procedure
- Knowing top managers by sight and by name

Ongoing Training

There is a need to conduct ongoing training for all employees, regardless of how long they have been members of the department.

There are two instances when additional training is needed:

- The purchase of new equipment, and
- Change in or unusual employee behaviour while on the job.

When new equipment is purchased, employees need to know how the new equipment differs from present equipment, what new skills or knowledge are required to operate the equipment, who will need this knowledge, and when. New equipment may also require new attitudes about work habits.

Employee behaviour while on the job that is seen as an indicator for additional training may be divided into two categories: Events that the manager witnesses and events that the manager is told about by the employees. Events that the manager witnesses that indicate a need for training are frequent employee absence, considerable spoilage of products, carelessness, a hig

Events that the manager might be told about that indicate a need for training are that something doesn't work right something is dangerous to work with, something is making work harder.

Although training is vital for any organization to function at top efficiency, it is expensive. The money and man-hours expended must therefore be worth the investment. There must be a balance between the dollars spent training employees and the benefits of productivity and high-efficiency performance. A simple method of determining the need for training is to measure performance of workers: Find out what is going on at present on the job, and match this performance with what should be happening. The difference, if any, describes how much training is needed.

In conducting performance analysis, the following question should be asked: Could the employee do the job or task if his or her life depended on the result? If the employee could not do the job even if his or her life depended on the outcome, there is a deficiency of knowledge.

If the employee could have done the job if his or her life depended on the outcome, but did not, there is a deficiency of execution. Some of the causes of deficiencies of execution include task interference, lack of feedback and the balance of consequences.

If either deficiency of knowledge or deficiency of execution exists, training must be conducted. The approach or the method of training may differ, however. Deficiencies of knowledge can be corrected by training the employee to do the job, then observing and correcting as necessary until the task is proficiently performed. Deficiency of execution is usually corrected by searching for the underlying cause of lack of performance, not by teaching the actual task.

Training Methods

There are numerous methods or ways to conduct training. Each method has its own advantages and disadvantages, which must be weighed in the light of benefits to be gained.

Some methods are more expensive than others but are also more effective in terms of time required for comprehension and proficiency that must be developed. Several useful methods of training housekeeping personnel are listed and discussed.

On-the-job Training

Using on-the-job training, a technique in which "learning by doing" is the advantage, the instructor demonstrates the procedure and then watches the students perform it.

With this technique, one instructor can handle several students. In housekeeping operations, the instructor is usually a GRA who is doing the instructing in the rooms that have been assigned for cleaning that day. The OJT method is not operationally productive until the student is proficient enough in the training tasks to absorb part of the operational load.

Simulation Training

With simulation training, a model room is set up and used to train several employees. Whereas OJT requires progress towards daily production of ready rooms, simulation requires that the model room not be rented. In addition, the trainer is not productive in cleaning ready rooms.

The advantages of simulation training are that it allows the training process to be stopped, discussed, and repeated if necessary. Simulation is an excellent method, provided the trainer's time is paid for out of training funds, and clean room production is not necessary during the workday.

Coach-Pupil Method

The coach-pupil method is similar to OJT except that each instructor has only one student.

This method is desired, provided that there are enough qualified instructors to have several training units in progress at the same time.

Lectures

The lecture method reaches the largest number of students per instructor. Practically all training programmes use this type of instruction for certain segments. Unfortunately, the lecture method can be the dullest training technique, and therefore requires instructors who are gifted in presentation capabilities. In addition, space for lectures may be difficult to obtain and may require special facilities.

Conferences

The conference method of instruction is often referred to as workshop training. This technique involves a group of students who formulate ideas, do problem solving, and report on projects. The conference or workshop technique is excellent for supervisory training.

Demonstrations

When new products or equipment are being introduced, demonstrations are excellent. Many demonstrations may be conducted by vendors and purveyors as a part of the sale of equipment and products. Difficulties may arise when language barriers exist. It is also important that no more information be presented than can be absorbed in a reasonable period of time; otherwise misunderstandings may arise.

Training Aids

Many hotels use training aids in a conference room, or post messages on an employee bulletin board. Aside from the usual training aids such as chalkboards, bulletin boards, charts, graphs, and diagrams, photographs can supply clear and accurate references for how rooms should be set up, maids' carts loaded, and routines accomplished. Most housekeeping operations have films on guest contact and courtesy that may also be used in training. Motion pictures speak directly to many people who may not understand proper procedures from reading about them. Many training techniques may be combined to develop a well-rounded training plan.

Development

It is possible to have two students sitting side by side in a classroom, with one being trained and the other being developed. Recall that the definition of training is preparing a person to do a job for which he or she is hired or to improve upon performance of a current job. Development is preparing a person for advancement or to assume greater responsibility. The techniques are the same, but the end result is quite different.

Whereas training begins after orientation of an employee who is hired to do a specific job, upon introduction of new equipment, or upon observation and communication with employees indicating a need for training, development begins with the identification of a specific employee who has shown potential for advancement. Training for promotion or to improve potential is in fact development and must always include a much neglected type of training—supervisory training.

Many forms of developmental training may be given on the property; other forms might include sending candidates to schools and seminars. Developmental training is associated primarily with supervisors and managerial development and may encompass many types of experiences. The various developmental tasks that the trainee must perform over a period of 12 months. Development of individuals within the organization looks to future potential and promotion of employees. Specifically, those employees who demonstrate leadership potential should be developed through supervisory training for advancement to positions of greater responsibility.

Unfortunately, many outstanding workers have their performance rewarded by promotion but are given no development training. The excellent section housekeeper who is advanced to the position of senior housekeeper without the benefit of supervisory training is quickly seen to be unhappy and frustrated and may possibly become a loss to the department. It is therefore most essential that individual potential be developed in an orderly and systematic manner, or else this potential may never be recognized. Even though there will be times that the trainee may be given specific responsibilities to oversee operations, clean guestrooms, or service public areas, advantage should not be taken of the trainee or the situation to the detriment of the development function.

Development of new growth in the trainee becomes difficult when the training instructor or coordinator is not only developing a new manager but is also being held responsible for the production of some aspect of housekeeping operations.

RECORDS AND REPORTS

Whether you are conducting a training or a development programme, suitable records of training progress should be maintained both by the training supervisor and the student. Periodic evaluations of the student's progress should be conducted, and successful completion of the programme should be recognized. Public recognition of achievement will inspire the newly trained or developed employee to achieve standards of performance and to strive for advancement. Once an employee is trained or developed and his or her satisfactory performance has been recognized and recorded, the person should perform satisfactorily to standards. Future performance may be based on beginning performance after training. If an employee's performance begins to fall short of standards and expectations, there has to be a reason other than lack of skills. The reason for unsatisfactory performance must then be sought out and addressed. This type of follow-up is not possible unless suitable records of training and development are maintained and used for comparison.

EVALUATION AND PERFORMANCE APPRAISAL

Although evaluation and performance appraisal for employees will occur as work progresses, it is not uncommon to find the design of systems for appraisal as part of organization and staffing functions. This is true because first appraisal and evaluation occurs during training, which is an activity of staffing. Once trainees begin to have their performance appraised, the methods used will continue throughout employment. As a part of training, new employees should be told how, when, and by whom their performances will be evaluated, and should be advised that questions regarding their performance will be regularly answered.

Probationary Period

Initial employment should be probationary in nature, allowing the new employee to improve efficiency to where the designated number of rooms cleaned per day can be achieved in a probationary period. Should a large number of employees be unable to achieve the standard within that time, the standard should be investigated. Should only one or two employees be unable to meet the standard of rooms cleaned per day, an evaluation of the employee in training should either reveal the reason why or indicate the employee as unsuitable for further retention. An employee who, after suitable training, cannot meet a reasonable performance standard should not be allowed to continue employment. Similarly, an employee who has met required performance standards in the specified probationary period should be continued into regular employment status and thus achieve a reasonable degree of security in employment.

Evaluation

Evaluation of personnel is an attempt to measure selected traits, characteristics, and productivity. Unfortunately, evaluations are generally objective in nature, and raters are seldom trained in the art of subjective evaluation. Initiative, self-control, and leadership ability do not lend themselves to measurement; therefore such characteristics are estimated. How well they are estimated depends to a great extent on the person doing the estimating. Two raters using the same form and rating the same person will probably arrive at different conclusions.

Certain policies on the use of evaluations should be established so that they are understood by both the person doing the evaluating and the person being evaluated. These policies must be established and disseminated by management. In order to establish such policies, the following questions, among others, must be answered and communicated to all those involved in the evaluation: What will evaluations be used for? Will evaluations influence promotions, become a part of the employee's record, be used as periodic checks, or be used for counseling and guidance? What qualities are going to be evaluated? Who is going to be evaluated? Who will do the evaluating? Reliable evaluations require careful planning and take considerable time, skill, and work.

An evaluation must be understood by the employee. Evaluation should be used at the end of a probationary period, and the employee must understand at the beginning of the period that he or she will be observed and evaluated. Each item, as well as what impact the evaluation will have on future employment, should be explained to the employee. People undergoing periodic evaluations, such as at the end of one year's employment, should also know why evaluations are being conducted and what may result from the evaluation. In both situations, the evaluation should be used for counseling and guidance so that performance may be improved upon or corrected if necessary.

Certainly, strong points should be pointed out. An employee should be made aware of good as well as not-so-good evaluations. Evaluations should be made for a purpose and not for the sake of an exercise. They should ultimately be used as management tools. Evaluations should be developed to fit the policies of the particular institution using it and the particular position being evaluated. The same evaluation may not be suitable for every position.

OUTSOURCING

In certain locales, such as isolated resorts, hotels are tempted to use contract labour because the local market does not support the necessary number of workers, particularly in housekeeping. Advocates of outsourcing are quick to point out the advantages of the practice. Scarce workers are provided to the property, and there is no need to provide expensive employee benefits. The entire staffing function is assumed by the contractor. There are no worries regarding recruiting, selecting, hiring, orienting, or even training the employees. Merely issue them uniforms and send them off to clean rooms. Some employers may even be willing to relax their responsibilities regarding employment law such as immigration and naturalization requirements. Management should never forget that once a contracted employee dons a company uniform, the guest believes that person is an employee of the hotel. The guest also believes the hotel has made every reasonable effort to screen that person in the hiring process to ensure that he or she is of good moral character, who has the best interest of the guest at heart.

Unfortunately, there have been several incidents in which the outsourced employees did not quite have the best interest of the guest in their hearts. There have been more than a few cases in which outsourced workers were wanted felons who inflicted considerable bodily harm on guests during the performance of their duties. A number of these incidents have resulted in lawsuits, with awards against the hotel in the millions of dollars. This author does not recommend outsourcing in housekeeping, and cautions operators who ignore this advice to keep their guard up and continue to meet their legal and ethical responsibilities regarding employees and employment law.

THE MAID'S CART AND THE SERVICE ROOM

Maid's cart also called as a room attendants trolley, or chamber maid's trolley, this is perhaps the most significance piece equipment in the housekeeping department. it is like a giant tool box, stocked with everything necessary to service a guest room effectively. Most such carts available now are made of metal, but sometimes wooden carts may be in use.

The cart should be spacious enough to carry all the supplies needed for a GRA to complete half a day's room assignments. Since the cart is large and may be heavily loaded, it must be easily movable as well.

The ideal cart would have fixed wheels at one end and castor-wheels at the other. The cart should be well organized so that the GRA's do not have to waste time in searching for supplies or make frequent trips back to the supply room. Also, if the cart is not stacked neatly, it will look very unsightly.

They are more useful than hand caddies when a large amount of supplies and items are to be carted or replaced. They are ideal for the efficient removal and carriage of smaller pieces of cleaning equipment, cleaning agents, linen and rubbish. They eliminate the time wasted in assembling equipment at the work location or moving them from one place to another.

LOCATION OF THE MAID'S ROOM

Maid's service room/floor pantry: these are located on each guest floor to keep a stock of linen, guest supplies and maid's cart and cleaning supplies for that particular floor.

Maid's service room stores a complete set of linen for the whole floor over and above what is already in circulation in the rooms. The maid's service room should be tucked away from guest's view and should be situated near the service elevators.

It should store all housekeeping items so that the housekeeping staffs do not have to keep going back to the housekeeping department or linen room for any item. It should have shelves and cupboards door linen and supplies, and sufficient area to park a room maid's cart.

It should have a sink with water supply. Since the maid's service room is used to stock expensive items such as linen, it should remain locked at all times when not in use.

The key to the floor pantry is kept by the GRA of that floor and a duplicate is kept with the floor supervisor. The following should be provided in the maid's service room:

- Cupboards to store guest supplies, cleaning agents and equipments
- Shelves and racks to store fresh room linen
- Linen trolleys to store fresh and soiled linen and for transporting/ dispatching the same to the linen and uniform room.
- A notice board to display information regarding expected arrivals, VIPs in house, extra bed, etc.
- A sink with hot and cold water facilities to wash or disinfect glasses, fill drinking water in flasks, and for flower arrangements
- Guest loan items such as rollaway beds, bed boards, baby sitters etc.

CARE AND MAINTENANCE

- All carts and trolleys need to be kept clean, wiped daily and stored locked.
- The room should be dry area and it should be well ventilated.
- The soiled linen bag and thrash bags should be emptied.
- A thorough cleaning may be done once a week.
- The wheels may be oiled during this cleaning for the smooth movement of the trolley.
- Carts and trolleys should be never used as general dumping grounds when not in use.
- All the linens and amenities should be well arranged when the shift is completed so that it will be easier to replenish extra items when necessary.

EASE PRESSURE

What's the first thing that comes to your mind when you think of the word hospitality? Is it a semi-clean home with an open-door policy? Is it a chicken spaghetti casserole on its way out the door for a sick friend? Hospitality can be all of above and none of the above. Often hospitality is confused with perfection. Perfection seeks to impress; hospitality seeks to put another's needs before your own. The word "hospitable" is derived from the word hospital, which means a charitable institution, a repair shop, a hospice or a shelter. Hospitality provides a shelter for the soul, a healing for the spirit.

Ultimately this is what we offer when we open our home in the true spirit of love or when we offer our time, gifts or talents outside of our home to reach others. If hospitality comes down to love and kindness, one of the ways we are kind to ourselves is by doing our best to stay healthy. If you're like most women, you probably don't sleep enough. You eat the crust off the peanut butter and jelly sandwiches as you feed your kids and run in a frenzy to "keep it together" each day. We have too much to lose by not being our best selves.

Be kind to yourself so you have the energy to be kind to others. Keep in mind that home sometimes can be the hardest place to extend hospitable kindnesses. Often at home, we're tired, overworked and grumpy. When we let our hair down, it has lots of tangles! Our goal is to freely give love and kindness to others, and our starting point is at home. Work together to solve issues, plan together to serve and listen to each other's concerns. Personal care of you+family+friends = the foundation for hospitality. For many of us, our friends are like our extended family. Life without them would just be dull. We need that connection to ease our soul.

A deep heart-to-heart talk with a cherished friend feels as comforting and soothing as a super-soft, oversized sweatshirt on a chilly day. Friends are important. A good friend is one who understands your world, the difficulties and triumphs. Thinking of my favourite friends always makes me smile because of all the love, laughter, tears, prayers and cherished moments. Hospitality begins with us sharing our hearts. It blossoms by us loving our families and cherishing our friends. The key to accomplishing hospitality is easier than you think: an open door, a cup of coffee and listening ears. Happy hospitality. Often our planned visits revolve around food. We meet at restaurants, at each other's homes for dinner or at a yogurt shop for a treat.

Life loses its richness without the opportunity to live it with friends. Have you scheduled time with friends lately? They offer joy, share the burdens and lighten the load. Patients who travel to Aberdeen Royal Infirmary for an operation the next day, or who need to stay for long-term treatment, will all be able to make use of the facility. NHS Grampian believes the hotel, which will be built in the hospital grounds, will ensure better treatment for those who need it. Dr Roelf Dijkhuizen, medical director with the health board, said:'We want a facility where people who make use of hospital services can stay overnight. The most obvious example would be someone who comes from the islands and is waiting for a flight home.'Another would be a cancer patient who needs treatment that is only available in the hospital over three consecutive days.

At the moment, we have to ask them to stay in hospital for those days, but with a hotel we can provide much more convenient and private accommodation at a much lower cost.' The hotel will be built in partnership with a private contractor. Aberdeen Royal Infirmary is seen as the perfect site for the development because it takes in patients from such a large area. At present, anyone travelling from Orkney and Shetland for a non-urgent operation is put up overnight in a fully staffed ward. Health bosses are growing concerned that this is taking away beds from patients who desperately need treatment.

They feel the freeing-up of the beds will ensure better levels of care for patients on the wards. The facility will operate in the same way as a normal hotel but people using Aberdeen Royal Infirmary services will be put up free of charge. Patients with relatives could also make use of it, as well as visiting health officials. Dr Dijkhuizen added:' If we invite colleagues from the U.S. to visit for a conference, we don't have to give away all the profit to another hotel.

We could put them up here.'This would be good for the hotel company and good for the NHS if we put the contract together properly.' But Aberdeen MSP Brian Adam is sceptical and has raised his concerns with NHS Grampian. He said:'I am not sure developing a hotel is the greatest use of NHS land, property or energies.'I think the fact they are calling it a hotel shows that these days the health service is all about privatising as many services as possible.'

Reported customer tips averaged about half the cash earnings of waiters and waitresses in hotels and motels studied by the Bureau of Labour Statistics during July through September 1983. The survey, covering 23 metropolitan areas, found employer-paid wages making up the balance. In most areas, these wages averaged between $2 and $3 an hour, largely reflecting the tip allowance employers can apply towards meeting the Federal minimum wage of $3.35 an hour. Customer tips also contributed substantially to the earnings of several other occupational groups.

For waiter and waitress assistant, tips commonly averaged 16 to 22 per cent of their earnings, 44 to 57 per cent for bell persons, 25 to 40 per cent for public bartenders, and less than 20 per cent for service usually had the highest employer-paid wages, ranging from $3.99 an hour in Dallas-Fort Worth to $10.16 in Las Vegas. Public bartenders, receiving tips to a greater extent than service bartenders, had wages averaging from $3.55 an hour in Miami to $9.83 in San Francisco-Oakland. Although service bartenders, who prepare drinks for waiters and waitresses to serve, usually averaged more in wages than public bartenders, this pattern was reversed when tips were included in the comparisons. Similar patterns occurred between other occupations, including waiters and waitresses and their assistants.

For example, table waiters and waitresses in full-course restaurants averaged less in wages than their assistants in each area surveyed-usually by 30 to 60 per cent. When tips were included in the comparisons, waiters and waitresses averaged more-usually by 40 to 70 per cent. Paid holidays, most commonly 6 to 8 days annually, were provided to at least three-fourths of the nonsupervisory, nonoffice workers in each area studied. At least nine-tenths of the workers in each area were also covered by paid vacations, typically 1 week after 1 year of service, 2 weeks after 2 years, and 3 weeks after 10 years.

Life, hospitalization, surgical, basic medical, and major medical insurance, were available to three-fourths or more of the workers in nearly all areas. Retirement pension plans were available to a majority of workers in 10 of the 23 areas. Also, food and beverage service workers typically received at least one free meal a day. The 2,050 establishments within scope of the survey employed a total of 356,000 workers during July through September 1983. Of this total, nonsupervisory, nonoffice employees represented five-sixths of the workforce.

Nearly one-half of these workers were concentrated in Las Vegas, Atlantic City, New York, Los Angeles-Long Beach, and Chicago. Corresponding employment in the remaining 18 areas ranged from about 14,000 in Dallas-Fort Worth, San Francisco-Oakland, and Washington to 1,750 in Buffalo. Nearly three-fifths each of the food service and other nonoffice workers were employed in hotels and motels with collective bargaining agreements covering a majority of such workers. The proportions, however, varied widely by area. For example, virtually all of the workers in Atlantic City were covered by labour-management agreements, but no establishment visited in Houston or Memphis had union agreements covering a majority of their workers. The Service Employees

International Union and the Hotel and Restaurant Employees Union, both AFL-CIO affiliates, were the major unions.

SERVICE ENCOUNTER

As the services sector becomes a larger component of our national economy, it becomes increasingly critical that the management of service operations is addressed systematically. One concern is the interaction of service employees and the technology making up the job design. Effectively matching job design and technology leads to effective service encounters, while mismatches cause short-run or long run problems for the organization. Organizational mismatches between job design and supporting infrastructure, specifically the information technology selected, can give rise to the use and exercise of judgment and discretion by service encounter employees that from the viewpoint of the organization or the customer is extraordinary, conflicted, or perverse.

Perverse judgments debilitate the organization and degrade the quality of the service encounter. Conflicted and extraordinary, judgments ultimately debilitate the organization and may degrade the quality of the service encounter if some customers should perceive others as having received preferential treatment. This paper explores dynamics in managing operations, technology, and human resources that give rise to the exercise of such judgments with the intent to construct a conceptual framework that will explain such judgments and the behaviours that issue from them. The importance of the service encounter to a service organization is well documented in the operations management and marketing literature. This encounter is often the only point of contact the customer has with the organization. It is the context in which the organization provides the customer with what is presumably of value. The customer assesses the value of what the service organization provides on the basis of how adequately it provides explicit and implicit benefits that meet customer needs and expectations.

It is thus incumbent upon a service organization to insure that its customer contact personnel are sufficiently supported through appropriate job design, training, and supporting infrastructure that can include an appropriate information technology. This better insures that the organization's customer contact personnel represent it in the best possible way to its customers. Job design defines the extent to which customer contact personnel must exercise judgment in meeting customer needs.

Ideally, the organization's infrastructure is sufficient to support the conformance of job design to customer needs. This paper will explore dynamics in managing operations, technology, and human resources that give rise to the exercise of problematic judgments with the intent to construct a conceptual framework that will explain such judgments and the behaviours that issue from them.

The authors have identified three types of problematic judgments that they label perverse, conflicted, and extraordinary judgments. Perverse judgments debilitate the organization and degrade the quality of the service encounter. Conflicted and extraordinary judgments ultimately debilitate the organization and may degrade the quality of the service encounter if some customers should perceive others as having received preferential treatment.

A conceptual framework that provides an adequate understanding of the dynamics that prompt such judgments being made permits more effective planning of the service encounter, the discovery and analysis of the nature of service quality gaps, and suggests actions that can be taken to close those gaps. In cases where these judgments occur, remedial actions can be taken that have both operational and strategic implications. Such a framework can benefit both the organization and the customers it serves.

This is divided into five parts. This review provides the motivation for critiquing the quality of service encounters as a technology management and subsequent organizational design issue. This part will touch on the increasingly important role of services in societal economies, the focus on the training of customer contact personnel at the expense of attending to the organizational infrastructure that supports those encounters, and how the introduction of IT into a service organization impacts its infrastructure.

THE ROLE OF SERVICES IN THE ECONOMY

The evolutionary course societal economies appear to follow involves a movement towards increasing organizational complexity. Technological innovations result in increased productivity and diversity in the extractive and manufacturing sectors of an economy which result in shifts of the labour force into other sectors. This shift is made possible only because of a simultaneous accompanying increase and expanding diversity of business, trade, infrastructure, social/personal, and public administration services. Without the direct and indirect linkages that exist between the material goods producing sectors and these service sub-sectors, increased productivity and diversity in the goods producing sectors would not be viable.

Adequately performing this increasingly complex function has resulted in the percentage of the U.S. workforce allocated to services steadily increasing at a modest exponential rate in this century. Since the 1960's, services have accounted for more than half of that labour force with no indication that the continued growth in this proportion has passed an inflection point. By 1995, service industries accounted for 75per cent of GDP and 78per cent of employment. Therefore, it becomes increasingly important that services be the focus of critical attention for the purpose of evaluating their functional effectiveness and efficiency. If not clone, our understanding of services for this time and the future may prove inadequate. Eventually, this inadequacy will lead to their practical mismanagement and the degradation of the effectiveness and efficiency required of services to contribute towards the realization of healthy activity of an evolving economy.

FOCUS ON THE SERVICE ENCOUNTER

Addressing the concerns for service quality and effectiveness has been done in several different ways. The most basic way is to analyse the service encounter, the interaction between the customer and the service delivery or customer contact personnel. Research on service encounters may focus on perceptions of the persons involved in the exchange. Hartline and Ferrell devised a model that addressed the management of service encounter employees based on the perceptions of the three groups that had previously been studied separately; managers, employees and customers. Their literature review and the literature search this paper's authors conducted inductively suggest that the preponderance of studies exploring service quality and effectiveness have limited themselves to issues related to micromanaging service encounters.

GLOBAL VIEWS OF SERVICE QUALITY AND EFFECTIVENESS MANAGEMENT

In addition to service encounter models, more global views of the management of service performance have been addressed. Bowen and Lawler stress that decisions concerning how to manage service employees should be based on five contingency factors. They state that an organization should consider its basic business strategy, the nature of the relationship to the customer, technology, business environment, and types of managers and employees. Thus, management of services is based on a set of variables that constitute settings in which service encounter perceptions are formed. Singh and Deshmukh advocate the application of Total Quality Management principles to the management of services. They stress that TQM is a systems approach to organizations in which every element interacts with every other element. Like Bowen and Lawler, they argue that service quality is not simply a function of what the manager wants the employee to do, or what the customer perceives, or how well trained the employee is. The success of a service organization is predicated more on the interaction of many its aspects. One systems approach to achieving service quality and effectiveness is found in Hauser's and Clausing's "house of quality."

Applying the "house of quality" to the service encounter, Fitzsimmons and Fitzsimmons show how marketing, design, engineering and manufacturing must be coordinated in order to actually meet the customer's desires. A global or systemic view is critical in managing an organization's adoption of a technology, particularly when that adoption directly involves the organization's operations. The manufacturing management literature of the 1980's and early 1990's, for example, is replete with discussions that advocate this perspective. This is so because its contributors found that the repercussions of introducing a new technology into a manufacturing concern ran through virtually every aspect of that concern's organizational structure. They further found that unless that concern accommodated the adoption of its new technology by reorganising itself so as to effectively exploit its new technology's capabilities, the end result was far more likely to be counterproductive and deleterious than beneficial.

Both Sciulli and Rodger and Paper argue that what has been said about manufacturing organizations and their adoption of new technologies holds true for service organizations as well, and their adoption of IT, in particular in both the banking and health care industries.

Their argument is in part supported by the work of a committee of the National Academy of Sciences that identified a phenomenon that it labeled the "information technology paradox." This paradox refers to the lagging growth in service sector productivity when compared to the growth in investments in service sector IT. The committee provided a list of several explanations for this paradox. At the top of its list was the mismanaged employment of information technology.

It does not however, discount the importance of the service encounter, that is, the interaction between customers and customer contact personnel. Rather, it regards successful service encounters as resulting from a coordinated convergence of organizational factors; customer contact personnel training, job design, the reward/punishment system, empowerment, and the manner in which IT is integrated with the rest of these factors forming an organizational infrastructure supporting those encounters. By rigorously analysing service operations and the encounters they produce as a function of the effectiveness with which technology and its adoption are managed, it may be possible to discover a basis for identifying types of service failures resulting from infrastructure design flaws integrating IT.

BUSINESS STRATEGY

Organizational strategy begins wish the organization's mission statement that identifies what service the organization provides. This implies an interaction between the target market segment and the service provided and an interaction between technology and personnel employed to produce and deliver the service and how the service package is designed.

The design of a job consists of what customer encounter personnel are expected to do based upon their skills and qualifications and organizational constraints. These expectations cannot, however, be divorced from the technology through which customer encounter personnel act. A service is produced as a response to an existing market that it can opportunistically enter, as an instrument that calls new kinds of markets into being, or as a combination of both.

The Internet auction company, eBay, is a recent example of such a combination. On-line auctioning existed prior to eBay's appearance. However, eBay took on-line auctioning several steps beyond what already existed to an interactive environment and redefined customer expectations. As a result, eBay has virtually monopolized the on-line auctions industry and has dramatically expanded the industry's market in which it is the dominant player, attracting new customers while holding its old ones. The nature of services is such that their production and consumption is simultaneous. Consequently, the production and delivery of a service constitute its encounter with the customer whose expectations are standards against which the efficacy of the service is evaluated.

How the production and delivery of the service are designed into the service package is therefore, critical.

The technology selected for the service package plays a part in that design. On the one hand, the service package is first designed to which a suitable and available technology is then attached. Such is the case, for example, with fast foods where IT systems are employed to open transactions and communicate customer orders to the back room. IT may be employed in the back room to monitor operations and bring the transactions to a close. On the other hand, technology may restrict how decision makers would like to design their service packages or it can open up the design of a package so as to include heretofore infeasible possibilities by which competitive advantages can be pursued. Such is the case, for example, in tele radiology.

Recent developments in IT and standardization in the way imaging equipment generates its images has made it technologically possible to physically decouple radiologists from the images they must read. As a result, access to radiological services has become decidedly more timely and widespread for potential customers than heretofore thought possible. Such developments have created opportunities to redesign the initial service package and revise customer expectations by reinforcing initial diagnoses with second and third opinions and exploiting subspecialization skills while at the same time, reducing the turn-around time to patient consultation.

SERVICE PACKAGE DESIGN

The widely accepted means of categorising service organizations is through the use of typologies. One of the most widely used typologies is Lovelock's that strategically profiles a service package. Of particular interest to the authors of this Study is Lovelock's typology that juxtaposes customization of services with [+ or-] exercise of judgement and discretion by customer contact personnel in meeting individual customer needs. A barber, for example, is expected to provide the customer more customised services than a home pest exterminator who has a finite set of programme modules from which to select and much less judgment to exercise.

Like the barber, an attorney also performs a customised service but the attorney must use and exercise judgement and discretion that exceeds the judgment and discretion a barber uses and exercises and certainly exceeds the judgment and discretion the home pest exterminator must use and exercise. It is expected that similar services will position themselves similarly in Lovelock's typologies. Technological innovations in service production and delivery can, however, lead to typological repositionings of a service operation and a consequent revision and redesign of its profile and service package. One must assume that such redesign of the service package is done to derive some competitive advantage or at least prevent the service operation from being competitively disadvantaged.

The various technologies an organization chooses to employ therefore interact with all the typologies that strategically profile it and contribute to the design of the organization's service package. The specific interaction between the employment of IT and the extent to which customer contact personnel are empowered or not empowered to use and exercise judgment and discretion to meet customer needs during the service encounter is this study's object of analysis. Working down the main diagonal of Lovelock's typology of customization and discretion, the more standardized the service, the less use and exercise of judgement and discretion by customer contact personnel is necessary. The more customised the service, the more use and exercise of judgement and discretion by customer contact personnel is necessary. In most cases customer contact personnel are the sole points of contact customers have with an organization providing them the service they seek. Their evaluations of it and decisions about future patronization of it are largely determined by how customer contact personnel manage to present the organization during service encounters. Thus, how the judgment and discretion customer contact personnel are empowered or not empowered to use and exercise and the IT they employ interact in the design of the service encounter can be decisive if the organization is to attract and hold its customers.

The extent of judgment and discretion customer contact personnel are expected to use and exercise understandably varies from service to service. However, what about situations that do not precisely conform to a given service for which the technology has been designed? Judgment and discretion used and exercised by customer contact personnel in such situations is important for at least two reasons. First, decisions including judgment and discretion or the lack of them may affirm or contradict organizational objective or policies. Furthermore, unacceptable decisions issuing there from will result in positive or negative encounters from the customer's viewpoint.

These decisions may be particularly important in achieving a service recovery when a service failure has occurred or is imminent. A service operation employs IT in order to increase and improve service efficiency and effectiveness in a way that is consistent with its competitive strategy. Fitzsimmons suggests that IT accomplishes this by creating another entry barrier, generating revenue, creating a database upon which empirically based decisions can be made, and enhancing productivity.

Customer contact personnel draw on and contribute to such a resource when they access IT to support their service encounter activity. Their access to the IT system can, however, vary. They may be restricted with respect to the range of information they can browse. They may also be restricted with the respect to the range of information they can input. Fast food customer contact personnel can browse virtually no range of information and the range of information they input into the system is restricted to the orders they take. Their job can be characterized as being almost completely circumscribed by the technology associated with their job. A customer wants, for example, a taco with allowable modifications.

A predetermined closed set of intermediate steps is synchronic with the outcome. The employee merely selects predetermined and technologically constrained choices, as one would push a stop or start button on a machine. Airline ticket counter personnel must, on the other hand, be able to browse routings, schedules, and ticket information for the entire industry in order to input the orders they take. The outcome of the order is something separate from the subset of intermediate steps that achieve it. Airline ticket counter personnel must create that subset. They use IT to expedite the construction and creation of that subset.

The IT they employ does not therefore, so nearly circumscribe their jobs as with the fast food order taker. Job design for service employees has been categorized as a "production line" approach or an "empowerment" approach. The production line approach, as its name implies, is based on a Tayloristic view.

It is based on four tenets-simple tasks, clear division of labour, substitution of equipment and systems for employees, and little decision-making discretion of employees. This design seeks to gain customer satisfaction through efficiency, consistency, and low costs.

The empowerment approach, on the other hand, allows employees to make decisions that in the production orientation would be reserved for higher-level management. In such settings, jobs are less simple and more broadly defined and employees are given more latitude. In order for employees in such a design to be effective, they must have access to needed information, knowledge about how to use the information, and sufficient power to meet customer requests during the service encounter.

The production line approach gains its low costs through consistency, which can be translated into lack of personal service. This means that as the service encounter is standardized, the choice of actions possible by the service provider is limited.

Attempts to provide personalized service in such a setting would drive up costs and violate the competitive advantage of the firm. In addition, while the customer receiving the personal service may be more satisfied, other customers who are receiving slower service because of it may be disgruntled. The empowerment design is slower, less efficient and more expensive to operate. It requires careful selection and extensive training of employees. This design could put a firm at a competitive disadvantage from a cost standpoint servicing encounters of a routine form. Companies must clearly define their business strategy and know the environment and the customer base they pursue in making a decision concerning job design for their employees.

INTERACTION OF JOB DESIGN AND INFORMATION TECHNOLOGY

It is imperative with the production line job design that IT is installed as a part of that design so as to facilitate matching it to the service encounters anticipated. The number and nature of the options from which the employee chooses should then be limited to matching the constraints on their decision-making authority. Any access to additional information would not only be of no use; it would actually deter efficiency. For example, if all hamburgers are prepared to the same degree of doneness, giving a customer encounter person the option of asking a customer how he/she would like the meat cooked would slow down the process.

In fast food, cash registers prompt order-takers through the decisions that are allowable. Thus, the more standardized the service the more easily circumscribed technologically it can be because the reality of the encounter is simple and presumed to be more easily captured than encounters in which provided services are customised and the outcome of any one such encounter is variable.

The more circumscribed technologically the service is, the more efficiently the service can be performed but the more dependent upon the circumscribing technology customer encounter service personnel become. In the case of the empowerment job design, use of judgment and exercise of discretion on the part of employees demands access to information.

If the employee is to provide personalized service, the IT system must provide access to information concerning options and their availability. Thus, if the service can be customised and the service provider has discretion, the information must be provided to enable that discretion to be used. This means that the less standardized the service the less easily circumscribed technologically it can be because the reality of the encounter is too complex and varied in individual outcomes to be easily captured.

This does not mean however, that these customer contact personnel are any less dependent upon the technology that less extensively circumscribes their job than their counterparts who provide standardized services. Rather, their dependence is different. They cannot effectively use and exercise judgment and discretion that, by definition, are parts of their job without IT.

A TYPOLOGY OF SERVICE ORGANIZATIONAL MISMATCHES

One may assume that for any given range of actions provided to customer contact personnel, protocols exist that prohibit, obligate, and permit selections of alternatives that depend on the encounter circumstances. Within this normative framework, the exercise and use of judgment and discretion can be extensive or limited to the point of being virtually nonexistent. Where their use and exercise are extensive, it is to presumably match and conform the job to the needs and expectations of specific customers. Where their use and exercise are virtually nonexistent, the job as it is designed and its supporting organizational infrastructure are presumably adequate to also match and conform the job to the needs and expectations of specific customers. Organizational mismatches, therefore, arise between the job design and its supporting organizational infrastructure when customer contact personnel are confronted with a service demand that cannot be met without their being at odds with how they are to do their job and/or with the goals and objectives of the organization.

This section provides a typology of such mismatches based on job design and IT as the significant infrastructural component of interest providing the contexts in which judgement and discretion are used and exercised. Violations of the job design can occur in a number of ways. First of all, do customer contact personnel follow courses of action that fall outside what the technology circumscribes for them? Examples of such behaviour are abundant. One can imagine an employee breaking open a cash register to make change for a customer because there is no sale with which to ring it open or no access to a key with which to unlock it.

One can also imagine a situation where a hotel guest is permitted to take a free muffin from the breakfast line because the cash register is not programmed with a "muffin" key. As job violations go, breaking open a cash register to make change is certainly more extreme than giving away muffins. Both cases, however, suggest that the customer contact job as it is technologically circumscribed may be inadequately designed to satisfactorily address every encounter for providing service that might come its way. Such design inadequacies typify mismatches. Such mismatches could lead to service failures that in some cases only the extraordinary use and exercise of judgment and discretion can repair.

Thus, the exercise of extraordinary judgment is a legitimate topic to examine. The job design/service package is totally circumscribed, consisting of other organizational inputs including customer encounter personnel who have no leeway whatsoever using or exercising judgement and discretion in their conduct of the service encounter. As long as these encounters are routine, *i.e.*, match the job's design, encounters are successful and customers are satisfied. Non-routine encounters, on the other hand, do not match the job design. From the viewpoint of the organization, such an encounter is a non-event. It is certainly not a success but neither is it a failure, for the organization has not defined the customer's need as something the job was designed to satisfy. From the viewpoint of the customer seeking satisfaction, however, it is hard to argue that the encounter can be anything but a failure.

The customer encounter personnel may, however, be able to satisfy a non-routine need and achieve a service encounter success attended by a mix of other results, but they must do so by abandoning altogether the use of the technology that is a fundamental functional part of their job's design. Violations can occur within the job as designed and technologically circumscribed. These violations involve judgments that disregard organizational protocols and lead to particular technologically-doable ends that the technology installed is not intended to support. Such judgments may be conflicted or perverse. The exercise of judgments that are conflicted may result in a service encounter success in the view of the customer and probably the customer encounter service person as well.

Take for example, a customer who wishes to make a last minute change to his/her discount fare airline ticket at an airport airline ticket-counter. Penalties for making such changes are part of the terms to which the customer agrees when he/she purchases such a ticket. Yet, the customer encounter service personnel at airline counters in airports rarely assess such penalties. Not only will they change flights for discounted tickets, they will even change airlines. They are perfectly capable of assessing such penalties, taking money, even making change. They have the IT available to do it, but they rarely do despite the fact that airline management directs them to the contrary. Apparently, such personnel are empowered to exercise a great deal of individual judgment and discretion in such matters as they weigh such issues as customer flow, acceptable aircraft load factors, and customer goodwill. The authors regard conflicted judgments as being made in situations where the customers can be better served even though providing such service could prove detrimental to the service organization. The job design/service package consists of a partially circumscribing IT and other organizational inputs including customer encounter personnel who have substantial leeway in terms of the judgement and discretion they can use and exercise in their conduct of the service encounter.

Given that non-routine/custom service encounters are within the realm of possibility, success certainly occurs when customer contact personnel use and exercise judgement and discretion only insofar as they choose to strictly adhere to organizational guidelines and policies. Thus an airline customer contact person could change a customer's discount ticket and assess the prescribed penalty and neither party would have any reason to regard such an encounter as anything but successful, for the desired change was made and the customer was assessed only the agreed-upon change fee. Such customer contact personnel can, however, use and exercise their judgement and discretion and not adhere to policies by choosing not to assess a customer a penalty for changing a discount ticket.

This also results in a successful service encounter from the point of view of the customer. It is, however, one that is lavish compared to assessing the customer a penalty for making the change. Furthermore, such a choice on the part of the customer contact person does not involve abandoning: the technology that is a part of his/her job design but putting it to use. The exercise of perverse judgments and the behaviours that ensue are often motivated by a perceived need on the part of various employees to "beat the system" and almost invariably jeopardize the success of the service encounter and well being of the service organization as well. A study the authors did of a well-known fast-food service franchise, referred to as Flex-Mex, serves as an example. Flex-Mex's market qualifiers were a number of competitive priorities, "mass customization" of its product and speed of service. Its employment of IT contributed to a great extent in making this possible. Flex-Mex's cash register transmitted orders through a computer to display screens located in its back room where ingredients were assembled into menu items and orders filled.

The assembly employee who completes the last step in filling the order removes it from the display screen. The screen then displays the next order in the queue. Screens may hold many orders at a time and rarely do they become overloaded. This is due in part to screen capacity and in part due to the fact that an order can be "bumped" at anytime.

Assembly personnel, therefore, do not necessarily need to wait until a customer physically receives his/her order to remove that order from the screen. IT, however, performed more than an order communication function for Flex-Mex. It was used to monitor order delivery speed performance and foodstuffs wastage.

Crews were rewarded for above-standard performance with half-price menu items for their meals and were denied half-price menu items for their meals and/or penalized individually with demotions or dismissal for sub-standard performance. As a result of this additional set of functions IT performed, assembly personnel would often "bump" an order before it was filled because that would stop the timer on that particular order.

Thus, assembly personnel were able to insure that no one order ever took an excessive amount of time quite independent of whether a customer had to wait an excessive amount of time for his/her order. Such a practice also resulted in misfilled orders since employees often carried as many as five different orders in their short-term memory.

Several other downside phenomena accompanied these service failures. First, the correct order had to be refilled. This took additional time but IT was not timing this activity. Second, the shelf life of these menu items is very short once prepared, less than five minutes in most cases.

Thus, a certain amount of foodstuffs had to be scrapped if no new customer came along shortly ordering the same item. The assembly crew could only compensate for this waste by shorting other orders by small amounts of the ingredients. The job design/service package consists of a partially circumscribing IT and other organizational inputs including customer encounter-personnel who have no leeway whatsoever in terms of the judgement and discretion they can use or exercise in the conduct of the service encounter.

What is noteworthy is that it is not an encounter with a customer that elicits a perverse use of the technology of which the job design is in part constituted, but the encounter with limited measures of employee performance upon which a system of rewards and punishments is based.

The encounter with the customer is irrelevant. Analysis of these cases can establish the utility of a conceptual framework to explain the use of judgment by customer contact service personnel when acting within the technology paired to their jobs. Thus, what would otherwise be anecdotal information can be processed into knowledge about the management of operations, technology, and human resources.

Such knowledge will permit decisions to be made as to the extent to which customer contact service personnel should use judgment and exercise discretion to the benefit of both the customer and the servicing organization. The first case involves two examples in the use of extraordinary judgment.

One is the example of breaking open the cash register to give a customer change. The other is the hostess who gives away breakfast muffins. Both examples suggest that the involved customer contact personnel are committed to effectively serving the customer.

Both, however, constitute organizational mismatches that derail the organization's pursuit of its goals. The circumscribing technology has not adequately comprehended all the different kinds of service encounters involving customer needs. Given that service operations management does not recognize needing change or wanting only a muffin as legitimate customer needs, the protocols in place are not adequately conceived. The ends of the organization and the ends of its customer contact personnel are at odds because the technology as employed by the organization is divisive.

Given the conceptual framework the authors have constructed several alternative courses of action that can be proposed. There may be very good reasons why customer contact service personnel are not allowed to make change. If management wishes to continue that restriction, the protocols must be very clear that customer contact service personnel are not so empowered.

If the failure to make change results in needless loss of goodwill, the most obvious alternative course of action would be to give the operator the cash register access key. Such a change in policy would invariably require additional protocols as to whom change can be given and when it can be given, thus empowering the register operator to use his/her judgment and exercise discretion in applying those protocols. Concerning the muffin give-away example, the most obvious failure is that the technology inadequately captured the range of service encounters. This failure should be easy to rectify by merely programming the register with alternatives to selling just the buffet.

This would further circumscribe the register operator's job and remove the need for extraordinary judgments from time to time. Given that part of the hotel's breakfast line consists so often of a breakfast buffet, there may be little incentive to go to that kind of trouble since little control would be exercised over breakfast buffet customers as to how many muffins they might take in the first place. Be that as it may, over time, the practice of muffin give-away could prove costly and, while the cost of operating a breakfast buffet line is partially subsidized by hotel registrations, there is little reason to carelessly add to its cost.

Despite upper management level directives urging airline ticket counter personnel to assess penalties more frequently, they continue to use and exercise their judgment and discretion in this matter and assess them much less frequently than upper management would prefer. They do this without fear of sanctions. This is a case of conflicted judgments and could of course be resolved by technologically circumscribing the process by which those changes are made. It would be an easy matter to programme for such changes so that the change could not be finalized until the penalty was assessed for the change. This would take the control of assessing such penalties out of the hands of the airline ticket counter personnel. Such programming has not however, been done. The reasons for not doing such programming could be several, the most likely one being that airline ticket counter personnel have as a primary task facilitating the movement of traffic through the terminal.

Anything contributing to impeding that movement must be regarded as undesirable and costly. Airline ticket counter personnel are, therefore, left to use judgment and exercise discretion in such matters since assessing penalties could prove time consuming.

On the other hand, changing discounted tickets disrupts the yield management schemes designed to optimize flight revenues. Changing discount tickets involves a cost for which airlines can make a compelling argument. Penalties are assessed to offset this loss. This conflict between what is practiced and the protocols in place suggests that from the standpoint of the conceptual framework the airline ticket counter personnel have not been sufficiently empowered.

They certainly have been sufficiently empowered in terms of their use and exercise of judgment and discretion. They have not, however, been sufficiently empowered to have a say in how the protocols are devised and applied. The higher levels of airline management would do well to so empower them. Working together on equal footing, both parties might be able to agree on protocols that would garner more revenue through penalties that would offset the organization's yield management shortfalls while keeping the traffic moving at an acceptable rate. The case of Flex-Mex provides a true-life example of the judgments service personnel make that are perverse. Unlike extraordinary and conflicted judgments that work for the most part to the benefit of the customer but are potentially debilitating to the service organization, perverse judgments are debilitating to the service organization including the quality of the customer service it provides. The conceptual framework the authors have constructed provides a basis for identifying the factors that contributed to the Flex-Mex mismatch and proposing alternative courses of action to remedy it. First, the extent to which technology circumscribed the jobs of the Flex-Mex employees, particularly those in the back room, was not extensive enough.

This resulted in Flex-Mex's reward/punishment system and its performance measurement method that were intended to motivate high performance actually leading to the contrary.

In addition, Flex-Mex's employees were not sufficiently empowered for management to be receptive to their observations concerning their dysfunctional work setting or suggestions they might submit as to how that work setting could be made more functional. Thus alienated, they acted in a way to protect their individual interest that put them at odds with some of the organization's goals and objectives. The conceptual framework constructed suggests several alternative courses of action Flex-Mex could pursue to remedy this mismatch. First, it could extend the application of its IT to more completely circumscribe the tasks of its employees.

This could include timing an order from when it is placed with the order taker to when it is placed on the customer pick-up portion of the front counter and not electronically permit back room employees to "bump" orders from their screens. The IT system could also be reengineered to account for redoing misfilled orders. Such changes in IT's application would certainly restrict the extent to which employees could make perverse judgments. It would also, however, undoubtedly further intensify the hostility of the work environment and could lead to other undesirable results. Flex-Mex could also consider empowering its employees in ways that could possibly even dispense with any need to reengineer its IT system.

Revising the incentive and performance measurement systems would be a start. Tying their rewards to the success of both their local operation and the organization at large might do better at gaining the loyalty and dedication of

Flex-Mex's customer service personnel than providing them half-price menu items. This would be especially so if these personnel had some say as to what those rewards would be and how their performance should be measured. This does not necessarily mean that the use of judgment and the exercise of discretion in doing their jobs would be increased.

These jobs require the use and exercise of little judgment and discretion. Rather, it would mean that Flex-Mex's customer contact service personnel had a stake in how well Flex-Mex does. This paper has provided a conceptual framework for exploring the dynamics that arise in managing the integration of operations, technology, and human resources. It has focused on how mismatched combinations of operations, technology, and human resources impact the use and exercise of judgment and discretion by customer contact service personnel and how these organizational anomalies can be eliminated.

The few examples presented in this paper hardly provide sufficient data to empirically validate this framework and the kinds of organizational mismatches it identifies. Furthermore, the off-diagonal categories have not been addressed. Therefore, further work empirically validating and perfecting this framework or developing one to more accurately categorize types of service organizations in order to better isolate types of intra-organizational mismatches is in order. Beyond that is the issue of determining from among a set of alternative courses of action the framework specifies which alternative is the most appropriate to pursue in eliminating organizational mismatches.

Thus, it will be necessary to identify, select, and develop measures as well as techniques to process these measures to rigorously determine the appropriate alternative course of action. This programme of applied research is both fruitful and valuable inasmuch as it addresses potential service operations ineffectiveness and inefficiency resulting from failures integrating technology and human resources and could contribute to sorting out the factors that have resulted in the "information technology paradox."

- This empirical observation, the Clark-Fisher hypothesis, explains employment shifts towards sectors of lower productivity.
- Cook, Gho, and Chung, researchers have developed different typologies to answer specific questions w a pragmatic consideration. Therefore, the authors believe that they have sufficient warrant to employ one of Lovelock's typologies because of its implicit usefulness to the question at hand.
- A competitive advantage can be achieved by providing a low-cost speedy standardized service to a large market segment with similar needs or by providing customised service to a segment whose needs are dissimilar. In the first case customising services would be inefficient, strategically contradictory, and possibly annoy customers delayed by the preferential treatment they perceive others receiving.

In the latter case, such customization would be strategically necessary because it would be what was expected.

- A totally circumscribed job design is one in which every organizationally sanctioned course of action customer encounter personnel can take as a part of their job is executed through the IT system.
- The extent to which a particular service is technologically circumscribed, if at all, depends of course on factors other than the mere fact that it can be done. Certainly the benefits gained and the costs incurred to so circumscribe a set of tasks are major considerations.
- From conversations with Delta, USAir, and TWA airport ticket/check-in counter personnel.

Bibliography

Anil Kathuria: *Hotel Management*, Sonali Publication, Delhi, 2008.

Ashim Gupta.: *Hotel Tourism and Catering Management*, Centrum Press, Delhi, 2011.

B B Vidyarthi: *Management of Hotel and Catering Industry*, Pearl Books, Delhi, 2007.

B.K. Chakravarti.: *Hotel Management Theory*, Vols. I and II, APH Publication, Delhi, 2009.

C.P. Yadav.: *Management of Hotel and Catering Industry*, Anmol Publication, Delhi, 2001.

D.K. Aggarwal.: *Housekeeping Management*, Aman Publication, Delhi, 2006.

D.K. Sharma.: *Perspectives of Hotel Management*, Pearl Books, Delhi, 2012.

Dahl, Crete M., Grace H. Woolley.: *Housekeepers' Guide to Selecting and Training Employees*, Stamford Conn: Dahl Pub. Co., 1949.

Dahl, Crete M.: *Housekeeping Management and Organization for Hotels and Institutions*, Stamford, Conn.: The Dahls, 1945.

Dahl, Crete M.: *Housekeeping Management in Hotels and Institutions; Purchasing, Upkeep, and Administration*, New York London: Harper & brothers, 1931.

Dinesh Tomar.: *Management of Hotel and Catering Industry*, Ankit Publication, Delhi, 2011.

Fleur Barrington.: *1001 Little Housekeeping Miracles*, Carlton Publishing Group, 2009.

G. Raghubalan, Smritee Raghubalan.: *Hotel Housekeeping: Operations and Management*, Oxford University Press, 2009.

Gaurav Gandhi.: *Hotel Management Diet and Nutrition*, Random Publications, Delhi, 2012.

Gaurav Gandhi.: *Hotel Management Food and Food Services*, Random Publications, Delhi, 2012.

H.C. Chaturvedi.: *Hotel Management*: Current Issues and Practices, Akansha Publication, Delhi, 2006.

J Mathews: *Hotel Management*, Pointer Publishers, Jaipur, 2008.

Jagmohan Negi, Gaurav M.J., Ritushka, Suniti: *Housekeeping Operation and Management: Procedure and Techniques*, Kanishka Publication, Delhi, 2011.

Jitendra K. Sharma.: *Contemporary Tourism and Hospitality Management*, Kanishka Publication, Delhi, 2006.

Jyoti. S. Sharma.: *Catering Management Practices*, Akansha Publication, Delhi, 2006.

K.S. Negi.: *A Textbook of Hotel Management*, Wisdom Press, Delhi, 2011.

Kumar Singh.: *Hotel Management*, Aman Publication, Delhi, 2006.

L.K. Sharma.: *Hotel and Catering Management*, Surendra Publications, Delhi, 2012.

M C Metti: *Catering: Housekeeping and Hotel Management*, Anmol Publication, Delhi, 2008.

N N Dahalia.: *Fundamentals of Hotel Management and Operation,* Pearl Books, Delhi, 2007.

Neeta Mehta.: *Fundamental of Hotel Management and Operations*, Random Publications, Delhi, 2012.

Nirmal Dubey.: *Hospitality Tourism and Hotel Management*, Sonali Publications, Delhi, 2011.

O.P. Kandari, Ashish Chandra: *Hotel, Tourism and Catering Management*, Shree Publication, Delhi, 2004.

Pallab Sengupta, Biswanath Bid.: *The Professional Housekeeping*, Naman Publication, Delhi, 2011.

R.K. Arora.: *Professional Housekeeping*, APH Publication, Delhi, 2010.

Ravi Aggarwal: *Housekeeping in Home and Hotel: System and Operations*, Sublime Publication, Delhi, 2008.

Ravindra Verma.: *Hotel Management and Tourism*, Centrum Press, Delhi, 2010.

Suchi Garg.: *Fundamentals of Hotel Housekeeping*, Alfa Publication, Delhi, 2006.

Vijay Kaushik.: *Management and Functions of Housekeeping*, Book Enclave, 2006.

Index